J. Franklin Jameson
and the Birth of the
NATIONAL ARCHIVES
1906–1926

J. Franklin Jameson, 1859–1937, father of the National Archives (National Archives)

VICTOR GONDOS, Jr.

J. Franklin Jameson and the Birth of the NATIONAL ARCHIVES

1906–1926

Foreword by
JAMES B. RHOADS

University of Pennsylvania Press
1981

Library of Congress Cataloging in Publication Data

Gondos, Victor, 1902–
   J. Franklin Jameson and the birth of the National
Archives, 1906–1926.

   Bibliography: p.
   Includes index.
   1. United States National Archives. 2. Jameson,
J. Franklin (John Franklin), 1859–1937. I. Title.
CD3023.G66   027.5'4 [B]   80–54050
ISBN 0–8122–7799–6   AACR2

Printed in the United States of America

Contents

Illustrations

Foreword

In 1968, when Victor Gondos, Jr. relinquished the editorship of *Military Affairs*, the chief historian of the Office of Military History described him as "soldier, architect, archivist, historian, author, editor, with truly significant accomplishments in each field."

Gondos served as editor-in-chief of the scholarly journal for seventeen years, a period in which his professional life was probably richer and more productive than at any other time. In addition to his editorial labors, he served successively as chief of four branches in the National Archives; he became well known as an authority and consultant on archival buildings and equipment; and he lectured and wrote extensively on the planning and design of archival buildings, archival administration, and history.

The background that he brought to bear on his varied professional career was unique, for he alone in the United States was professionally qualified as both architect and archivist. Add to that his life-long fascination with the military and his deep love of history, and one may begin to discern the forces that shaped and motivated his life.

Gondos graduated in 1925 from the School of Architectural Engineering at the University of Michigan. While at Ann Arbor he was also a dedicated member of the Reserve Officers Training Corps, and upon graduation he was commissioned a second lieutenant. For the next fifteen years he pursued an architectural career in Philadelphia and regularly engaged in summer service with the Coast Artillery Reserve. He was commissioned a captain in 1930, but rheumatoid arthritis eventually cut short his military career, and he was retired for physical disability in 1940.

At about the same time, his long-standing interest in history caused him to contemplate seriously a change in his civilian career, as well. He enrolled as a graduate student in history at the University of Pennsylvania, was granted a master's degree in 1941, and in the following year joined the staff of the National Archives in Washington, D.C. There he served initially as a records appraiser, and later as the editor of microfilm publications. In 1948, he was selected as chief of the Business Economics branch. Subsequently, he became chief of the Old Army and the Civil War branches, and at the time of his retirement from the federal service in 1965 he headed the Army and Navy branch.

During his nearly quarter-century of service at the National Archives, he maintained a full and demanding "extracurricular" career. Until the early 1950s, he was active in the Reserve Officers Association, serving as its national historian during 1951 and 1952. An early member of the American Military Institute, he served as associate editor of *Military Affairs* during World War II, and, as noted earlier, was editor-in-chief from 1951 to 1968. The institute chose him as its first fellow in 1961. Gondos was also active in the Pennsylvania Historical Junto and the Columbia Historical Society.

Gondos joined the Society of American Archivists, and served as chairman of its Committee on Archival Buildings and Equipment from 1943 to 1965. His contributions in that capacity led to his selection as a fellow of the society in 1957. During this period he wrote a number of articles on facilities and equipment for archives, as well as *Edificios para Archivos,* said to have been the first work on its subject published in Spanish. In 1970, after his retirement, the society published his *Archives and Records Center Buildings.*

As though this rich and varied professional life were not enough, Gondos began, in the late 1950s, to take coursework at the American University for a doctorate in history. Within a few years he was beginning to define his dissertation topic, and his architectural background, coupled with his archival career, quite naturally led him to consider a study of the long struggle to have the federal government's permanently valuable records housed in a building in Washington specially designed for their protection and use. Initially, he had thought to include an account of the design and construction of the building in his dissertation, but it soon became apparent that this would lead to too lengthy and unwieldly a narrative.

In 1971, Victor Gondos, aged sixty-nine, completed his dissertation and was awarded the Ph.D. He hoped to see his study published and then to commence work on its sequel, a study of the design and construction of the National Archives Building. He talked to me about both of these objectives and I gave him my support. I felt then, as now, that the archival literature would be enriched by the publication of *The Movement for a National Archives of the United States* and that Gondos was uniquely equipped to write a definitive account of the National Archives Building and its construction.

After Gondos's death in 1976, his widow, Dorothy Gondos Beers, discussed with me various possibilities for the publication of the dissertation. It was a pleasant surprise, therefore, when, after my retirement as archivist of the United States, the University of Pennsylvania Press and Mrs. Beers asked me if I would consider editing the manuscript for publication. I accepted the task as an opportunity to further an objective that I had supported for nearly a decade.

This book differs in minor ways from the dissertation that Victor Gondos wrote. It has a new title, is a bit shorter, is organized differently here and there, is less heavily annotated, and has undergone some stylistic revision. These changes were carefully reviewed by Dorothy Gondos Beers, and her incisive comments and questions have been immensely helpful in producing the finished work. If the process of revision inadvertently has altered the substance or conclusions of the author, the editor bears full responsibility.

James B. Rhoads

Preface

The term *archives,* derived from the Greek word *archeion,* has long carried the dual meaning of both a body of records and the building that houses the records. This study is concerned solely with the housing of the records. More specifically, it is concerned with describing the long struggle to obtain proper housing for the archives of the government of the United States of America. Preeminent in this struggle was a professional historian whose name became a household word among historians and archivists, John Franklin Jameson.

In the Pennsylvania Avenue lobby of the National Archives Building there is a bronze plaque describing Jameson as the one "whose persistent and wise guidance led to the establishment of the National Archives." Although the prominent part played by Jameson in the movement for a National Archives of the United States is known and acknowledged, the details of the history of that enterprise have become ever dimmer with the passing of the years. In brief, Jameson and the movement for a national archives were becoming a legend, without the foundation of historical documentation. There are numerous references to the movement and to Jameson in annual reports, in archival books and articles, and in correspondence and memoranda, but there existed no full-length detailed study of the struggle to implement the idea of a national archives.

One of the initial projects authorized by the first archivist of the United States, Robert D. W. Connor, was "the making of as complete collection as possible of the [documents concerning the] care and preservation of the official records of the United States Government."[1] This project was partially completed in 1939 but never published. It is a collection of twenty-four loose-leaf volumes of typescripts, facsimiles, and photostats, compiled under the direction of Percy Scott Flippin, entitled, "The Archives of the United States Government: A Documentary History, 1774–1934."

Soon after Solon J. Buck succeeded Connor as archivist of the United States, he too went on record as favoring the compilation of a documentary history of the movement. Leo F. Stock, long-time associate of Jameson, suggested transferring to the "National Archivist" certain correspondence at the Carnegie Institution concerning the part played by Jameson and his staff in the effort to establish a national archives. Buck replied to Stock that "the papers . . . would be a valuable addition to the materials on the movement for a National Archives."[2] In the succeeding years, there was much talk of the compilation of a definitive history of the movement for a national archives, but that history still remained to be written.[3] It was not until the early 1960s that I fully realized the lacuna in archival literature.

In March 1964, I had a number of talks with Waldo G. Leland. My notes show that Leland was highly gratified to learn of my intention to undertake a study of the movement for a national archives. He stated to me the following:

Although a number of excellent article length studies have been made . . . there is very definitely a need to do a book length study, bringing together the roots of the movement . . . and bringing into balance and proportion the several contributions. . . . Admittedly . . . J. Franklin Jameson became the leader of the movement . . . but there were lines of force flowing into his orbit and flowing out again which have not been adequately dealt with or more than hinted at in other writings.[4]

The temporal scope of the movement to be treated definitively in this study is limited to the period 1906–1926, from Jameson's first appearance on the Washington scene to the date of the first major congressional appropriation, which ensured the construction of the National Archives Building. Significant and apposite events prior to 1906 and after 1926 are summarized in the first and the concluding chapters.

The pursuit of basic research on the project was rendered possible in 1965 and subsequent years by the concurrent opening to public access of three vitally important groups of papers: the papers of J. Franklin Jameson at the Library of Congress, the papers of R. D. W. Connor in the Southern Historical Collection at the University of North Carolina, Chapel Hill, and the papers of Miles Poindexter at the University of Virginia Library, Charlottesville. The relevant correspondence and memoranda of Waldo G. Leland, as he himself informed me, were found interfiled with the Jameson Papers. Other principal sources included the Flippin Collection at the National Archives as well as various National Archives record groups; the American Legion Archives in Indianapolis,

Indiana; the American Historical Association Archives in the Library of Congress; the long series of annual reports of the AHA; and, of course, the annual reports of federal departments and agencies, as well as the many congressional serials, such as the Senate and House documents, hearings, committee reports, bills, and the completed acts of Congress.

Naturally, a scholarly study of this nature requires the aid, knowledge, and cooperation of others. Foremost, I owe particular thanks to Professor Arthur A. Ekirch (then of the American University and now of the State University of New York at Albany) for his advice and criticism during the years of research and writing. Professors David J. Brandenburg and Carl G. Anthon of the American University also rendered valuable guidance and counsel. Thanks are also due to a number of leading American authorities on archives and manuscripts, namely, the late Waldo G. Leland, Oliver W. Holmes, the late Ernst Posner, and Frank B. Evans, all of whom offered insight and counsel. Finally, three successive archivists of the United States, Wayne C. Grover, Robert H. Bahmer, and James B. Rhoads, each in turn expressed appreciation of and support for my project.

In interviews, correspondence, and searches, this work utilized the knowledgeable cooperation of many others too numerous to mention individually. Nevertheless, I desire to express specific appreciation to the following persons and institutions: to David C. Mearns, then chief of the Manuscript Division, Library of Congress, who expressed his deep interest in the project by obtaining permission for me to microfilm pertinent correspondence and memoranda in the Jameson Papers; to the late James W. Patton, director of the Southern Historical Collection at the University of North Carolina, who placed all the recently arranged Connor Papers at my disposal and obtained permission from Henry Groves Connor to allow me to scan briefly the then-restricted Connor diary; to Edmund Berkeley, Jr., curator of manuscripts at the University of Virginia Library, who assisted me on the Miles Poindexter Papers; to the American Legion Archives and Library in Indianapolis, Indiana, and Washington, D.C., particularly staff members Thomas V. Hull, Richard O'Keeffe, and Patricia O'Connell; to Buford Rowland, George P. Perros, Charles South, and James C. Brown of the Legislative branch of the National Archives for prompt and courteous services in searching the records of the U.S. Senate and House of Representatives; and, last but not least, to Camille Hannon and Geneva Penley of the library of the National Archives. To the host of unnamed persons interviewed and corresponded with in connection with the project, I can offer only my profound appreciation and gratitude.

Victor Gondos, Jr.
Washington, D.C.

President Herbert Hoover laying the cornerstone of the National Archives Building,
February 20, 1933
(National Archives)

1
Prologue

LAYING THE CORNERSTONE

Herbert Hoover, thirty-first president of the United States, troweled the mortar as the cornerstone of the National Archives Building was lowered into place. The day was February 20, 1933; the hour was 2:30 P.M. At that moment the American people were immersed in the worst depression in the nation's history. Yet that very afternoon the distinguished gathering of cabinet officers, Supreme Court justices, senators and representatives, Washington business leaders and newspaper editors, members of the Treasury's Board of Architectural Consultants and of the Advisory Committee on the National Archives, and other concerned citizens was witnessing the fulfillment of a hope, constantly recurring over the preceding century and a quarter, of governmental and historical leaders.

Before taking trowel in hand, the president addressed the assemblage concerning the meaning of the occasion:

There is an especial significance in this ceremony, coming within two days of the celebration of George Washington's birthday. The soil on which we are standing is part of the original tract acquired by President Washington for the Nation's Capital. The building which is rising here will house the name and records of every patriot who bore arms for our country . . . there will be aggregated here the most sacred documents of our history, the originals of the Declaration of Independence and of the Constitution of the United States. . . . The romance of our history will have living habitation here in the writings of statesmen, soldiers, and all the others, both men and women, who have

1

builded the great structure of our national life. This temple of our history will
. . . be one of the most beautiful buildings in America. . . . It will be one of the
most durable. . . . Devoutly the Nation will pray that it may endure forever
. . . the repository of records . . . of our beloved country.[1]

The Marine Band, led by Captain Taylor Bronson, added color to the
occasion with its music and flourishes; and a detail of the Coast Guard
escorted the president. After the invocation by the Right Reverend
James E. Freeman, bishop of the Episcopal Diocese of Washington,
Ogden L. Mills, the secretary of the Treasury, whose department had
supervisory control of the plans, construction, and contractual disbursements for the new edifice, gave the opening address. Appropriately, the
secretary spoke in more mundane terms than would the president. He
observed that the "completion of the building and the final transfer of
the archives will mark the culmination of many years of effort on the
part of Government officials and historical associations" in order to
"safeguard the priceless records of the Nation." The dangers to the
archives that then existed were "too distressing to contemplate," he
said, "for these papers include among others the support for titles to
millions of acres of land, thousands of patent rights, the documents
necessary to protect the Government against all manner of claims, the
whole series of papers covering our dealings with other nations," and
other documents constituting "a written record of our national life."[2]
The exercises were closed with a benediction by the Most Reverend
John M. McNamara, auxiliary bishop of the Catholic Archdiocese of
Baltimore.

The VIPs departed, the onlookers vanished, the music was stilled, and
the bunting was removed. It was now the task of architect John Russell
Pope, builder Matthew McCloskey, and the Public Buildings branch of
the Treasury Department, and all their myriads of associates, techni-
cians, artists, and workmen, to bring the dream to reality. Two years
later, when the roof of the new archives proudly graced the skyline of
the Federal Triangle in the national capital, the newly appointed first
archivist of the United States, R. D. W. Connor, in a national radio
broadcast told the American public

The erection of the National Archives in Washington marks the consumation
of a movement . . . that was launched more than a century ago. Like the ebb
and flow of the tide, this movement at times ran with great rapidity and power,
at other times it has been sluggish and weak, but never since Congress in 1810
appropriated money for the building of a fireproof depository for the "preservation and orderly arrangement" of "the ancient public records and archives of the
United States," has it entirely subsided. In the erection of the National Archives
Building the movement reached its high water mark.[3]

The presidential laying of the cornerstone took but a moment. This
is the story of the decades of struggle that made that moment possible.

After more than twelve decades, during which the records grew astronomically in volume despite time's ravaging hand, a monumental structure was reared from a vast excavation between Pennsylvania and Constitution avenues, halfway between the Capitol and the White House, an edifice that would realize the vision of the founding fathers, that the record of their works and those of the nation they established be perpetually preserved.

THE ARCHIVES OF THE EARLY REPUBLIC

Conscious of the importance to posterity of its proceedings, the First Continental Congress, at its first meeting on September 5, 1774, unanimously chose Charles Thomson as secretary to the Congress. Thomson began the duty as a temporary affair, but by common consent he continued to serve throughout the revolutionary and confederation periods.[4] To him we owe the careful custody and preservation of the archives of the Continental Congress and of the central government under the Articles of Confederation. After the organization of the federal government in 1789, those archives were deposited in the custody of the State Department where they remained until they were transferred to the Library of Congress, in 1903, and to the National Archives decades later.[5]

As the capital of the United States was moved from New York to Philadelphia and then to the District of Columbia, the papers of the old and the new governments likewise were successively transferred. Some 170 years later, Wayne C. Grover, the third archivist of the United States, noted that "no one could have been a more careful record-keeper than Charles Thomson, Secretary to the Continental Congress, and no one more solicitous for the safety and preservation of these prized records than George Washington."[6] Unfortunately, other high officials of the early nineteenth-century republic were not so careful.

Fires were especially frequent in those days of open hearths and wooden floors and roofs. When the government moved to the Potomac in 1800, the first executive offices were two companion buildings situated on a line with the southern facade of the White House, one of them 200 yards to the east and the other a like distance to the west. The easterly site, then as now, was occupied by the Treasury Department. The westerly site was occupied by the State, War, and Navy departments. The Treasury structure was started in November 1798, and its western companion was begun in July 1799. Both were ready for use in 1800.[7] Misfortune struck almost immediately. On November 9, 1800, fire destroyed most of the valuable records of the War Department; and two months later, January 20, 1801, fire damaged records at the Treasury.[8]

Congressional concern about the safety and care of the government records mounted during the ensuing decade. In 1810, on the motion of a Massachusetts representative, Josiah Quincy, a congressional committee was appointed to inquire into the condition of the "ancient public records and archives of the United States." The committee reported that the early records were "in a state of great disorder and exposure; and in a situation neither safe nor convenient nor honorable to the nation." This investigation led to the first act for housing federal records, signed by President Madison on April 28, 1810, "providing for the better accommodation of the General Post-Office and Patent Office, and other purposes." It called for an appropriation of $20,000 for fireproof rooms for the deposit of "all the public papers and records of the United States . . . in the custody of the state, war or navy departments."[9]

The next event of significance in the early history of the federal records was the British military incursion into the national capital in August 1814, the burning of certain public buildings, and the consequent loss of some archives and currently used records. Actually, losses due to the invasion appear to have been minimal. A secret journal of the Congress and property of the Library of Congress were lost because of the negligence of a couple of clerks. Most of the departments had had the foresight to hire and commandeer wagons and horses, and they removed the records from the city several days before the battle of Bladensburg.[10]

Signing of the Treaty of Ghent precluded further damage from British attack, but the universal enemy of records, fire, remained an ever-present danger. As a partial solution to this problem of records preservation, the federal government, like the states of the Union, during the nineteenth century supported the publication of selected documents. Ebenezer Hazard set the pattern for this type of endeavor when, in 1792–1794, with some government aid, he published two volumes of selected documents, *Historical Collections,* covering the period from early colonization to the end of the New England Confederation. Later followed Jared Sparks's more ambitious enterprises in four major series, which comprised a total of thirty-eight volumes. Sparks assembled copies of documents from the archives of the thirteen original states, from foreign archives, and from private collections.[11]

In the three decades before the Civil War, the government also sponsored the publication of a compilation of documents covering the period 1789–1838, which was produced by the publishing firm of Gales and Seaton and entitled *American State Papers: Documents, Legislative and Executive.* Produced in the second quarter of the nineteenth century, also with government subvention, were two other well-known series of documentary publications: *The Annals of Congress of the United States,* in forty-two volumes, covering congressional debates during the period 1789–1824; and, between 1837 and 1853, Peter Force's nine-volume compilation of documents of the American Revolution, known as *American Archives . . . a Documentary History of . . . the North American Colonies.*[12]

This collection and publication of selected documents made portions of the national historical source materials widely available, but it also tended to obscure the need for a national archives comparable to those of Europe. It was little understood that subjective selectivity, no matter how conscientiously attempted, was quite alien to the concept of archives.

Perhaps no one ever stated more succinctly the justification for preservation of permanently valuable public records than a New Englander, Richard Bartlett, who wrote, "To provide for the safe and perfect keeping of the Public Archives is . . . one of the first and most imperative duties of a legislature." Everything that can be procured by money, he continued, "sinks into insignificance in comparison with the original records."[13]

When the public buildings in Washington, burned or damaged during the brief British occupation, were reconstructed after 1814, those on either side of the president's mansion were rebuilt first and were completed by 1820. But several decades after 1820, these buildings proved to be far too small. The onrushing tide of westward expansion, culminating in the war with Mexico and the conquest of California and the Southwest, caused unavoidable growth of the federal government. Between 1820 and 1860, eleven states were admitted to the Union, and the nation's population more than tripled from 10 million to 31 million persons.

As far as the government's records and space were concerned, to the problems of growth were added those of recurring conflagrations. One of the dramatic fires of the first half of the century destroyed the first Treasury Building at the end of March 1833, and another damaging fire in 1836 destroyed the Post Office and Patent Office. The severe losses of irreplaceable records underlined the need for constructing better buildings, and the ideal of fireproof construction permanently preoccupied government officials and builders.[14]

Louis McLane, who had succeeded Roger B. Taney as secretary of the Treasury, headed the committee of inquiry into the Treasury fire, and within a fortnight reported to President Jackson that there was then "no proper security for the public archives" and that the State, War, and Navy departments were in buildings that were "altogether insecure." The Treasury building, he said, had "contained some fireproof depositories, in which a portion of the records were preserved." He recommended a large fireproof building to accommodate "all the public offices under the same roof" and to allow for expansion rendered necessary by the "growth of the country . . . for some years to come."[15]

Acting on this recommendation, President Jackson requested that Congress "authorize the erection of suitable depositories for the safekeeping of the public documents and records." In the meantime, he directed Robert Mills, the eminent architect, to draw plans for a new Treasury building. Congress authorized the building by an act of July

4, 1836, and Mills, who had plans ready for the new Treasury structure, was immediately placed in charge of the design and supervision of public buildings.[16]

Postmaster General Amos Kendall now put in a plea for safe quarters for the General Post Office whose "valuable books and papers" were "daily exposed to destruction."[17] President Jackson promptly sent a message to Congress that in view of the surplus in the treasury it was expedient to provide a "fireproof building for the important books and papers" of the Post Office Department.[18]

The Congress had hardly received this message, and had had no time to act upon it, when catastrophe struck. At three o'clock in the morning of December 15, 1836, fire broke out in the basement of the City Post Office, which within an hour spread to the rooms occupied by the General Post Office and the Patent Office. By daybreak nothing was left but the bare walls. Fortunately, most of the books and papers of the General Post Office were saved, though the entire contents of the City Post Office and the valuable models and papers of the Patent Office were consumed by the flames.[19] President Jackson at once reiterated to Congress his recommendation for an immediate appropriation "for the construction of a fireproof General Post Office."[20]

Work on the Treasury structure was temporarily halted in 1838, as materials destined for the state wing of the Treasury were transferred to the new Post Office and Patent Office buildings.[21] At the conclusion of the Mexican War in 1848, Secretary of the Treasury R. J. Walker again called for the completion of the Treasury building. The structure was not finished until the Lincoln administration, which continued the construction to completion as a symbolic act of faith in the permanence of the nation.[22]

HALL OF RECORDS EFFORTS

In the seventh decade of the nineteenth century, with the onset of the Civil War, the construction energies of the federal government were naturally concentrated on measures needed for survival. This meant, among other things, the building of many temporary wooden structures for training camps, supply depots, hospitals, and the like.

The Civil War also marked the beginning of a new epoch, during which the power and activities of the federal government were greatly expanded. The first archivist of the United States, R. D. W. Connor, has noted that during the seventy years from 1789 to 1860, the total accumulation of archives of the executive departments amounted to only 108,000 cubic feet. But "during the fifty-five years from 1861 to 1916, 923,000 cubic feet of records were added."[23] This growth naturally intensified the problem of properly housing government records.

Prior to the structural changes in the political, economic, and social life of the nation wrought by the war, officials viewed records preservation in parochial terms. Primarily, they had asked for some fireproof rooms in their respective departments. After the Civil War the concept of a central records repository or warehouse for the government as a whole began to emerge.

In July 1870, the secretary of war appointed a board to examine "the existing methods of keeping the records . . . of the War Department and its Bureaus." The board reported that many records were of insufficient value to justify their preservation. Similar conditions were reported by other departments. The secretary of the Treasury recommended the construction of a brick fireproof building south of the Treasury for housing the records.[24] The army quartermaster general in 1875 recommended that Congress authorize the destruction of worthless papers.[25] But voices for either storage or disposal of records continued to be singularly ineffective, and Congress manifested little interest until the second half of the decade of the 1870s.

As a result of the fire of September 24, 1877, which destroyed part of the Interior Department Building, President Hayes appointed a commission to consider and report on the security of public buildings in Washington. The commission rejected records disposal for the relief of overcrowding and called for a large fireproof structure to accommodate government archives, and at a location removed from the immediate vicinity of other buildings.[26]

Spurred to action by these developments, Quartermaster General Montgomery C. Meigs, in a report dated October 9, 1878, submitted to the secretary of war the first design for a hall of records. The building was to be built quickly of brick and to cost about $200,000. Secretary of War G. W. McCrary approved Meigs's project and "earnestly recommended its adoption."[27] In his annual message for 1878, President Hayes launched the movement for a hall of records, recommending the Meigs plan to Congress, and he again referred to it in his annual message for 1879.[28]

Congress took no action until another fire occurred in the War Department on February 8, 1881. Two days later the Senate passed bill S. 1889, which had been introduced by Sen. Justin S. Morrill of Vermont, calling for an appropriation of $200,000 for a hall of records. As happened with so many similar bills thereafter, it was never considered by the House.[29]

Bill S. 1889 was the forerunner of a long list of bills introduced in the Senate or the House. In the decade 1882–1891, bills similar to that of Senator Morrill were introduced repeatedly by a new champion of the hall of records concept, Sen. George W. Vest of Missouri, chairman of the Committee on Public Buildings and Grounds.[30] All these bills passed the Senate, and despite the favorable recommendations of presidents Arthur and Cleveland, all of them failed of passage in the House. The failure in the House was at least partly due to the rival interests of local real estate men.[31]

Meanwhile, the heads of the various departments and bureaus, in their annual reports, continued to urge relief for their space and records security problems. Virtually yearly, the supervising architect and the secretary of the Treasury continued to recommend the project.

In the spring of 1886, Rep. Ezra Child Carleton of Michigan attempted a partial solution of the records problem with a bill that called for extending the Winder Building. He proposed to appropriate $100,000 for the construction of a "fireproof building, to be known as the Hall of Records," for the use of the War and Treasury departments. This bill too failed of passage.[32]

Two other developments in the attempts to solve the problems of documentary preservation as well as dissemination occurred in the latter half of the nineteenth century. One was the continuing publication of selected documents for historical use. The other was the granting of statutory permission for destroying "useless papers" for space relief. Official publication of government documents steadily increased. The congressional series continued to grow; the State Department in 1861 inaugurated its famous series known as *Foreign Relations;* and in 1880, the War Department published the first of 130 volumes of *The War of the Rebellion: A Compilation of the Official Records of the Union and Confederate Armies.* [33]

But publication was highly selective. As more and more American historians were trained in historical research at German universities, the subjectivity of selective publication was increasingly condemned. Moreover, publication was expensive and time-consuming, and it was hardly a substitute for proper archival preservation and research availability.

Another records problem with its roots in the Civil War was the passing of large-scale pension legislation, beginning in 1879, which forced a pioneering effort at records management. Constituents complained to Congress early in the 1880s that their pension payments were being delayed. The War Department was flooded with claims requiring verification. The logjam was broken by Capt. Fred C. Ainsworth, chief of the Record and Pension Division of the Surgeon General's Office, who created a name index card file that abstracted the information in over nineteen thousand bound volumes containing medical data relating to over 2 million Union veterans.[34]

The urgent pleas from the bureaus at last aroused Congress to the magnitude of the records crisis. A select committee of the Senate, headed by Sen. F. M. Cockrell of Missouri, was established to "Examine the Methods of Business and Work in the Executive Departments." But rather than seek a solution through the creation of a central archives, Congress passed a bill on February 16, 1889, which set the precedent

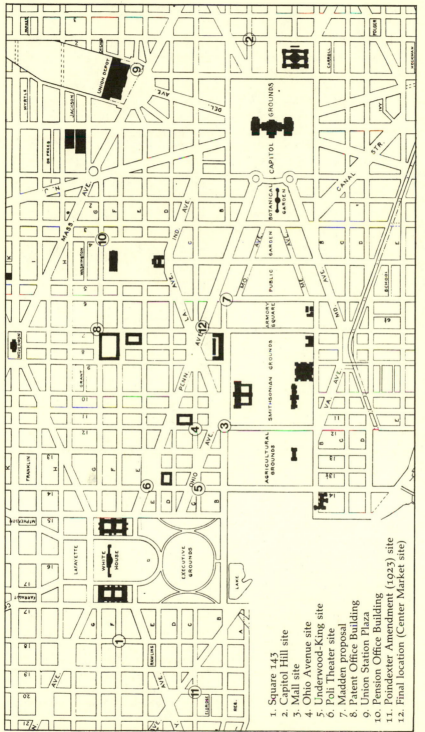

Sites considered for the National Archives Building

1. Square 143
2. Capitol Hill site
3. Mall site
4. Ohio Avenue site
5. Underwood-King site
6. Poli Theater site
7. Madden proposal
8. Patent Office Building
9. Union Station Plaza
10. Pension Office Building
11. Poindexter Amendment (1923) site
12. Final location (Center Market site)

for authorizing the disposal of certain records. Thus from 1889 on, the departments annually submitted to a joint committee of Congress lists of records proposed for disposal.[35]

Nevertheless, departmental agitation for a central records depository continued unabated. Between 1889 and 1903, some thirty bills relating to a hall of records were introduced in one or the other house of Congress. The bills were for the authorization either of a site and the construction thereon of a building or merely for the purchase of a site. These bills were regularly referred to the committees on Public Buildings and Grounds, from which they rarely emerged. One proposed purchasing the Corcoran Gallery of Art for a hall of records.[36]

The monotony of inaction was broken by a clause in the Sundry Civil Expenses Appropriation Act of June 11, 1896, which directed the secretary of the Treasury to submit plans giving the size and general characteristics of a hall of records. In pursuance of the act, Secretary of the Treasury Lyman J. Gage made a report in January 1898 which for the first time mentioned as large a figure as 4 million cubic feet of ultimate capacity for a hall of records to cost $1.2 million, but he also submitted an estimate of $450,000 for a smaller structure of 1 million cubic feet capacity to be built initially.[37]

On March 3, 1902, Secretary of the Treasury Leslie M. Shaw, in a letter to the Senate Committee on Public Buildings and Grounds, noted that the "events of the year 1898 had already begun to exhibit a marked effect upon the growth of the files." Therefore, he said, for design purposes it would be preferable to use a new estimate of 5 million cubic feet, which the supervising architect advocated. Shaw estimated the cost of the site and a suitable hall of records thereon at $3,025,000.[38]

In the second session of the Fifty-seventh Congress the matter of a central records repository was at last paid more than lip service by the national legislature. With the powerful aid of Sen. Charles Warren Fairbanks of Indiana, the acquisition of a site for a hall of records was incorporated in the omnibus Public Buildings Act of March 3, 1903. The Deficiency Appropriation Act of the same date carried an appropriation of $400,000 for the acquisition of square number 143, in Washington, D.C., "as a site for the hall of records."[39]

In December 1904, Secretary of the Treasury Shaw reported that the designated site for the hall of records had been acquired, and he recommended that Congress pass an appropriation of $150,000 for preliminary work for the construction of the building. The secretary repeated this recommendation in his annual reports for 1905 and 1906, forcefully emphasizing the importance of a hall of records.[40]

After agitation for more than a quarter of a century, by federal cabinet officers and departmental officials, and numerous members of Congress, this was where the hall of records matter rested in 1906, prior to the advent on the scene of a historian, J. Franklin Jameson.

In the meantime, in the final decade of the nineteenth century, a new force, the American Historical Association (AHA), began to interest itself in the problem of records preservation. "It seems . . . to be one of the fundamental facts in American archival development," observed Ernst Posner, "that it is a response to the . . . insistently presented demands of the scholarly world." European archives, on the other hand, owed their origins to the "continuously developing specialization of government functions,"[41] namely, to the felt need for a central depository over and above the individual agency registries.

Within a decade after it was organized in 1884, the American Historical Association began grappling with the problem of the administration, preservation, and accessibility of public records in the United States, both state and federal. The historians, however, tended to follow the lead of federal officials in thinking of a national government repository as a hall of records, in effect a storage warehouse in which the records deposited by each agency would remain within that agency's legal control.[42]

In 1893, the World's Columbian Exposition made Chicago, Illinois, the center of great popular interest, and the AHA decided to hold its ninth annual meeting at the Chicago Art Institute from July 11 to 13. Ellen Hardin Walworth of Saratoga, New York, read a paper at the first morning session on "The Value of a National Archives to a Nation's Life and Progress." She noted that the "archives hold the evidence of facts; what the Bible is to the theologian, and what statute law is to the lawyer the state archive is to the historians." Long-standing tradition, "the common law of historians, cannot be ignored," she stated, but for public affairs and individuals the earnest student must authenticate the facts and "seek the official evidence that will prove his statements." For such evidence, Mrs. Walworth declared, the researcher must turn to the archives of a nation.[43]

Two years later J. Franklin Jameson, who had studied European archives and manuscript collections, submitted a program to the Executive Council of the AHA for the systematic collection, organization, and selective publication of source materials of American history. As a result the Executive Council established the association's first standing committee, the Historical Manuscripts Commission, and appointed Jameson as its chairman. This development was salutary for the archival cause. As one noted scholar observed many years later, "The commission's work quickly accentuated the difference between private papers and public archives."[44]

Thus, by 1899, the association recognized the need in the area of public archives and established a separate Public Archives Commission. This commission, in turn, enlisted the cooperation of some thirty advisers in the individual states, who had the mission of inquiring into "the character of the historical archives of the Federal Government and the individual States and reporting on the provisions made for their maintenance and accessibility." The commission's surveys of state archives,

1900–1917, were published in the annual reports of the AHA. The capstone product was the publication in 1904 of the Van Tyne and Leland *Guide to the Archives of the Government of the United States in Washington.* "These surveys," commented Professor Posner, "offered an impressive picture of archival holdings in America, such as the archival establishments of Europe had never achieved."[45]

As a consequence of the developing activities of its Public Archives Commission, the association, at its seventeenth annual meeting, passed its first resolution for a hall of records on December 30, 1901. This resolution diffidently followed the concept of government officials as to the nature of such a central repository and closed by drawing the "attention of Congress to the importance for American history that such a hall of records would possess."[46]

The resolution of 1901 was the first step taken by the historians' association to influence the national legislature on the central records repository issue. The most that can be said for it is that it was a beginning. It may have been of some slight use to federal officials and to congressional sympathizers in persuading Congress, at long last, to appropriate funds for a hall of records site. Yet the acquisition of that site, square 143 (rather ironically, now the location of the headquarters building of the General Services Administration), became so highly controversial that it impeded the historians' later movement for a national archives.

2

Jameson Establishes A Base
in the National Capital

AT THE CARNEGIE INSTITUTION

The future leader of the movement for a national archives of the United States, J. Franklin Jameson, came to the national capital in October 1905 to assume the post of director of the Bureau (later Department) of Historical Research of the Carnegie Institution of Washington.

The idea for an office of historical research at the newly created Carnegie Institution was inspired by a suggestion of Frederick J. Turner "for a historical school for graduate students in Washington." The council of the American Historical Association, which was favorable to the idea, appointed a committee to explore the matter. The committee consisted of Jameson, Charles Francis Adams, Jr., and Andrew C. McLaughlin. The study of the committee resulted in the establishment in March 1903 of the Bureau of Historical Research, with Jameson's committee colleague, Professor McLaughlin, as the first director.[1]

Jameson, it appears, was keenly disappointed, as he had desired the position for himself, partly because he wanted to implement the new bureau's program and partly because he wanted to escape what to him was the uncongenial atmosphere of Chicago.[2] McLaughlin, after a couple of fruitful years at the Carnegie Institution, which included the publication of the noted *Guide* to federal archives in Washington by Van Tyne and Leland, resigned in 1905, to accept the chair of history at the University of Michigan.[3] Jameson then succeeded McLaughlin at the Carnegie Institution.[4]

For more than two decades following his arrival in Washington, Jameson labored purposefully to accomplish the program recommended

13

in 1902 by the advisory committee of historians. The four main points of this program were to maintain a national clearing house for historians, publish documentary materials, explore European archives for materials relating to American history, and edit the *American Historical Review.* [5]

Given Jameson's scholarly interests, his proximity to the AHA headquarters, and his keen interest in all matters pertaining to the historical profession, it is not surprising that he became involved in many activities not specifically included in his duties as director. When a lobbyist was needed by the historians, Jameson, as a Washington resident, was always at hand, "willing, informed, and persuasive."[6] Two principal projects were to test Jameson's perseverance and promotional capacities to the limits: one, the establishment of a government commission for national historical documentary publications, which was at best only marginally attained; and the other, the establishment of a national archive (he always referred to it in the singular). The latter goal, the subject of this study, Jameson superimposed on the original Carnegie Institution program. After many despairing defeats, the National Archives Building became Jameson's enduring monument.

What were the elements in Jameson's background that prepared him for his life's work? He was versed in the principal classical and modern European languages. In his undergraduate days at Amherst College he won a number of academic prizes for proficiency in Latin, Greek, German, and mathematics. His many letters to Waldo G. Leland through the years attest to his knowledge of French.[7]

In the later years of the nineteenth century, the next step one took after college was foreign study, most often in Germany, the place of origin of the Ph.D. program in American universities. Jameson desired to do likewise, but his family could not afford it, and he was not able to raise the several thousand dollars which he considered necessary for a stay of several years. Instead of study abroad, in September 1879, he started teaching at the high school in Worcester, Massachusetts. A year later, on the advice of Herbert Baxter Adams, he began graduate work at the new Johns Hopkins University. In two years he received the university's first doctorate in history, and he stayed on as a teaching assistant for six years.[8] In the spring of 1888 Jameson found an opportunity to leave Johns Hopkins for Brown University, where he remained for thirteen years. Then for four years, from 1901 to 1905, he was professor of history and head of the department at the University of Chicago.[9]

During his years at Johns Hopkins, Jameson became a founder and charter member of the AHA. While at Brown, he became, in Donald Mugridge's words, "the first and greatest editor" of the *American Historical Review,* which was established in 1895.[10] Except during the four years he was in Chicago, Jameson edited the *Review* until 1928.

After assuming his post at the Carnegie Institution, he made the first of numerous inspection and survey trips to Europe, where he became well acquainted with both British and continental archives and archivists, as well as scholars in history and the humanities. From March until the middle of July 1906, he visited the chief European archives, particularly in Italy, Switzerland, and Germany.[11]

Jameson returned home, refreshed and strengthened in his determination to make available to scholars all possible primary documentary sources—manuscripts, archival holdings, printed documents—the first requisites for a "scientific" history of the country.

HALL OF RECORDS TO NATIONAL ARCHIVES

The year 1906 may be characterized as a landmark. In addition to the advent of Jameson on the Washington scene the year marked a watershed, on one side of which was the simple hall of records proposal and on the other the emerging concept of the national archives, a professional and scholarly institution of national significance. The latter idea was not the sole property of Jameson. It was actually fathered by none other than Henry Cabot Lodge, with a New England genealogist, Lothrop Withington, as the deus ex machina.

Before Jameson's arrival, the need for a fireproof records repository had been felt by various cabinet officers, chief clerks, and others in the federal hierarchy. As previously noted, in their annual reports and messages they always referred to such a building as the hall of records. In their minds the idea involved little more than a storage warehouse for records no longer in active use. The hall was envisioned as a large building in which the various agencies would have ample storage spaces assigned and would retain control over their respective records holdings. The building itself, of course, would be maintained by a superintendent who would have physical but not legal custody of the records. Legally, the respective records would remain the property of each agency. Obviously, although it would have relieved the federal departments of crowding and accessibility problems, such a concept provided little for scholarly research needs.[12]

As early as the 1890s, committees of the American Historical Association had sent memorials to Congress urging recognition of the need for the proper care of the scattered and neglected historical records of the government.[13] In 1899, in an effort to prompt some visible improvement in American governmental archives, the AHA had established its own Public Archives Commission, which initially turned its attention to the state governments but also took an active part in the movement for a federal archives building in Washington.[14]

All this agitation, from governmental and historical sources, at last moved Congress to some action—the purchase of square 143 as a site for the building. This square, situated between Eighteenth and Nineteenth and E and F streets, N.W., in Washington, D.C., and containing a little over three acres, was recommended by Secretary of the Treasury Lyman J. Gage as a site for a hall of records. It was considered suitable because of its convenient location near other government departments, because it had a sufficient elevation to "secure the papers and records from injury or destruction by dampness," and because "there were few buildings to be removed."[15] But, as Elihu Root told Jameson years later, "Nobody seemed to take interest enough in the subject to have the building put up after the land was bought."[16] This inaction proved costly to the national archives movement in the early 1920s. Time and again, in congressional debates, proponents of an urgent need for an archival building were confronted with the lack of action following the site acquisition of 1903.

In June 1906, the secretary of the Treasury (the cabinet officer most consistently interested in the records problem through successive administrations) again called the attention of the Senate "to the importance of an appropriation for a hall of records" and emphasized that "an appropriate site for a hall of records was purchased two or three years ago." He deemed it "of great importance that a suitable building be authorized." Secretary Leslie M. Shaw recalled to the Senate that for many years such action was recommended in every annual report of the Treasury head. He concluded with the suggestion that $2 million be authorized as "a tentative limit of cost."[17]

The only result was that on June 29, 1906, the House of Representatives approved a resolution that the secretary of the Treasury make a survey and report to the House at the next session on how much floor space for office use would be gained by removing all files that were not needed for current reference and storing them in a suitably constructed building; and, further, the amount of rent that could be saved if the records were removed to a suitable building.[18]

This exercise resulted in the usual spate of dutiful letters from agency heads, contributing data which were promptly filed and forgotten.[19] However, one man, unconnected with the government, did take an interest in the archival problem and wished to do something about it. He was Lothrop Withington of Newburyport, Massachusetts, and he discussed the matter with his senator, George F. Hoar.

Senator Hoar, who was then seventy-seven years of age, and died shortly afterwards, was known as a friend of history and scholarship and therefore was sympathetic to Withington's concern about the inadequate care of the federal records. But, as he no longer felt able to act, he advised Withington to seek active aid from his Massachusetts colleague, Sen. Henry Cabot Lodge.[20]

Senator Lodge, who at one time had taught American history at Harvard College and had many historical, biographical, and political writings to his credit, had acquired the popular appellation of "the scholar in politics." He readily understood the need for the proper preservation, arrangement, and accessibility of the national archives and agreed to introduce a bill in the Senate to be drafted by Withington. As the latter himself said, he "carefully adapted" a bill "from the act of the first of Victoria [the organic act of the English Public Record Office, August 14, 1833] which established the magnificent glory of historic scholarship in London."[21] This bill, in its provisions, turned out to be a landmark, indeed.

Although the word *archives* does not appear anywhere in this six-page bill, its clauses are the forerunners of those in the National Archives Act of 1934. It represents the watershed between the two concepts, that of the hall of records and that of the national archives. The measure, had it become law, would have created a Board of Record Commissioners, with sole legal custody of all records over eighty years old; and, if so ordered by the president, by any cabinet department head, by the president of the Senate, by the Speaker of the House, or by the chief judges of federal courts, the board could also assume legal custody over records less than eighty years old. Other provisions made it unlawful to destroy any record pertaining to government business except by "express authority of the Board"; agents of the board could inspect records in any federal office and arrange for their security; the Record Office, under the board, was to be headed by the record keeper, assisted by first and second deputy record keepers with cognizance over the executive departments; and the judicial and legislative branches were to have, respectively, one judicial deputy record keeper, and one legislative deputy record keeper. These officials were to be appointed by the president and confirmed by the Senate. All other staff and assistants were to be appointed by the record keeper and confirmed by the Board of Record Commissioners. Provision was made for receiving in legal evidence copies of documents attested with the seal of the record keeper or the special seals of the four deputies. To give concrete effect to these provisions, a "Record Office Building" was to be built in Washington, D.C., to house the records in the board's custody; the physical needs of the searchers and historical and other scholars were explicitly recognized in instructions to the record keeper that he shall provide "ample accommodations" for them.[22]

The Lodge bill, however, went beyond the later provisions of the National Archives Act in according the record keeper authority to purchase collections of historical manuscripts in private hands, which had a "substance similar to public records"; and the record keeper was authorized to receive in custody "ancient records of the several States including judicial and local records," provided the states transferred legal custody of them. The record keeper was also to provide quarters for, and cooperate with the work of, any United States historical commission established by special act. Current expenses of the establishment were to be provided in annual appropriations of Congress.[23]

Referring the Lodge bill to the Senate Committee on the Library was the logical procedure. Unfortunately, it was never reported to the floor of the Senate for either passage or rejection.

It is interesting to note that Withington saw quite clearly that the librarian and the archivist were professionally not identical. He believed that there was quite enough work to absorb the capabilities and energies of each in a separate library and archives and that "the intensely circumscribed and highly technical task of the professional archivist needs a quite detached foundation."[24]

Anticipating the views of Jameson and Herbert Putnam, the librarian of Congress, Withington thought that the site of the record office "by every administrative and aesthetic reason" should be the "twin plot north of the Library of Congress." He hoped to see "a fellow palace to the Library of Congress sitting beside it, and housing not only our record office, but our historical commission." He thought such a juxtaposition of the two institutions would greatly improve upon the situation of similar institutions in London and Paris. "Every student," he asserted, "is well aware of the advantage which would ensue if the public record office and the British Museum were side by side in London, and Les Archives and the Bibliothèque Nationale in Paris."[25]

Withington thought as keenly about the archival problem in its various aspects as Jameson did later. He even foresaw the obstacle to the side-by-side placement of the library and the record office:

Our lawyers have long had an eye upon this ground for the new Supreme Court building, but there is no special reason for placing the Supreme Court there, and every reason for putting the record office there as a mate to the library and to include all its historical manuscripts.[26]

The Lodge bill of 1906 went the route of historical might-have-beens, but with the perspective of time one can perceive that it made an important contribution. Although it was entitled "A Bill to Establish a Record Office," its terms were equally relevant to a national archives. Lothrop Withington's draft of the Lodge bill therefore deserves full recognition.

THE COMMITTEE OF THREE

It was a year or two after the Lodge-Withington effort had failed that Jameson became actively concerned with the archival housing problem. His assistant, Waldo G. Leland, led off with a paper on the federal government archives, which he presented to a meeting of the Columbia Historical Society of Washington, D.C., early in 1907.[27] This was a forerunner of the numerous propaganda efforts of Jameson and Leland to educate the historically minded public, on the one hand, and the national legislature, on the other, to the need for adequate housing of the government archives in the nation's capital.

In the paper, Leland told how a hall of records had been "urgently recommended since 1879"; about an ex officio commission of 1887, directed to report on archives, but not known to have ever met; about the report on the condition of government archives in 1900; and about the report of the Advisory Committee on History of the Carnegie Institution, in 1902, which, in turn, led to the Van Tyne and Leland *Guide* of 1904. He then described at some length the records holdings in the executive departments.[28]

Even though at this time he was primarily concerned with the campaign for a historical publications commission, Jameson could not resist the impulse to take some action on behalf of the archives, probably with Leland's prodding, as the latter, through his governmentwide archives survey in 1903 and 1904, had become acquainted with the parlous state of the records. As the president of the United States was the only one who could speak with authority to Congress on behalf of all government agencies, Jameson decided the best course was to take up the matter directly with President Roosevelt.

Accordingly, early in December 1907, Jameson wrote to Roosevelt and referred to a "conversation with which you were so good as to favor me yesterday," in which Jameson had raised the question of the "creation of an adequate archive-building." He told the president that it was his understanding that Roosevelt agreed that a national archives building was a desirable objective but that he did not think it could be consummated soon. Jameson agreed that this view of the situation was undoubtedly correct; nevertheless, now that he had put his hand to it, he would stick with it as long as necessary, "because I believe my present office calls on me to further in any way that I can any movement likely to result in great benefit to national historical interests."[29]

At the moment, he told the president, there was little he could do other than to have some "private discussions with members of Congress" to "keep the matter before their minds." But to leave it at that was hardly in keeping with Jameson's activist nature, and he took "the liberty to suggest as a first step that the President might ask the heads of departments to furnish data" on the amount of space each department would require in an archives and the annual growth of these requirements. Roosevelt fell in with this suggestion and sent a copy of Jameson's letter to each department head, instructing them to reply to the president. These replies were then forwarded to Jameson and became a part of his files.[30]

Some agency heads were not interested. Secretary of Agriculture James Wilson, for example, was of the opinion that the Department of Agriculture "need not be considered in the building of a Hall of Records." The department had relatively small scientific laboratories, and the secretary could not foresee huge administrative demands for space.[31] Chairman of the Interstate Commerce Commission Martin A. Knapp was likewise of the opinion that the commission "would not need any space in the Hall of Records," and he could not conceive that its records "would be of great value to national historical interest."[32] The secretary of the Smithsonian Institution, Charles Walcott, stated that the "Institution is now able to take care of all its own papers," but he estimated that "a space of 6,000 cubic feet would meet all requirements for fifty years or more."[33]

The heads of the larger departments, of course, took a different view. Their problems with respect to space were often urgent. Attorney General Charles J. Bonaparte was among the first of the department heads to reply affirmatively. He stated that "some of the Department's older records . . . now stored in basement rooms, could well be transferred to a Hall of Records." Space then being used for storage amounted to two rooms, each about twenty feet square, and he estimated that for future growth a provision of a few hundred square feet annually would be ample.[34] Postmaster General George von Lengercke Meyer, reflecting the ever-space-hungry Post Office Department, asserted that the space occupied by noncurrent records then totaled 111,600 cubic feet and estimated that 125,000 cubic feet of storage space, in addition to the initial increment, would "cover increasing demands of the Department for the next ten years, provided a careful elimination of all unnecessary records . . . be made each year."[35]

Naturally, among the biggest space consumers were the military agencies. Acting Secretary of War Robert Shaw Oliver told the president that his department could use 279,677 cubic feet in a hall of records, and he estimated an average yearly increase of 3,505 cubic feet.[36] Secretary of the Navy Victor H. Metcalf seemed somewhat testy, remarking that Congress had made provision "for the collection, indexing, carding, and preparation for publication of the records relating to the personnel and operations of the United States Armies" but had made "no like provision . . . for the Navy." As to the navy records, these were "scattered through various offices and bureaus." The secretary thought that "the logical method of procedure would be to form in the Navy Department a Division of Records (or Records and Pension) to collect, catalogue, index and prepare for publication all naval records." Thereafter, he asserted, it could be determined what should be sent to the hall of records. In short, he wanted to use the hall of records project as a vehicle for a project parallel to the War Department's *Official Records* series. As the navy bureaus reported their space requirements variously in terms of cubic feet, square feet, and lineal feet, it was difficult to get a firm figure, but the total approximated 100,000 cubic feet, with an annual increase of 2,500 cubic feet.[37]

Beekman Winthrop, assistant secretary of the Treasury, explained that "governmental business increases enormously every year" and that the Treasury was unable to properly provide for accumulating records "unless a building of the character mentioned is erected." He emphasized that Congress had granted authority to purchase "Square No. 143, for a Hall of Records." The last parcel in that site, he said, "was secured by deed recorded August 6, 1906." He noted that "although recommendations have been made yearly, the Congress has . . . made no appropriation for the erection of a building."[38]

It remained for the librarian of Congress, Herbert Putnam, to make the most significant observations to the president. First, he gave a summary of the Public Buildings Act of March 3, 1903, as it related to square 143; then he cited Senator Fairbanks's bill of 1904, directing the secretary of the Treasury to erect a hall of records on the selected site, and the letter of the secretary of the Treasury to the president of the Senate, requesting that $2 million be authorized for the building. Finally, he came to the meat of what he wished to say: "It appears to me," he wrote, "that the President may desire to know how far the adopted function . . . of the Library of Congress, as the depository of certain historical material in the possession of the Government, would affect the question."[39]

Putnam stressed the difference of function between the library and the proposed archives:

I would report very emphatically that this function of the Library does not in the least diminish the necessity for a building, and a very large one, for the accommodation of the administrative records of the various departments which [because they are permanently valuable] ought not to be destroyed, but which are not appropriate for the collections of the Library.[40]

Putnam emphasized the difference between manuscript collections and archival holdings, stating that "there is a clear distinction between . . . manuscript collections . . . and these records which are accumulated from the ordinary operations of the various executive departments." The librarian noted that the latter were "far beyond the existing capacity of the government buildings." This situation had created pressures leading to "the destruction of great masses of them." There remained "other masses which should be preserved." These, however, should not be preserved in administrative offices but, as "under other governments, national and local . . . set aside in a building especially constituted for their accommodation." In such a building they should be accessible "not merely to the several departments in which they originated, but to the investigator at large."[41]

Putnam thus gave his support to the movement for a national archival repository and affirmed that its functions must not be added to the Library of Congress. As these communications at the top levels of government clearly indicate, the thought and emphasis were still on a place for records storage. Jameson, with the thought of making the records more secure uppermost, at first would have been content to see a hall of records, with the hope that it would mature, in time, into a true archival institution. In thinking, speaking, and writing of the proposed institution, Jameson invariably began to refer to it as the "National Archive," but it took several years of educational effort to get others habitually to use the term *National Archives.* [42]

Jameson's educational program got under way in the spring of 1908. Its first fruit was the establishment by the American Historical Association of the "committee of three," which eventually came to be known as the AHA's Committee on the National Archives. On November 27, 1908, the Executive Council of the AHA approved a resolution "to draw the attention of the President and of Congress" to the importance of a hall of records to preserve and make available the "Government's earlier materials . . . for researches in American history" and also emphasized that "several heads of executive departments of the Federal Government . . . in recent years made urgent representations to Congress of the need of a hall of records." In the last of four paragraphs, the resolution states the following:

Voted that a committee of three be appointed to present the above resolution to the President and to present an appropriate memorial upon the subject to Congress. [43]

One month later, this action of the council was officially reported at the annual business meeting of the American Historical Association, held in Richmond, Virginia. With President George Burton Adams in the chair, it was announced that a committee had been appointed to present the resolutions to the president and to Congress. As he was the prime mover, Jameson was naturally appointed chairman, with Prof. John Bach McMaster of the University of Pennsylvania and Rear Adm. Alfred T. Mahan, the noted naval historian, as his committee colleagues.

Jameson lost no time in getting his committee started on its long road to the designated objective. Early in December 1908, he wrote to McMaster and Mahan, apprising them of the formation of "a committee of three to take up with the President and with Congress the question of a Hall of Records in Washington . . . to contain at least the overflow of public papers from the departments, and likely to result in the formation of a national archive establishment." One can see in these initial letters, in which Jameson coupled the two alternative designations of the proposed records repository, his increasing determination to effect a revolution in the nomenclature as well as the orientation of the establishment he wished to see created. He asked both of his fellow members to meet with him in Washington in late December. With his usual careful preparation, he informed them that he was compiling a statement that he would send to them a week before the meeting. The statement would give them "first, a history of the legislation and executive recommendations . . . within the last twenty or thirty years" and, second, "a summary . . . of the data respecting the needs of the departments . . . which the President at my suggestion last spring elicited from their respective heads."[44]

Mahan replied by return mail that he could not "go to Washington for this purpose."[45] McMaster, on the other hand, answered that he expected to be in Washington "on Monday the 29th early. . . . Any hour you select will suit me."[46] Jameson informed McMaster that Mahan was not coming, but the two of them could meet at the "Round Table"[47] at one o'clock on the twenty-eighth and he would also "get Leland, who knows the seamy side of the archives here in Washington more extensively than anyone else, to give a little statement on some of the most striking infelicities of the present situation." Jameson also planned to have a talk with the secretary of the Treasury, who "of all members of the Cabinet," was "the one most interested in the thing."[48]

Concurrently, Jameson addressed Secretary of the Treasury George B. Cortelyou, informing him of the existence of the AHA committee of which he was chairman, and of which Professor McMaster and Admiral Mahan were members. Although the committee, as a working unit, was actually Jameson alone, he always mentioned the other two because their names carried prestige not only with scholars and officials, but also with the intelligent reading public. As noted in a letter written some ten years later,

The Committee was practically nothing more than a convenience for me to refer to whenever there seemed to be any question of what business I, as an outsider to the government, had to meddle in the matter.[49]

Jameson had his initial interview with Cortelyou on the same day as his meeting with McMaster at the Round Table, December 28, 1908, and provided him with a copy of his "History of the Movement for a National Hall of Records," in which he had summarized the departmental and legislative efforts since the latter part of the nineteenth century. Rather shrewdly, Jameson, in his talks with public officials, generally placed primary emphasis on administrative needs which, if satisfied, would also be helpful for historical and other research requirements. Thus he told Cortelyou that he realized that "the exigencies of public business would have main weight in bringing about the erection of such a building . . . and that the historical interests are quite secondary."[50]

Jameson found Cortelyou "warmly in favor of the erection of such a building," and, to further the cause, the secretary advised him to get in touch with Sen. Nathan W. Scott, then a power on Capitol Hill. In his talks with Cortelyou and Scott, Jameson found that they agreed there was no immediate prospect for an appropriation for the building but "the more likely possibility was for a provision to permit the drawing of plans."[51] Hearing that the supervising architect of the Treasury Department was working on plans for a hall of records, Jameson wrote to him inquiring in "what stage of advancement . . . the plans may be?" If plans were indeed in progress, he wished to get in on the process as he had relevant data to contribute. His department at the Carnegie Institution, he said, had "collected some information and some printed material, with views and plans, respecting the best archive buildings in Europe." Though he felt apologetic about offering "our small stock of information, still less advice, to the Supervising Architect," and though historical interests would be only of secondary consideration in planning, he wanted it known that "we have such information," which could be placed at the disposal of the planners.[52]

The supervising architect's reply was curt and to the point:

So far as I know the statement in the newspaper that our office is working on plans for the Hall of Records is entirely wrong. . . . I can state positively that at this time no work is being done on the building and no work is contemplated under any appropriation now provided for.[53]

Though his initial ventures into the realm of archival design were nonproductive, the process of educating others went on apace. At the annual meeting of the AHA in December 1909, Jameson's two most knowledgeable associates, Leland and Marion Dexter Learned, gave the members comparative analyses of European and American archival problems. Learned, compiler of the guide to materials for American history in German archives (then about to be published by the Carnegie Institution), told the assemblage that American archival problems were quite different from those of leading European countries, due in the main to the decentralized form of government in America. Learned thought that "we are far behind in the care and treatment of documents," compared with German state archives. He felt that "it is high time that the historical societies and the State should work hand in hand . . . toward the systematic organization and administration of our archives, State, municipal, and private." He believed that the Library of Congress, in conjunction with other historical agencies, could do much in improving archival conditions.[54]

Leland, too, thought "our task was more difficult because of our form of government." He pointed to France and other countries with a highly centralized form of government, where it was enough to provide for a single central administration which had full power over the archives of the communes and the departments as well as of the national government. This was impossible in America, where "instead of one archival administration we must always have at least 47 (and more as new States are added), all mutually exclusive of each other." Efforts to secure effective legislation must therefore be widely distributed. But first Leland wanted to concentrate efforts on the national government. In Washington, records were scattered in over a hundred repositories, and many of these were harmful rather than helpful for the preservation of records. The Library of Congress, he observed, had "done something to mitigate the evil" by transferring to the Manuscript Division some material of "especial historical interest." He thought, however, that "it is a serious question to what extent . . . archives should be transferred to a division of manuscripts in a library. . . . There is much to be said against it." So, Leland concluded, there is "no satisfactory solution . . . short of a national archive depot."[55]

At this same meeting, Leland and Jameson helped to create another arm of the American Historical Association. It will be recalled that in 1899, the Public Archives Commission of the AHA was established mainly with a view to fostering better archival conditions in the states. In 1904, the Conference of Historical Societies had been organized to afford a forum at AHA meetings for the historical societies of the nation. Now, in 1909, at the initiative of Leland, Jameson, and other members of the Public Archives Commission, the Conference of Historical Societies organized the annual Conference of Archivists, also affiliated with the AHA. This conference proved useful in the consideration of common problems of state archivists and others having custody of public and institutional records of permanent value, and in systematizing their experiences and thoughts. One writer referred to it as "the first self-conscious body of archivists in the United States, and its founding marks the beginning of a new profession." The annual conference of archivists remained in existence until 1937. It was then dissolved and succeeded by the formal official body of the profession, the Society of American Archivists.[56]

3

Jameson, Poindexter, Sheppard, and Taft

THE AHA RESOLUTION OF 1910

With the advent of the Taft administration, Jameson began to make strenuous efforts to profit from the groundwork for a national archival repository which he had laid in 1908 and 1909. In the following two years he continued his policy to effect a change of thought and terminology from a hall of records concept to that of a national archives. He also managed to acquire powerful congressional supporters in the persons of Sen. Miles Poindexter and Rep. Morris Sheppard. He also tried repeatedly but unsuccessfully to get President Taft to mention the archives project in his annual messages to Congress.

Two fires that occurred in 1910 and 1911 gave dramatic publicity to the importance of records preservation. The first occurred in the Geological Survey on July 31, 1910,[1] and the latter in the New York State House on March 29, 1911.[2] Fortunately the Geological Survey fire was not serious, but it endangered a unique collection of 65,000 volumes, 85,000 pamphlets, and 25,000 maps. As George O. Smith, director of the Geological Survey, observed, it was "the most complete collection of geological works and maps in this country if not in the world."[3]

The Albany fire, on the other hand, was a truly traumatic experience. An incalculably valuable store of the historical records of New York State, dating back to its colonial period, was lost forever. This fire left a profound impression on public men and on legislators, as well as on historians and archivists.[4]

Jameson always used the occurrence of records fires as a means of dramatizing the vital question of records safety. Now he decided on a frontal attack on the problem through President William Howard Taft. From his customary summer retreat at North Edgecomb, Maine, Jameson wrote the president's secretary, Charles D. Norton, about "the possibility of laying before the President a suggestion . . . for use in his annual message to Congress." His impression was, Jameson said, that "however heartily the project is approved by . . . heads of executive departments, it will not be taken up in earnest by Congress until their attention is pointedly directed to the matter by the President." Therefore, he hoped "that the President might be persuaded to insert in his next annual message a brief recommendation upon the subject." He further offered to go to Beverly, Massachusetts, where Taft was summering, "to supply any further information." Moreover, he was of the opinion "that the time is fully ripe for the Government to take the initial steps toward concentration of archive material in proper repositories . . . which most European governments have carried to a greater or less point of advancement."[5]

Two months later, Norton got around to answering Jameson's request. He told the latter that "your letter of September 7th . . . had careful consideration, and I am taking it with me to Panama, together with a comment made upon it by Assistant Secretary Hilles of the Treasury Department, and will see that it is laid before the President." Norton suggested that on his return from Panama Jameson should see him in the White House. He concluded by asking if Jameson thought "that the organization of the present Library of Congress might be an effective one through which to classify, index and store these valuable records?"[6]

Jameson was bemused by the query. There is a fair copy of the Norton letter in Jameson's files, which he intended to send to someone, probably Leland, for at the bottom of the copy he had penned

The hand of Joab is in this thing. I'd like to know how the Library got wind of my correspondence with Taft and talk with Hilles. It doesn't much matter who bosses the job, perhaps, so it is done.[7]

In his reply to Norton, Jameson did not tackle the question head on, but rather discussed the pros and cons of the "centralization" of an archives administration. He thought that too sudden and too tight a central control of the records on deposit would be harmful. He believed that in a new archives repository it would be better to start off gradually, with each agency retaining control of its own records. As time passed and confidence was generated in the new repository, all would come to agree on the practical wisdom of centralizing the administration of the holdings. He cited the precedent of the Public Record Office in London, which was at first a place of deposit, "in which each ministry retained the jurisdiction over the papers which it had deposited. After a few years a unified administration was created . . . under the general supervision of the Master of the Rolls, in the hands of the Deputy Keeper of the Public Records." Jameson concluded that he would be willing to place the archives temporarily under the general supervision of the librarian of Congress, but organizationally separate from the library. In the long run, however, the archival agency should be independent.[8]

In his second annual message to Congress, the president did make a general statement on public buildings, but it concerned his desire to improve on the method of appropriating for buildings. There was, he said, "too little study of the building plans and sites with a view to the actual needs of the Government." He proposed a commission of government experts to prepare a report to Congress as a basis for legislative action.[9] Jameson sent a copy of the Taft message to Leland, but complained that "he did not mention an archive building." Jameson was disappointed in the president's remarks on the problem of expenditures for public buildings, telling Leland that "the message as a whole . . . struck people as disappointingly tame. It sounds like the work of a supremely capable administrative chief, who had no inspiration to convey respecting political conduct."[10]

The year 1910 terminated, as was and is the custom, with the annual meeting of the American Historical Association. The annual Conference of Archivists also met at this time and discussed the paper offered by Dunbar Rowland of Mississippi on the advantages of concentrating both state and national archives in central repositories. Rowland declared that "the State owes a duty to . . . make public records accessible." The "great body of public records" in the United States, "especially at the National Capital," are "of little use to the historian because of the chaotic conditions" and the lack of a systematic plan for the care of records in scores of widely separated buildings. Facilities for the use of the archives were lacking, Rowland stated, "because of the failure to concentrate the nation's archives in a suitable building, planned . . . for an archive repository."[11]

Gaillard Hunt, chief of the Manuscript Division of the Library of Congress, and just returned from the International Congress of Archivists and Librarians at the Hague, followed Rowland. He dwelt upon the need of a "proper national archives building in Washington" and gave a rapid survey of the best points in the archives repositories of Europe. Although he fully agreed with Rowland on the need for concentration, he cautioned archivists that government papers "are put in archive houses primarily for government administrative purposes," and the needs of the scholar must be subordinated to the needs of the government itself. In passing, he referred to the Public Record Office in London, the *Archives nationales* in Paris, the Royal Archives at The Hague, the new building being built in Berlin to hold the central Prussian archives, the new building at Dresden for the Kingdom of Saxony, and the excellent condition of the archives in Italy at Florence, Venice, and

Rome. He reserved his greatest praise for the Vienna Imperial Archives, completed eight years earlier. He termed it the "most elaborate new archive building in the world," with well-arranged stacks and safes for the archives, and "highly artistic" entrance and offices; a building of which the "Austro-Hungarian Government is reasonably proud."[12]

Hunt drew five lessons from his observations abroad: (1) all the foregoing governments made special provisions for the collection and preservation of their archives, whereas the United States government did not; (2) every central archival depository had a research room for those using the archives, whereas in Washington there was none; (3) each government established rules for the use of archives created before an established date—for example, records in London that were dated before 1837 could be examined, in Paris those before 1848, in Dresden those before 1832, and in Vienna those before 1847—however, in America there was no clearly defined policy on access; (4) most foreign archives had reasonably adequate inventories of holdings; and (5) every foreign archives was in the charge of trained archivists, which was not the case in America. Then Hunt told the archivists' conference why the movement for a national archives must come from outside the government:

Each department . . . is loath to have any of its functions taken away from it, even when it does not perform in the best way. It would rather have these archives under its own administration, care, and authority than to have them taken away from it. All of the departments are crowded; all anxious for new buildings that will relieve some of the congestion of the old buildings. So any great movement for an archive house in Washington must come from the outside—from you gentlemen here—rather than from the city of Washington.[13]

In concluding the Conference of Archivists, Jameson noted that in the current session of Congress he hoped for nothing. "It is a slow matter to get anything done in the large manner we wish," he noted dolefully, "but the end will be accomplished sometime."[14]

Pursuing the usual course of associations, the AHA once again adopted a resolution. It consisted of a single paragraph petitioning the Congress to erect in the city of Washington a "national archive depository, where the records of the Government may be concentrated, properly cared for, and preserved."[15]

"NEVER, NEVER SAY HALL OF RECORDS"

Early in 1911, Jameson wrote his two committee colleagues, Professor McMaster and Admiral Mahan, identical letters reminding them of the duty they had assumed in December 1908, to promote the objectives of the AHA council resolution "in favor of the erection of a National

Archive Building." He had not called upon them much, as "the time seemed not then ripe for formal action, or for anything more than occasional consultations and conferences with official persons here in Washington."[16]

Now, he informed them, the time for serious action had arrived, because at its recent meeting a resolution had been formally adopted by the association as a whole. Jameson therefore proposed to request Senator Lodge to present the AHA resolution, together with a more detailed memorial from the committee, in the upper house, and to get a representative to present it in the lower house of Congress. "Of course no action will be taken in the present Session," he admitted, "but the campaign of education must be started . . . so I wish to have the matter presented in both Houses this month."[17]

Within ten days both McMaster and Mahan advised Jameson of their approval of the memorial he had drafted and the procedure proposed.[18] In acknowledging Mahan's signature of the memorial, Jameson cautioned him:

This is of course but the first step. It will have to be reintroduced next December, and followed up the rest of my natural life or until the building is agreed upon.[19]

Sen. Henry Cabot Lodge was Jameson's pipeline to the Senate. On February 23, 1911, he obligingly presented the resolution and the memorial in the Senate. Concurrently, Rep. George P. Lawrence, also of Massachusetts, presented the documents in the House. The longer, explanatory memorial, signed by Jameson, Mahan, and McMaster, delineated six points supporting the AHA resolution:

1. that government papers were scattered in a hundred different depositories;
2. that access was difficult as the papers were crowded together and "stowed away in places where the papers are deteriorating" from dampness and heat;
3. that overcrowding in department buildings caused large masses of archives to be stored in unsuitable buildings at large rents;
4. that papers "declared to be useless" and subsequently destroyed might have high value for present and future historians, even though they may be without administrative value;
5. that valuable records already destroyed by fire, at various times, entail for the government the loss of millions of dollars in claims; and
6. that the remedy for these conditions, as in other countries, is the erection of a suitable building, where government records can be filed in an orderly and systematic way, in safety, with guides for convenient use, a treasure to both the administrator and historian and "a national archive commensurate with the greatness of the country and the importance of its history."[20]

In a supporting action, the *Nation,* an influential national magazine, ran an editorial on "Our National Archives." Using the Geological Survey fire as a departure point, the editorial noted that it was "now fully twenty years since Congress was first asked to build a storehouse for the national archives" and that "some years ago a site was purchased; but there the matter was dropped." The *Nation* hazarded a guess that government agencies were "more concerned to get new buildings . . . than to relieve . . . congestion in the old buildings. Their first interest is in getting good offices for men rather than good housing for records. Moreover there is a feeling that a central depository might diminish the functions of the departments."[21]

Displaying a technical knowledge which could have come only from an expert source, such as Leland or Jameson, the magazine contended that "the erection of more department buildings will not solve the problem of caring for the archives," because "the architectural problems in designing a building for archives and a building for offices are quite different." For archives, the editorial said, "there must be tier upon tier of stacks," with lower ceiling heights, "and great areas of space must be left unoccupied . . . for future expansion."[22]

In discussing the records situation in the several departments and in the Congress, the *Nation* bore down hard on the lack of accessibility to the records, especially at the War Department, which permitted

. . . no one to examine its records. They are kept in greater secrecy than surrounds the archives of any European country, the reason assigned for this policy being that there is no space in the War Department where investigators might work. It may be remarked, however, that there is no space provided for investigators in any government office in Washington, except the Library of Congress.[23]

The shameful conditions of archives in America were contrasted with their conditions in Europe, and the magazine observed that "all American scholars who visit European archives bring back one story—that ours is the only great government which has made no provision for the care and preservation of its records." The *Nation* concluded with the joyous news that the "American Historical Association, numbering three thousand members, has . . . appointed a committee . . . to urge upon the authorities in Washington the need of preserving the archives, and, at the recently held meeting at Indianapolis, had adopted a resolution stating the matter succinctly."[24]

Another publicity channel utilized by Jameson and Leland was the managing editor of the New York *Evening Post,* Edward G. Lowry, with whom they were on friendly terms. Several days before the appearance of the *Nation* editorial, the *Evening Post* published a similar long editorial on the condition of the government's archives. Two months later Lowry, realizing the value of using the Albany State House fire as a text for further publicizing the archives movement, visited Jameson to obtain additional ammunition. In informing Leland of Lowry's visit, Jameson voiced his concern about the difficulty of exorcising the old terminology and the older concepts of a records repository and admonished him that in his dealings with journalists and others he should "never, never say Hall of Records."[25]

RECRUITING POINDEXTER AND SHEPPARD

Always on the lookout for congressional adherents to the cause, Jameson in 1911 recruited one of his staunchest allies who, for a dozen years, led the fight in the national legislature for a national archives building. The man was Miles Poindexter. Though born in Tennessee, on April 22, 1868, he received his education mainly in Virginia, graduating in law at Washington and Lee University in June 1891. A few months after acquiring his diploma, young Poindexter began the practice of law in Walla Walla, Washington. In 1897, he moved to Spokane, where he served successively as assistant prosecuting attorney for Spokane County, from 1898 to 1904, and judge of the superior court from 1904 to 1908. A member of the Republican party, he was elected in 1908 as a representative to the Sixty-first Congress. In the election of 1910, he was advanced to the U.S. Senate, where he eventually served two terms.[26]

Jameson became acquainted with Poindexter during his brief service in the House through the fortuitous circumstance that the congressman was a neighbor and friend, in Spokane, of Frederic Elmendorf, Jameson's nephew.[27] Soon after his arrival in the Senate, Poindexter was assigned to the Senate Committee on Public Buildings and Grounds. Sensing an opportunity for personal influence on this strategically important committee, Jameson went to work on the senator from Washington.

Evidently Jameson relished the job of recruiting Poindexter, remarking to Leland that "I have been putting it up to him that he ought to immortalize himself by becoming the father of the National Archive Building." Jameson said he was "feeding him with information on the subject in chunks as large as he can masticate at a time. He rather takes to the idea."[28] Poindexter's conversion was complete and wholehearted. Years of subsequent failure would not shake his confidence in ultimate victory. He became Jameson's most zealous co-worker and legislative ally.

In the House, Jameson had also acquired a powerful friend for the archives movement in the person of Rep. Morris Sheppard of Texas, who could always be counted on, both as congressman and later as senator. Sheppard was born in Morris County, Texas, on May 28, 1875. He graduated from the University of Texas at Austin in 1895, and studied law both there and at Yale University, where he received his law degree in 1898. He practiced law in Texarkana, Texas. His long congressional career began in 1902, when, on the death of his father, Rep. John L. Sheppard, he was elected to fill the vacancy. He served in the House until 1913, when he was elected to the Senate, where he was destined to serve until his death on April 9, 1941.[29]

By the summer of 1911, Poindexter and Sheppard both believed that the time had come for action. They asked Jameson to draft appropriate bills for introduction. Jameson's correspondence with interested members of Congress, with the Office of the Supervising Architect, and with all those that he thought might abet the movement was extensive then as later. He sought for pressure to be exerted on Congress from many directions. As Elizabeth Donnan and Leo Stock state in the introduction to their selection of his correspondence, "Jameson proved to be not only a tireless but also an ingenious lobbyist."[30]

On June 12, 1911, Jameson submitted to his congressional sponsors drafts of a bill "for an archive building." He submitted a shorter and a longer draft. The shorter assumed that the government already had a site for the building, the controversial square 143. The reason for the longer draft, he explained, was to provide a plan for choosing a new site, "acceptable to the chief contributing departments," if the committee felt that "by reason of the provision of the public buildings act of June 25, 1910, assigning the lot to the Geological Survey," square 143 was "no longer available for an archive building."[31]

Jameson had cleared the short form of the bill through the law officer of the supervising architect and, later, the acting supervising architect, James A. Wetmore, who had duly amended it. Jameson therefore told both Poindexter and Sheppard that the shorter form should be adopted unless they or their respective committees thought it would be "better to begin the process over again for the archive building" in view of the "movement on behalf of the Geological Survey."[32]

Jameson was especially concerned about the site problem because of the square 143 problem. He consulted with Elihu Root, then a senator from New York. Root told him that, although he personally favored the archives project, he wanted to leave no doubt in Jameson's mind that the square 143 matter had left some very ruffled feelings in Congress. In sending him a letter of introduction to Hamilton Fish, he told Jameson that "quite a number of years ago the government bought and paid for a square for the purpose, and there the matter stopped. Nobody seemed to take interest enough in the subject to have the building put up after the land was bought." Now that the land had been assigned for the Geological Survey building, Root observed, "There appeared to be a good deal of feeling about this old hall of records transaction and I am afraid it would prove a serious obstacle to a new movement." Nevertheless, the senator was of the opinion that "such a movement . . . certainly ought to be made."[33]

Jameson, thanking Root for his counsel, was optimistic in the opinion that progress was possible, stating that he thought there was "a good hope of something being done by the present House of Representatives."[34]

In the meantime, on the motion of Rep. Burton L. French of Idaho,[35] the House Committee on Public Buildings and Grounds invited Jameson to address it "on this important subject of the preservation of historical records."[36] Jameson promptly accepted the invitation.[37] In the hearing before the committee on May 12, Jameson gave an introductory statement about himself and his work. He said he would have preferred to have Leland there but he was in Paris. He then described the confusion created in the records by the changes of bureaus and consolidations and alterations of systems; the losses from fires since 1800; and Leland's description of the thousands of volumes stored in places so damp "the moisture drips from the roof . . . until the bindings become moldy and the leaves stick together," while other records are open to plunder by passersby. In many cases "Mr. Leland had to have a searchlight . . . going about in the archives," Jameson declared. He also deplored the indiscriminate destruction of so-called useless papers, stating that "two voices as to uselessness" should be heard, that of "someone who had regard for historical interests, as the head of a national archives system . . . would," as well as that of the agency administrator. Several representatives questioned Jameson at length about experience in other countries, desirable site locations, and building capacity needed. Rep. Richard W. Austin of Tennessee asked him whether he knew anything about the use for archives storage of the old building of the Bureau of Engraving and Printing. Jameson replied he had never heard of that idea and knew nothing about the building. Upon conclusion of the hearing he left with the committee copies of the AHA memorial signed by himself, Mahan, and McMaster, and the paper of Gaillard Hunt on "European Archive Buildings," which Hunt had read at the recent annual meeting of the AHA.[38]

Jameson was pleased with his performance at the House hearing. On the same day he wrote Leland,

Since beginning this letter I have held the House Committee on Public Buildings and Grounds spellbound for an hour with my eloquence on the archive situation. The eloquence consisted mostly of the facts which you conveyed to me orally and in writing. I gave due credit to the gifted author at these points. The Committee bore the whole with exemplary fortitude, and it is not impossible that before we die an archive building may be erected in Washington.[39]

He also reported on a talk with George P. Wetmore, the senator from Rhode Island, who declared himself favorable to the project. However, Jameson cautioned that he had found that "three other buildings have the right of way," but, he thought, "the Albany matter" may put the national archives "fourth in the bread line."[40] Several days later he told

Leland that no public buildings bill would be introduced until December or January.[41]

The day after the hearing, in a more subdued tone, he commented to Gaillard Hunt "that the House Committee seemed interested in the general subject. The Albany matter has waked people up temporarily." He also asked Hunt for "any illustrations there may be in Washington of the exteriors and of the interior plans of the best archive buildings in Europe."[42] In reply, Hunt gave Jameson advice on the archives at The Hague, at London, at Vienna, and at Magdeburg, but he considered the archives for the Kingdom of Saxony at Dresden "the most intelligent effort at construction for archival purposes" due to the "co-operation between the State Archivist, Dr. Posse, and the State Architect, under the Department of Finance." Both of them, he thought, would be willing to "furnish an American architect with the fullest information." Hunt strongly advised that when Congress "makes provision for our building," it should provide for an archivist on the building commission, as "his science is a peculiar one and . . . there is no American architect who has had any experience in constructing archives." Furthermore, Hunt stated, "the American architect who should undertake the planning should familiarize himself with the archives buildings of Europe."[43]

Several days later, Jameson informed the American ambassador in Germany, David Jayne Hill, who was himself a scholar and former university president, that

What with the desire of the new House of Representatives to amend matters, and with the deep impression which has been made by the dreadful destruction of historical material in the state capitol at Albany, the Congressional mind seems to be taking . . . a strong interest in . . . a . . . National Archive Building.[44]

Mindful of Hunt's advice, Jameson told Ambassador Hill that several members of the House and Senate committees "expressed a desire to know more concerning the best European designs of archive buildings," and therefore he requested the envoy to obtain and send him "plans of new archive buildings in Berlin and Dresden." He assured Hill that the committees on Public Buildings and Grounds would be highly appreciative of the information.[45]

Other measures Jameson took at this time were to ask Charles Moore, a scholar and eminent city planner, to come from Detroit to Washington "within a month" to advise on the procedure of securing a national archives building.[46] Jameson also had an interview with Rep. James Campbell Cantrill of Kentucky, chairman of a subcommittee of the Committee on Public Buildings and Grounds.[47] And he endeavored to enlist the aid of Comptroller of the Currency Lawrence O. Murray, and through him the secretary of the Treasury and the president himself, with a view to persuading them to exert pressure on the two congressional committees on Public Buildings and Grounds. Both Cantrill and Murray promised support, and Moore counseled him on procedure.[48]

Indicative of his frame of mind at this juncture, Jameson had observed to Moore that "it is not sensible to attempt to make the National Archive Building a handsome and expensive architectural monument, worthy of a place on the south side of Pennsylvania Avenue," though, of course, in the secret recesses of his heart he wished it could be so. Moore agreed that it need not be ornamental and recalled a remark once made to him by one of the most eminent of American architects, Charles Follen McKim, designer of the Columbia University Library and partner of the celebrated Stanford White, who said "it was the one building he would like to build to see what he could do with brick and mortar and plain surfaces."[49]

As to procedure, Moore said that "the best way to go about the matter would be to get some member of the House Committee on Public Buildings and Grounds interested in the subject; have a bill prepared and get him to introduce it and make it his hobby for the time being." This is precisely what Jameson had already proceeded to do. Moore promised to aid him as much as he could, and he kept that promise. "Any way," he said, "the Senate would be easy."[50] Although plenty of tribulations developed in the Senate too, on the whole, time proved Moore to be right.

In any case, Jameson thought the national archives building should "fit in with the general plans of the Park Commission"; and as for "the movement in its favor," he observed, this "ought to be in some way articulated with the efforts of those who are trying gradually to execute that Commission's plans for the city."[51]

At the end of May, Jameson again had an opportunity to meet with the House Committee on Public Buildings and Grounds. The committee held hearings on the preservation of government records from fire, on what to do to protect existing government buildings, and on how to plan future structures for greater safety. This investigation, too, was sparked by the fire in Albany. One of the principal witnesses, W. H. Merrill, president of the National Board of Fire Underwriters of Chicago, testified that the government owned more than $300 million worth of buildings and each year was spending more than $20 million for new structures. He placed his principal emphasis on adequate inspection. In view of the loss of $250 million and thousands of lives each year by fire in America, he urged that the government provide an example in the care of its properties that all property owners in the country would follow.[52]

The other principal witness, George W. Babb, president of the National Board of Fire Underwriters of New York City, placed his emphasis on building structure, testifying that "the principal defect in any building is the floor opening." He recommended solid fire-resistive floors and fire-resistive windows and walls; and, furthermore, he recommended that all stairways and elevators should be contained entirely in fire-resistive towers, with all openings from them guarded by fire doors.[53]

When these hearings had begun, earlier in May, Jameson had written Leland that the committee was "poking around the public buildings to see about dangers from fire," and, he asserted, "I have been trying with indifferent success to sic them on the trail of the archives."[54] But he certainly had success with the nationally circulated *Scientific American,* which, early in June, ran an editorial on the "National Archives in Danger." The magazine echoed a recent issue of the *New York Times,* which called attention to the storage on wooden shelves of documents such as the Declaration of Independence, the U.S. Constitution, the Articles of Confederation, and the bound volumes of the laws of the United States. The State Department had asked Congress for an appropriation of $10,000 for steel shelving, but the national legislature had done nothing about this "petty appropriation."[55]

The cumulative impact of Jameson's efforts became evident when, on June 19, 1911, Morris Sheppard introduced a bill, H.R. 11850, directing the secretary of the Treasury to prepare designs and estimates for a national archives building in the District of Columbia. This bill was based on a draft prepared by Jameson. It called for a fireproof national archives building of "modern library-stack type of architecture, containing not less than 1,500,000 cubic feet of space . . . for the orderly storage of records . . . accumulated in the departments and executive offices, and in the files of the Senate and the House" and "not needed for current use." The building was to be designed so as to be "capable of subsequent extension without impairing its architectural appearance to a capacity of 4,000,000 cubic feet." It was to be placed on a site large enough to accommodate extension to the ultimate size. Jameson calculated that for the initial structure, with a height of forty feet, a ground area of 40,000 square feet would be needed. For the ultimate 4 million–cubic foot building, a ground area of 100,000 to 120,000 square feet would be required, as well as space for approaches and lawns.[56]

Following the introduction of Sheppard's bill, there were various memorials, petitions, editorials, and news items backing the proposed archives project. Two of these are mentioned here.

On July 11, 1911, the scholarly senator from Mississippi, John Sharp Williams, presented a memorial in the Senate on which a hearing had been held the previous day before the House Committee on Public Buildings and Grounds. It was jointly signed by the directors of the departments of archives and history of the states of Mississippi and Alabama, Dunbar Rowland and Thomas M. Owen, respectively. It was a rather elaborate affair of four printed pages. Under four subheadings it dealt with the "Unsatisfactory Conditions" for the care and preservation of the federal archives; the deliberate "Destruction of Records," because of overcrowding in the executive departments; the "Remedy for

Existing Evils," namely, a central national repository; and the "Advantages of Concentration" of the national archives, under which half a dozen points were specified, including the orderly administration of public affairs and better facilities and access for scholars.[57]

A few months later, on December 1, 1911, the Executive Council of the American Historical Association met in New York City and approved a memorial to Congress, drafted by Jameson. It reminded Congress that "a committee acting for this body addressed a memorial to Congress upon this subject . . . presented in the Senate last February by Mr. Lodge, and in the House by Mr. George P. Lawrence." Among other points it was noted that the only place in Washington where manuscripts were cared for was the Library of Congress. A summary of records in the various departments and in the Senate and House was given, and access to the materials was requested. The memorial closed with these words:

In short, these scattered, unorganized, and ill protected archives contain a greater part of the materials for United States history than is to be found in all other places put together. Speaking in the name of all who work in American history, and of all who care for it, we . . . request decisive action in the present session of Congress.[58]

But though absorbed in its concern to spur Congress to action, the American Historical Association did not forget its appreciation of the congressman who introduced bill H.R. 11850. Professor C. H. Haskins presented the resolution at the annual meeting, on behalf of the Executive Council and the Public Archives Commission:

Resolved, That the American Historical Association has seen with satisfaction the introduction in the House of Representatives, by the Hon. Morris Sheppard, chairman of the Committee on Public Buildings and Grounds, of a bill (H.R. 11850) intended to take the preliminary steps to the establishment of a central depository for the national archives and urges upon Congress the passage of this . . . bill.[59]

The resolution concluded by instructing the secretary of the association, Waldo G. Leland, to send a copy of the resolution "to the President of the United States, the President of the Senate, the Speaker of the House of Representatives, and the chairman of the Committee on Public Buildings and Grounds of the Senate and House."[60]

PRESIDENT TAFT'S MESSAGE OF 1911

Jameson's struggle for a national archives building extended through the administrations of five presidents—Theodore Roosevelt, Taft, Wilson, Harding, and Coolidge. As he had a healthy respect for the power of the presidency in the advocacy of causes and policy, he made every practicable effort to obtain the support of each of them. Amidst his other activities during 1911, Jameson never lost sight of his tactical objective to get the chief executive himself to declare in favor of the archives project in his annual message to Congress.

Jameson explained to his fellow committee member, Professor McMaster, that in September and October 1910 he had endeavored to get Taft to insert a paragraph in his annual message "recommending the erection of such a building." Charles Hilles, the assistant secretary of the Treasury, to whom the president referred the matter for study, "was strongly interested." So Jameson had left with him a detailed written statement of the dangers "of the present want of system" and also a "history of the movement from 1879 to 1910." Hilles had advised Jameson that "it would contribute greatly to securing the President's consent" for a pronouncement on the archival problem if the AHA committee of three would have a formal interview with him on the subject. Accordingly, Jameson recommended to McMaster and Mahan that the three of them see the president at his summer place at Beverly, Massachusetts, in September or, if that was not mutually convenient, then in Washington in October.[61] McMaster, as usual, was all compliance. He was agreeable to calling on Taft at a time that was most convenient to Mahan and Jameson. He was ready to go to either Beverly or Washington.[62] Mahan was more difficult to move. Although he thought he could make it to Beverly in September, he preferred to visit the president in Washington in October.[63]

The time of the proposed meeting with Taft was resolved by Hilles, who, in mid-June, informed Jameson that the president was going on a western trip, but was expected to return to Washington in the second week of October, so he suggested that they get together after his return. Jameson, in acknowledging Hilles's letter, confirmed that he and his committee would plan on having the interview with President Taft in mid-October.[64]

Jameson told Hilles that he thought there was an excellent chance for the House Committee on Public Buildings and Grounds to report in favor of an archives measure in December or January due to the fact that, "under the influence of the Albany disaster" and of the committee's own subsequent "search for fire traps" in government buildings, it had developed a "considerable interest in the proposal" for a fire-safe archival repository. Jameson also told Hilles that he had enlisted Senator Poindexter and Representative Sheppard in the cause and had drafted an appropriate bill for their use. Jameson believed that all these factors made it even more urgent than before that the president adopt the archival repository as an "administrative measure" by urging the building in his next annual message.[65]

There was further correspondence between Jameson and Hilles later in the summer. Taft, it seems, had delayed his return to Washington until the first of November, and then there was a second postponement.[66] In reporting to McMaster and Mahan on these discouraging developments, Jameson wrote,

When the President prolonged his absence . . . to November 15, it appeared . . . that this made it impossible to think of an interview with him . . . with any notion of its having any useful effect upon the preparation of his annual message. Going over to the White House to inquire, I found that this was distinctly the case. . . . So I prepared a letter and left it, with some documents . . . to be forwarded to the President, which has been done.[67]

President Taft, in a long annual message to Congress, which was issued in four parts over the period of December 5 to 21, 1911, addressed himself to antitrust matters, to foreign relations, to the reports of the U.S. Tariff Board, and to the business of the Treasury Department and other executive departments and agencies; nowhere did he mention public buildings, and certainly not the need for a national archives.[68]

4

The Educational Campaign

GRASS-ROOTS SUPPORT

With the opening of the new year, 1912, Jameson, now at the national capital for six years, at last felt ready to put all his might into the campaign for a national archives. He concentrated on getting grass-roots support from the patriotic societies, particularly from the Daughters of the American Revolution (DAR), the historical societies, and the news media, mainly newspapers of national note.

His first act was to address a circular letter to state regents and officers of the DAR. He reminded them of the address he had delivered at the preceding year's Continental Congress of the DAR on the topic of historical work appropriate for their organization; in this address he had especially emphasized the need for a proper national archives building in Washington and the effective aid which the DAR could render in securing it.[1] "A bill looking toward the erection of such a structure," he said, "has been introduced in the House of Representatives by the Chairman of the Committee on Public Buildings and Grounds, and is now before that Committee for consideration." Although all members of the committee, he thought, favored the bill, the measure nevertheless would encounter opposition "based on the desire for an economical session." Then he appealed to each individual to write to her members of Congress in behalf of the measure, for "the proper time has now arrived."[2]

The response was quite heartening and probably made Jameson feel more optimistic than was warranted. For example, the New York state regent, Mrs. William Cummings Story, wrote, "I am heartily in favor of a National Archive Building" and would be "happy to do what I can."[3] The Virginia state regent, Mrs. Samuel W. Jamison, stated that she was writing to Carter Glass, her congressional representative, and to friends in Lynchburg.[4] The state regent of Maine, Mrs. Edwin A. Richardson, expressed herself as "delighted to help," and said that in addition to writing to her representative she would write to the others on Jameson's list to influence passage of the bill, "as we Daughters are truly patriotic and believe in the practice as well as the preaching of patriotism."[5] Mrs. Chalmers Meek Williamson, the state regent of Mississippi, recalled with pleasure Jameson's "splendid address before the Continental Congress of the DAR" and pledged the "cooperation of the Mississippi Daughters" in writing to members of Congress and in passing appropriate resolutions at the annual state conference in February. She noted that "Mississippi has been most active in the past—through our Dunbar Rowland—in this special work of the American Historical Association, and will continue to urge that Congress provide a National Archives Building."[6]

The response from the officers of local chapters was similarly enthusiastic. Mrs. W. S. Moore, the corresponding secretary of the Washington Heights, New York, chapter, for example, reported that at a recent chapter meeting at Washington's headquarters, "your letter . . . was read and received the approval of the Chapter," and it was voted that a letter be sent to Rep. John J. Fitzgerald, "urging him to endorse and support the bill."[7] Other chapters around the nation similarly supported Jameson.

To the president general of the DAR, Mrs. Matthew T. Scott, Jameson sent a full package of material which included a copy of Morris Sheppard's bill; a copy of the letter he had sent to all the chapters of the DAR; and articles from the New York *Evening Post* and the *Review of Reviews*. He also noted that he had asked the clerk of the House Committee on Public Buildings and Grounds to send her "a copy of the Hearings before that committee last May in which, besides the evils . . . the nature of the remedy is set forth." He frankly told Mrs. Scott that he did not expect action at this session as the majority caucus had voted against a general public buildings bill, but he expected better results from the next session of Congress, "provided sufficient efforts are put forth to influence public opinion and the minds of Congressmen." In this matter, Jameson believed, "the efforts of the Daughters of the American Revolution can be very powerful." He thought the effect could be heightened if the DAR went on record as a corporate body.[8]

Nearly two months later he followed up by requesting an interview with Mrs. Albert B. Cumming, who chaired the Committee on Legislation of the National Society of the DAR, to discuss the legislation relating to a national archives building. He reminded Mrs. Cumming that many of the Daughters had gone on record as individuals, but the DAR Committee on Legislation had not yet taken any official action. He offered his help in furnishing information to lay before the forthcoming Continental Congress.[9] Through the years the DAR did manifest its corporate will to the Congress.

Throughout the year 1912, Jameson kept up a steady barrage of correspondence with individuals and organizations to promote the archival idea. Among these he did not lose sight of the large Catholic constituency. He wrote to Prof. Charles H. McCarthy of the Catholic University of America, inquiring as to what progress he had made with the Knights of Columbus "in respect to a National Archive Building." He hoped the professor would let him know "how they seem to be disposed."[10] At the fifteenth annual meeting of the National Association of State Libraries (NASL), held in Ottawa, June 27 to July 2, the national archives cause was duly supported. The state librarians of Massachusetts and Connecticut reported to Senator Wetmore, chairman of the Senate Committee on the Library, that the NASL had "heard of the efforts . . . to establish a Hall of Archives for the preservation of the records . . . of the United States Government at Washington," and that it was "well known that most of the governments of the Civilized World are now engaged in providing adequate fire-proof buildings for the protection of . . . records" and are also providing "skilled experts to care for and properly classify and arrange" them. The NASL had therefore resolved "that this association heartily endorses the suggestion of providing a Hall of Records for the historical papers of the Government." It was further resolved that a copy of the resolution should be sent to the Senate and the House, with the request that action be taken at the "earliest possible moment" in order that the papers may be protected from catastrophes such as had recently taken place in Albany.[11]

To encourage newspaper and magazine publicity, Jameson told the editor of the *Washington Times* that if the House Committee on Public Buildings and Grounds proposed to renew efforts for a public buildings bill in the next session, "let it push for a National Archive Building, rather than a lot of little post-offices in local districts." With some wry satisfaction he observed that

the one good feature of the present situation is that no real steps toward improvement . . . having been made, we have carte blanche to erect here in Washington the finest National Archive Building in the world. We ought to have it. We ought to draw upon all the experiences of European countries . . . and to add all the improvements that American ingenuity, long exercised on . . . public libraries, can devise.[12]

He went on to observe that Great Britain was then "overhauling her whole archive system," because in the initial planning of the Public Record Office "she did not look forward into the future." America need not "make the same mistake."[13]

To J. Stewart Bryan, editor of the Richmond, Virginia, *News-Leader,* Jameson wrote that he had been laboring for two or three years with the House Committee on Public Buildings and Grounds on behalf of an archives repository. In the coming session of Congress, he thought, if some pressure from public opinion could be brought to bear, the committee would "take a decisive step" in the advancement of the project. Bryan replied that he was "greatly interested in the protection of our national archives" and would gladly assist the cause.[14]

The *Nation,* in the late fall of 1912, publicized Waldo G. Leland's views. Leland estimated that "5,000,000 cubic feet of space are already in use for records in the District of Columbia, with an annual growth of 60,000 cubic feet." Yet the bill then before the Senate called for a building of only 1.5 million cubic feet, and he posed a rhetorical question: "Where else than in Washington are abandoned car-barns deemed proper housing for records not only indispensable to the historian, but often vitally necessary to the proper conduct of official business?" Turning to the important question of the control of the records, once they are properly housed, Leland emphatically urged that they then come into the legal custody of the archivist. Any other course, he thought, would "involve such a tangle as to be unthinkable." But he expected that determined efforts would be made "to reserve to the various departments complete jurisdiction of their archives," a system which, he said, "failed lamentably in England." Central control of the records was essential to efficiency and to the authentication of documents. Leland favored legal control vested in an Archives Commission, with an archivist at the head of the actual work. Such an archivist, he thought, would naturally keep in closest touch with the Library of Congress, "which must remain the proper place for the preservation of private and historical manuscripts, and also with the proposed Commission on National Historical Publications to control the printing of such archives as warrant publication."[15] Here one sees the germination of ideas incorporated in the National Archives Act of 1934.

Among the historical societies, that of Wisconsin was the first to extend support. Jointly with the Department of History of the University of Wisconsin, the society sent a petition to Congress, urging that steps be taken "to erect, in the city of Washington, a national archive depository where the records of the government may be concentrated, properly cared for, and preserved."[16] Among the nine signatories were Carl Russell Fish, Frederic L. Paxson, and Reuben G. Thwaites.

In mid-November Jameson distributed circulars to historical societies throughout the United States calling for aid in inducing Congress, during the short winter session, to legislate for a national archive building. Throughout the remainder of the year he received encouraging promises of support. Clarence W. Alvord, then editor of the collections of the Illinois State Historical Library, stated that he had written the governor, would ask the trustees of the historical library to pass and forward a resolution to Congress, would ask the University of Illinois to put itself on record, and would send a resolution to members of the Executive Committee of the Mississippi Valley Historical Association.[17]

Herman V. Ames of Pennsylvania was somewhat difficult. He replied to Jameson that "I am in doubt . . . which one of several societies to which I belong you have in mind when you use the phrase 'your society.' " He wanted to know if Jameson referred to the Pennsylvania History Club or to the Pennsylvania Federation of Historical Societies, for both of which he was the president that year, or to the Historical Society of Pennsylvania of which he was a member. He could attend to the first two, but Jameson would have to address the executive council of the latter. Jameson promptly answered that he was interested in all of them and asked Ames to contact the executive council as he was not acquainted with its members. Three weeks later Ames informed Jameson that he had taken up the matter with Professor McMaster, who presented the topic to the council, but, Ames said, as "nothing had been prepared in the way of a resolution, they postponed action."[18] One can appreciate Jameson's infinite patience, confronted with such lack of resourcefulness.

R. D. W. Connor, secretary of the North Carolina Historical Commission, was not inclined to be led by the hand. Acknowledging receipt of Jameson's letter, he assured him that he would "have a suitable memorial adopted by our State Library and Historical Society, which meets here December 3 and 4," and he would have "a similar memorial adopted by the State Historical Commission," which was to meet soon.[19] O. G. Libby of the Department of History of the University of North Dakota thanked Jameson for the "opportunity for being useful" in the cause and informed him that "every department of history in the state institutions" of North Dakota was interested in the proposed national archives.[20] William MacDonald of Brown University guaranteed the support of the Rhode Island Historical Society in this "great undertaking . . . in which," he said, "I have long been interested."[21] The director of the Alabama Department of Archives and History, Thomas M. Owen, responded that he would "do everything possible" and that he would write to all members of the Alabama congressional delegation. He told Jameson to "command me . . . in this behalf in any particular way."[22] Franklin L. Riley of the Mississippi Historical Society was equally enthusiastic and hastened to assure Jameson "that the Mississippi Historical Society will be glad to cooperate with you in this movement." He would have the officers and executive committee of the society sign an appropriate memorial, have each write a personal letter to the members of the House Committee on Public Buildings and Grounds, and would "try to enlist the editor of the *Memphis Commercial Appeal,* a personal friend, in this cause."[23]

Reuben G. Thwaites, superintendent of the State Historical Society of Wisconsin, although he already had been instrumental in having a petition sent to Congress in April, again responded to Jameson's call, telling him that "I certainly shall do all I possibly can in behalf of your project," that although it was not practicable to call a general meeting of the society as the members were scattered, he would see that members of the executive committee endorsed it, and that he would get in touch with the Wisconsin congressmen the first week in December. He also asked for copies of Leland's article, "The National Archives: A Programme," to assist him in his efforts. Several weeks later he happily announced to Jameson that he had personal letters from several Wisconsin congressmen, all in favor of the proposed national archives building.[24]

In contrast to the usual tenor of communications from the states, the secretary of the Historical Commission of South Carolina, A. S. Salley, Jr., responded by dolefully remarking that he could get little or no cooperation of the kind needed. Furthermore, he had an "immense amount of work piled on him by the State without an assistant of any kind, not even a stenographer." Nevertheless, he would "do his best ... in influencing" the South Carolina delegation in Congress. As he was in Columbia and the headquarters of the historical society was in Charleston, he could do very little in the way of personal contacts, and "when I write a letter I seldom get a result." He thought, however, that most of the South Carolina representatives and Sen. Benjamin R. Tillman would support the archives bill.[25]

Other substantial support was promised by way of resolutions, letters to legislators, and the like from historical societies across the nation.[26] Come what might, Jameson could well feel that democracy was on the march and that Congress must listen and, perhaps, act.

PUBLICITY AIDES

Notably aiding Jameson's campaign of 1912, and his later efforts, were the writings of two publicists, one of whom, Waldo G. Leland, is well known to American historians and archivists. The other, Rosa Pendleton Chiles, was a comparative unknown, of whom Jameson thought so highly that he insisted she have a seat of honor at the laying of the cornerstone of the National Archives Building on February 20, 1933.

Miss Chiles, a freelance magazine writer, became concerned about the lack of care given to the government's archives in Washington. She personally made a survey of conditions, poking through attics, basements, carriage houses, and the like, and compiled the draft of an article which she sent to Jameson for comment and advice. Jameson was deeply impressed. In November of 1911, he wrote to the celebrated S. S. McClure, publisher of *McClure's Magazine,* and to Albert Shaw, editor of the *Review of Reviews,* requesting that they consider publication of the article.[27]

Jameson told McClure that he had had some talks with Miss Chiles during the past month when she was getting the material and drafting the article. She "has got together a great quantity of interesting facts, solid as far as my knowledge extends, and going beyond my knowledge to the extent of making a showing that really surprised even me, though I thought that I knew the worst. It is a very strong and convincing presentation."[28]

Jameson assured Shaw that he did not ask its publication on account of Miss Chiles, but "on account of the cause." He hoped for congressional action at the next session, "but the movement," he asserted, "needs every help it can get." He reiterated that "Miss Chiles has gathered her facts with a great deal of industry and care, and her statements can be regarded as perfectly solid and not in the least exaggerated." Then he appealed to Shaw's scholarly instincts, hoping he could print it in the January or February issue, as "it will be splendid ammunition for a mighty good cause, and one which surely must appeal to a distinguished former member of the historical department" at the Johns Hopkins University.[29] Shortly after the turn of the year, Shaw informed Jameson that Miss Chiles's article would be used in the February 1912 number of the *Review.* Jameson happily ordered "fifty separate prints of the article."[30]

Shaw was as good as his word, and by the end of January the Chiles article had appeared, somewhat abridged, and Jameson had sent copies to key members of Congress.[31] Rep. Burton L. French of Idaho suggested to Jameson that he obtain the consent of the publisher to have the full text incorporated in forthcoming hearings of the House Committee on Public Buildings and Grounds.[32] Shaw agreed, and within two weeks the full text of the article was printed in the appendix to the hearings of February 14.[33]

Chiles's opening paragraph is a classic statement of the parameters of the government's responsibility concerning archives:

One of the chief functions of any government is to preserve its archives; it is in the business of government for that purpose. Handling the people's affairs, it can only fully protect their interests and its own integrity by carefully guarding its records.[34]

Miss Chiles's article vividly described the intolerable conditions in the filing and care of records, the confusion caused by department reorganizations, bureau transfers, and the countless variations of filing and indexing of the "enormous volume of records." Papers were temporarily transferred from one office to another and never returned. Most of the papers were kept "in destructible receptacles . . . in wooden cases or on open wooden shelves." Often these shelves were twelve feet high and so close together "that there is barely room to walk between them."[35]

As better examples of care, she discussed the records in the State Department, which, she conceded, had an "excellent filing system," and the records in the War Department which were "the best cared for and arranged files in the Government." She was more critical of the Treasury Department, "where every voucher for every cent disbursed is under its custody . . . millions of them . . . yet these vouchers are stored in nonfireproof buildings, on wooden shelves . . . in places so dark that an electric lantern has to be used to find them . . . some in damp cellars . . . some in attics undergoing dry combustion." Then she described the Treasury fires of 1801, 1814, and 1833, and recounted the handling of Indian treaties, land patents, and Geological Survey records. But she absolved government officials, saying,

Executive officers should not be blamed . . . as a rule it is their faithfulness and caution that afford the only protection given to the Government papers. . . . But even the most faithful public servant is limited by the means placed in his hands, and, as a rule, it has been only by careful saving out of lump-sum appropriations that the heads of departments and bureaus have been able to afford even the inadequate protection . . . now given to the Government records.[36]

In calling for "the erection of a national archives building for . . . papers . . . out of current use," the author referred to the efforts of the AHA, particularly its "Jameson Committee." She quoted the memorial to Congress and the president in February 1911, as well as the Sheppard bill, and declared that now "that the President, heads of departments, and historians have been busy over the matter" for years, "it is time for the country to become more fully aroused than it has been." In conclusion, she asked, "What will Congress do?" And she wondered if a couple of million dollars for an archives building, diverted from the $126 million for the navy, voted in the last session of the Sixty-first Congress, "would not have been spent for better purpose?"[37]

Throughout his long and fruitful life, Waldo G. Leland was an eminent contributor to American archival and historical literature. He spent the years 1907 to 1914 and 1922 to 1927 in Paris, researching and compiling his *Guide to the Materials for American History in the Libraries and Archives of Paris.* Yet during his pre–World War I years abroad, he also functioned as secretary of the American Historical Association and somehow managed to collaborate with his mentor, Jameson, in promoting the movement for the creation of a national archives of the United States.

At Jameson's request, Leland produced in 1912 some of the most important promotional literature to advance the archival cause. Perhaps the most significant and popular of Leland's contributions was the article he compiled for the *American Historical Review* entitled, "The National Archives: A Programme." At Senator Poindexter's request, it was later reprinted as a Senate document.[38] Jameson distributed this document far and wide to senators, representatives, historical societies, government officials, and to whoever requested it. In sending a copy to Rep. Oscar Callaway of Texas, Jameson summarized Leland's seminal article in the following five points: (1) that the federal archives were of great value "not only as the most important source of national history, but also as protection of the government against improper claims in all matters of international controversy"; (2) that great masses of records were stored "where they run great danger . . . by fire, damp, dirt, vandalism, and other accidents"; (3) that this state of affairs was "constantly growing worse," and had been repeatedly called to public attention "by high officials of the government"; (4) that the only adequate remedy was the erection of a "suitable structure for the housing of archives, and providing proper administrative machinery for their control"; and (5) "that failure to make such provision is wholly out of accord with the dignity of the government, and entirely contrary to the practice of all other civilized nations."[39]

Clearly, without these two able publicists, Rosa P. Chiles and Waldo G. Leland, Jameson would have been severely handicapped in his great effort of 1912.

THE POINDEXTER AND LODGE BILLS

On February 8, 1912, Senator Poindexter introduced the first of his many measures for a national archives building. It was S. 5179, a bill that directed the secretary of the Treasury to prepare designs and estimates for a national archives building. The bill essentially paralleled the Sheppard bill. The following characteristics were specified: modern, fireproof, library stack architecture; not less than 1.5 million cubic feet of space initially for "the orderly storage of records"; location in Washington on a plot of land large enough for a building ultimately "embracing 4,000,000 cubic feet"; the construction cost, including heating, ventilation, elevators, and approaches "not to exceed one million dollars." Before the designs were completed, the best modern archives in Europe were to be inspected. When the designs and estimates were approved by a commission consisting of the president of the Senate, the Speaker of the House, and the secretaries of the departments of Treasury, War, and the Interior, the secretary of the Treasury was then authorized to purchase or condemn for public use a site for the building. A sum of $5,000 was authorized to be expended for preparing preliminary designs and estimates "from the appropriation for the construction of said national archives building."[40] Concurrently with the introduction of S. 5179, Senator Poindexter presented "a statement of the proceedings

that have already taken place for the . . . erection of an archive building
. . . prepared by . . . the Carnegie Institution."[41]

The following day, F. W. Fitzpatrick, a consulting architect, compli-
mented Poindexter on his initiative, but shrewdly noted the difference
between the old hall of records proposal and the new concept, stating
that "we old time advocates had a vastly different conception of the
requirements than yours." He explained,

We advocated a *great warehouse* for all those overflow records, a handsome building but one without gew-gaws and frilly ornament, fitted solely for its very
practical purpose, a perfectly fireproof building . . . divided into the smallest
possible . . . compartments, so that fire originating in any one of them would
not only be confined there but could do but trifling damage in that one compart-
ment.[42]

Fitzpatrick thought that the senator "must contemplate a wonderfully
ornate monumental structure," and concluded with the advice that "if
so monumental and costly a building was desired why not divert the
Lincoln Memorial fund thereto?" He thought it would "make that monument of some practical value and certainly more fitting than the mean-
ingless mausoleum . . . they are now discussing."[43] This appears to have
been the first time, but not the last, that the suggestion of such a use
for the Lincoln Memorial obtruded.

Another interested observer of the new effort in the Senate was none
other than Lothrop Withington, author of Senator Lodge's bill of 1906.
As he happened to be in Washington, he called at Senator Poindexter's
office but did not find him in, so he wrote him the following:

I was much pleased on Friday in Washington to learn that you have just
introduced a Bill for preparing plans for a long much needed Record Office for
the United States. You call it National Archives, but the building is the thing,
not the name.[44]

Rather appositely, Withington was in the capital for the purpose of
asking Senator Lodge to reintroduce his old bill. Despite the prior introduction of the Poindexter bill, Withington did prevail upon his Massachusetts friend. The senator placed the bill in the hopper on February
14, but it never got beyond referral to the Senate Committee on the
Library.[45]

Jameson, in his turn, expressed gratification to Poindexter for introducing the national archives bill in the Senate and inquired whether he
thought it advisable to hold a hearing during the current session even
though the House would not act on it then, or whether it would be
better to "defer such hearing until the next session," as after election
day, November 5, "the House may be less rigidly devoted to economy."
In his reply, Poindexter handsomely acknowledged that the bill he

submitted "is identically as prepared by you." In answer to Jameson's questions, he thought that "favorable action by the Senate during this session is possible," but the House was not likely to pass the measure because of the House caucus decision not to have a public building bill, in line with the economy policy of the House leadership. Nevertheless, Poindexter was in favor of getting Senate action on the measure, both to keep the matter before the public and because favorable Senate action would be a precedent for the future. He further advised Jameson that he had arranged with the Senate Committee on Public Buildings and Grounds to give Jameson and others a hearing on March 1.[46]

Jameson spent the latter half of February preparing the program for the hearing and marshaling his forces. He wrote to Charles M. Andrews of Yale; to Admiral Mahan and Professor McMaster of his committee of three; to Herman V. Ames, chairman of the Public Archives Commission of the AHA; to Gaillard Hunt of the Library of Congress; and to Rosa Pendleton Chiles. Others asked to attend were Waldo G. Leland, Fred Dennett, commissioner of the General Land Office, and James L. Wilmeth, chief clerk of the Treasury Department.[47] Andrews, whom Jameson asked to come and shed light on the "Public Record Office and . . . the recent work of the Royal Commission," accepted the invitation and said he would dine with Jameson that Friday evening.[48]

Ames was embarrassed at the high value Jameson placed on his testimony. Jameson very much wanted him to be present because, he said, "one who has for ten years been chairman of our Public Archives Commission will be listened to with respect." He even offered to pay his fare from Carnegie Institution funds. Ames truthfully replied that although he knew "considerable about the situation in general," he did not have "any very thorough knowledge of the details of the equipment of the several state depositories." In fact, he was "inclined to think" that Jameson was informed about such matters "probably more than myself." Nevertheless, if Jameson felt he could not spare him, he would come. Upon further consideration, Jameson decided to excuse him.[49]

Whatever may have been *The Influence of Sea Power Upon History,* the title of Mahan's famous work, the admiral's personal influence on the work of Jameson's committee of three was hardly perceptible. He flatly told Jameson, "you must not expect me in Washington." He had decided that he "would not leave home . . . unless the occasion was of great necessity"; and although he recognized the importance of the bill, he thought that Jameson's presence was sufficient.[50]

By the end of February, Jameson had completed his arrangements for the hearing and informed both Poindexter and Sen. George Sutherland of Utah of the program. He would make a brief preliminary statement, giving the qualifications of the various persons invited to participate and then follow with the testimony of Wilmeth, Dennett, Chiles, Hunt, Leland, Andrews, and possibly the supervising architect of the Treasury.[51]

The Senate committee met as scheduled, with Senator Sutherland in the chair. After Jameson's introductory statement, Chief Clerk Wilmeth of the Treasury explained the difficulties with records in his department, stating that "the absolute need of an archives building" had been "keenly felt for a long time" and that "in eight years at the present rate the files would be doubled." Wilmeth, his testimony shows, was still thinking in terms of the old hall of records concept, where each department would take care of its own records. He thought 1 million cubic feet was hardly enough, but that the ultimate goal of 4 million cubic feet was closer to the requirements. Commissioner Dennett, the next witness, also confined himself to the practicalities of figures. He said that in the Land Office they had "60,000 running feet of filing space in use . . . about 20,000,000 individual files."[52]

Rosa Chiles related her chamber of horrors. The files are so crowded, she said, "as to be utterly inaccessible." She berated the filing system, as "nearly all the old papers are filed folded, so that they crumble" on being opened, and advocated the adoption of "a flat system . . . for the old and new files." In answer to Sen. Claude Swanson's question, she said that the worst conditions were "in the Land Office, the Treasury, the Post Office, and the outlying rented buildings." At the Treasury, under the roof, there was real "danger of spontaneous combustion. . . . The files are on the top floor," she stated, "and when I went through them I almost fainted." In the Winder Building, owned by the War Department, she found that "in all the rooms where the files are kept there is a network of electric wires not inclosed in metal." She also thought that the building "could not stand another pound of weight on the floors." At the Court of Claims Building the records were in an annex, the floors of which were so wet due to heavy rains that she had to walk on shutters floating on the water as she was examining records of the Panama Canal. But the principal evil in her judgment was the failure of the government to provide fire protection. The federal government, she said, "has no fire inspection and the city fire department has no authority to go into any Federal building to make any examination at all. They only go in by invitation."[53]

Gaillard Hunt compared American and European archival conditions. As "writing upon parchment and paper is an art about two thousand years old, and the records in America only begin from about 1609 . . . we have an excuse for our backwardness," he asserted. Nevertheless, Hunt declared, "We are the only country in the world that does not make some sort of provision for its archives." Although conditions in Europe varied, all in all they were better than in the United States. As for the question of the location of an archives building, he stated that a central location was not regarded as vital in Europe. It was more important to have sufficient space for adequate additions to the building.[54]

Leland, after declaring that "the life of any business, and especially that of the public business, is in its records," emphasized the need to avoid crowding of records to ensure accessibility. He related how, at times, it took a clerk "several days or even a week to locate documents." Crowding also induced misfiling. "The clerk," he said, "hunts around . . . until he finds the documents he wants." But if conditions are difficult he seldom puts them back where he found them. He referred to Europe and Canada as affording examples of better, if not perfect, care of records. "In Canada," he said, "they have recently erected a building for the Dominion archives, which . . . provides a safe place for keeping records . . . they are also open to investigators." Leland favored a clause in the bill that would require the inspection of European archives before the architectural plans for an archives building were completed.[55]

As to the size of the proposed building, Leland explained that the modest request for one of 1.5 million cubic feet was based "upon an estimate of the amount of records . . . the departments would be willing to transfer . . . in the near future." In answer to a query from Senator Poindexter, he thought "that a building that would provide 5,000,000 cubic feet . . . would probably provide accommodations . . . for 10 or 25 years," provided further, that "there should be a [systematic] destruction of records."[56] At this point in Leland's testimony, Jameson interposed to observe that, by way of comparison, the Library of Congress contained a total of 10 million cubic feet, and Senator Wetmore added that the aggregate of all stacks was about 2 million cubic feet.[57]

Professor Andrews of Yale University addressed himself to his experience with the English Public Record Office. It was desirable, he said, "that no makeshift should be adopted." England had tried to adapt the attic of the new Houses of Parliament, built in 1834, to the needs of the Public Record Office. After several years of experience, it seemed that a new building was needed, one large enough to accommodate the records the departments offered. But "England made one very great mistake." It began with too small a building in 1851, and again built on a small scale a few years later, adding sections from time to time, including a large section in 1892 and 1893. "Anyone may see the effects of that piecemeal construction upon the Office," asserted Professor Andrews. "Everything is on a small scale . . . very inconvenient" and constantly calling for "unnecessary effort upon the part of those who work there."[58]

But Andrews had some good words, too. Although built on a small scale, the Public Record Office "made provision for a very wide range of work." There were separate offices devoted to different types of researchers, such as lawyers, government experts and officials, and the public, so that those who were using the records for legal, official, and historical or literary purposes were physically separated and did not come into contact with one another. He thought this concept should be incorporated in American plans. Andrews noted, however, that "this haphazard method of construction" forced the appointment of a Royal

Commission on Public Records to consider "the whole question of the organization of the record office . . . of space and of ventilation . . . suitable accommodations for students and other workers, and [the] larger question of future expansion." His conclusion was that the plans for an American national archives should provide not only for immediate needs, but also for orderly expansion on a site of sufficient size.[59]

Lothrop Withington was not on the program for the hearing, but, as Jameson remarked to a correspondent, he "requested permission to 'butt in' and did so with very good effect, infusing into the proceedings a little of that warmth of rhetoric and imagination in which historical students are so deficient."[60] Withington boldly stated that he did not advocate a *"departmental junk shop":*

I wish to . . . induce you to build a democratic palace and a thing with a soul in it . . . a companion building to the Library of Congress. . . . I regard this building, record office or national archives building, it does not matter what we call it, as a companion to the Library of Congress. Every student of European archives knows of the extreme advantage in having the archives building beside the library. In Paris and London it is a serious physical disadvantage to have their great libraries . . . away from their two very famous . . . archives, and it would be a very great honor for the United States to inaugurate this reform.[61]

Withington declared that the archives building should not only provide for the proper storing of documents but should also act as "a college of archivists." Citing his decades of experience with European repositories, he said that every European national archives "is a college for archivists." The building he had in view "might cost eight or nine million dollars," which was, he said, "a trifling sum for the United States to expend," considering that it would "become a center of life and a credit to our people in the future."[62]

Withington also ventured an opinion on records disposal. He was surprised that "Professor Jameson put the historical phase" of the archival question "into second place." He believed that "nothing . . . can put history in second place, and those old papers constitute our history." What should be done "in the way of destruction of papers," he said, "is to dispose of the duplicates." Archivists "should have a special aptitude for saying what can be really destroyed as duplication, and what should not," because the people "in . . . current business in the departments have neither the time nor the ability" to determine what should be preserved. "We genealogists laugh," he said, "at the inefficiency of regular historians who know nothing about the real sources of human history."[63]

Withington, however, did misconstrue Jameson's intent. The latter's strategy throughout the years of struggle with Congress was not to belittle history but to recognize the cold fact that if an archives building ever came into existence it would do so "more for reasons of administrative efficiency than for reasons of history." Therefore, he always urged the administrative need for an adequate archival establishment but never failed to couple it with the historical needs of the world of scholarship. As to the size of the proposed building, Jameson observed that "we have to reconcile on the one hand the desire . . . not to spend the money of this generation for interests that will come up 20, 25, or 50 years from now, and on the other hand, the desire to provide for an adequate building for future purposes." He concluded by voicing his belief that a building adequate for current needs should be built upon a lot large enough to accommodate future extensions.[64]

Despite Withington's advocacy of the site on Capitol Hill adjacent to the Library of Congress, the perennial problem of square 143 remained. Senator Wetmore queried Chief Clerk Wilmeth of the Treasury Department whether square 143, supposedly acquired for an archives building, was a convenient site. Wilmeth replied that it was not the most convenient site. He thought a better site "would be . . . near the Record and Pension Office," located in Ford's Theater,[65] which, he said, "would be about the center of the official group" of government buildings. Senator Poindexter interposed to say that his bill, S. 5179, contemplated the purchase of a new site, as square 143, though originally purchased for an archives building, was never used for that purpose, and the site was now covered by an act of Congress providing for the erection on that land of a building for the Coast and Geodetic Survey.[66]

The chairman adjourned the three-hour-long meeting at 1:00 P.M. The matter rested in committee for the remainder of the year, as, indeed, did Lodge's bill. At the annual meeting of the American Historical Association in December 1912, Jameson reported on the hearing and said that the "matter was now being considered by committees of both House and Senate" and, further, that "a systematic effort had been made . . . to secure support . . . from various historical societies in the country."[67] On Christmas Eve, Jameson, exploiting the spirit of yuletide, called on Lodge's good offices to present the memorial of the Massachusetts Historical Society, emphatically endorsing the archives bill "now before the Senate and House." Lodge acceded, but plaintively observed that he had introduced bills to that effect before but had never been able to secure action. Nevertheless, he said, he would be pleased to present the memorial to the Senate and have it printed in the *Congressional Record.*[68]

PRESIDENT TAFT'S MESSAGES

When Jameson started in earnest on his archival quest, William Howard Taft had recently succeeded the first Roosevelt as president of the United States. During those early years of the Taft administration, Jameson made repeated efforts through the president's secretaries to persuade the chief executive, in one of his annual messages, publicly to place his imprimatur on the movement for a national archives. The president, however, failed to mention the archives in his first three annual messages.

Taft was sympathetic, but he had numerous official headaches that monopolized his attention, such as the Payne-Aldrich tariff fight in the Congress; the Ballinger-Pinchot controversy on conservation of natural resources; and various aspects of the Dollar Diplomacy policies, notably the attempted Trade Reciprocity Treaty with Canada in 1911, the attempt to maintain John Hay's Open Door policy in China, and treaties with Central American states that failed in the Senate. All this and more was followed, in 1912, by an open break with his predecessor and benefactor, Theodore Roosevelt. So Taft may be excused for not considering the matter of archives at the top of his agenda.

Several weeks before the third annual message, Jameson had addressed a lengthy letter to the president, detailing the deplorable situation of the government's archives and the many efforts that had been made to improve conditions. He concluded with the following:

The fire in the Albany State Capitol and other causes led the House Committee on Public Buildings and Grounds, in the last session, to take a more serious interest in this problem than ever before. A bill (H.R. 11850) was introduced by the chairman of that committee and referred to the committee, but proceeded no further. I earnestly hope that the President may see fit to bring the matter forcibly to the attention of Congress and the country by a reference to it in the Annual Message.[69]

Although no mention appeared in the message, Jameson's persistent and solemn adjurations began to have an effect. After the turn of the year, in a special message to Congress concerned mainly with the work of the Department of the Interior, President Taft declared that "I can not close this message without inviting the attention of Congress . . . to the necessity for the erection of a building to contain the public archives." The president further stated that "the unsatisfactory distribution of records, the lack of any proper index or guide to their contents, is well known. . . . The land has been purchased and nothing remains now but the erection of a proper building." To be sure that the legislature had the facts straight, he closed with this statement:

I transmit a letter written by Professor J. Franklin Jameson, director of the department of historical research of the Carnegie Institution of Washington, in which he speaks upon this subject as a member of a committee appointed by the executive council of the American Historical Association to bring the matter to the attention of the President and Congress.[70]

Jameson was naturally elated and touched. "I wish to express gratification at the action which you have taken," he told the president, "in drawing the attention of Congress to the matter of a National Archive Building." He also noted that Taft had honored him "in referring publicly to my letter on the subject." He then made lengthy reference to the dual aspect of the archival problem, "the matter of the disposition of useless papers, the need for passing upon their historical value," in addition to the administrative determination of value by the executive departments. He suggested that the departments be required to submit disposal lists to the chief of the Manuscript Division of the Library of Congress.[71]

Realizing the need for factual information, Taft went a step further. In July, he issued an executive order directing department heads to obtain from their field offices outside of Washington data on the "extent, condition, accessibility, and historical nature and value of the archives of the Government." The president stated that the librarian of Congress would furnish detailed instructions to them for the preparation of the reports, and as the department heads received the reports from the field they were to be sent to the librarian for processing and editing.[72]

Months earlier Senator Root had told Jameson that it had occurred to him "that some very useful data might be secured as to the amount of space in the executive department buildings . . . devoted to file cases . . . necessary for the storage of the old documents which would go into a new archives building." He realized that the departments were overcrowded and were renting outside space for some of their work, at great inconvenience and expense. Root felt that increased efficiency would result from the "removal of dead material from the buildings," as these facilities should be devoted to active work only.[73] Taft had a high regard for educated men of the stamp of Root and Jameson, and their opinions were assured of a sympathetic hearing.

But as the year wore on, Jameson became increasingly concerned over the fate of the measures pending in the Senate and the House, and he once again addressed Taft:

A report in a Worcester [Massachusetts] newspaper shows me that at the centennial anniversary of the American Antiquarian Society . . . you spoke warmly concerning the need of a National Archive Building in this city. I write to ask whether you will not think it fitting to make a definite recommendation toward this end in your next annual message.[74]

The president responded by inviting Jameson to an interview in the White House, which occurred on November 25. The upshot of it was that Taft told Jameson to write to him "respecting a National Archive Building" as a topic for inclusion in his annual message to Congress.

Jameson did so. He thought there was a "very good disposition toward . . . such a building on the part of all the members of the Committees on Public Buildings and Grounds in both House and Senate." He

therefore strongly hoped for the passage "of one or the other of the bills
. . . before the two houses." Furthermore, Jameson thought headway
would be lost if the matter went over to a succeeding Congress, in large
part because Morris Sheppard, chairman of the House Committee on
Public Buildings and Grounds, was leaving the House to take his seat
in the Senate. In the short session of Congress, assembling in early
December, "a strong impulse from the Executive," he believed, was
"peculiarly timely" and would probably "carry the measure through."
Jameson, with some temerity, concluded with an admonition on terminology. "May I also suggest that, in anything . . . said in the matter,
the term 'Hall of Records' should be avoided. That term has been
. . . much used . . . here in Washington, but it is unsuitable . . . and
misleading to many minds."[75]

The president took note of this admonition, apparently with his customary good humor, by splitting the difference. In his last annual message as chief executive he invited the attention of Congress to a "Hall
of Archives," which, he said, was "badly needed, but nothing had been
done toward its construction."[76] Thus, on both the legislative and executive fronts, Jameson's educational campaign had made itself felt.

5

The Era of the Three Archival Acts

AUTHORIZATION FOR A NATIONAL ARCHIVES

The single-term presidency of William Howard Taft was rapidly drawing to a close, yet nothing had been actually accomplished by the team
of Jameson and Poindexter. With former President Theodore Roosevelt
undercutting his protégé Taft by dividing the Republican party into
regular and progressive (Bull Moose) factions, and running for the presidency on the latter ticket, the election of the Democratic candidate,
Woodrow Wilson, in the national election of November 1912 was
ensured.

Jameson, as a resident of the District of Columbia, was not a regis-
tered voter, but as a man descended from New Englanders he was
inclined to have Republican sympathies. Nevertheless, he viewed the
probable outcome of the presidential campaign with ambivalent feelings. Woodrow Wilson had been a classmate at Johns Hopkins. The
Democratic candidate also had a reputation as a scholar and, presumably, would be sympathetic toward archival matters. At any rate, Jameson did not lose the opportunity to renew his ties with Wilson. At the
time of the Democratic nominating convention, July 1912, Jameson was
again in Europe on one of his periodic visits. Though engrossed in his
archival pursuits, he continued to watch events at home. In late August
he wrote to Wilson, complimenting him on his speech accepting the
Democratic nomination for president:

I wish I had many votes to give. As a citizen of Washington, I have not even
one; but I can add one voice to the applause of the inaugural speech, three or

59

four spectators for the procession, and can always be counted upon as a warm supporter of the administration, albeit only in conversation.[1]

Jameson was decidedly a pragmatist. He always did the best he could within the framework of the political realities. He was on very friendly terms with both Roosevelt and Taft, and now he sought to be on at least as friendly terms with Wilson. He even adjured his Cosmos Club mate, Henry Adams, that he hoped "no result of the election" would seem to Adams "so calamitous that you cannot continue to enjoy this town."[2]

Determined to make headway before the expiration of the Taft administration, Jameson in mid-November distributed circulars to historical societies throughout the nation giving the facts of the archival situation, and he urged them to petition Congress for action. Throughout the remainder of November and early December, letters, petitions, and memorials of support flowed into Washington.

Charles Francis Adams, president of the Massachusetts Historical Society, addressed a letter to the Senate and House, urging "the erection of a national archive building in . . . Washington, and the transfer to it from time to time of such archives" as are not needed "in administrative and legislative routine." The Adams letter was presented by Senator Lodge, and "there being no objection," it was referred to the Committee on the Library and ordered printed in the *Congressional Record.*[3]

At the beginning of the new year, 1913, President Frank W. Hackett of the New Hampshire Historical Society presented a memorial to the Senate, which stated that at a meeting on January 9 "the society voted unanimously in favor of an appropriation by the Congress . . . for the erection of a building for the national archives at Washington."[4] The Pennsylvania Federation of Historical Societies, "comprising thirty-two historical societies with a membership of ten thousand persons," endorsed the bills pending before the Senate and the House and requested the Pennsylvania senators and representatives to vote for them.[5]

The preliminary barrage of countrywide historical society support was followed by the reporting out of bill S. 5179, with amendments, by Senator Poindexter, acting for the Senate Committee on Public Buildings and Grounds. The amendments served to increase the requirements: the space requirement was raised from 1.5 million cubic feet to 3 million; the ultimate size predicted for the overall design was raised from 4 million to 8.9 million cubic feet; the initial cost was raised from $1 million to $1.5 million; and for preliminary plans the sum of $5,000 was "appropriated out of any funds in the Treasury not otherwise appropriated."[6] In the original text this last item was merely authorized to be expended from appropriations to be made for a national archives building. This amendment, altering the original authorization language for preliminary plans to an outright appropriation, is attributable to Jameson's impatience to speed up the process of getting at least some sketches on paper. As the ploy flew in the face of established congressional practice, it ultimately did not succeed.

In the meantime, the congressional proponents of an omnibus public buildings bill had their devout wishes fulfilled. Garnering public works for the home district is important for the vote-getting strength of every congressman. From time to time innumerable individual bills for public buildings and works accumulated in the files of the House Committee on Public Buildings and Grounds. Rather than deal with these in individual pieces of legislation, the committee occasionally combined them into a single all-inclusive legislative package known as an omnibus bill.

In the judgment of the House committee, seconded by the House leadership, the time for an omnibus bill had arrived. Accordingly, on February 15, 1913, Rep. John L. Burnett of the Committee on Public Buildings and Grounds presented the bill to the House and declared that he was directed by the committee to "move to suspend the rules and pass H.R. 28766, the omnibus public buildings bill."[7] The bill was passed on February 17, under suspension of the rules, and the House clerk was instructed to request the Senate's concurrence.[8]

The Senate passed the bill, with amendments, on February 27. As the House disagreed with the Senate amendments, a conference committee was called. It required three successive conferences to get the House and the Senate to agree on all provisions of the bill. The item on the national archives generally followed the Senate version: the original designs were to be for 3 million cubic feet of space, expansible ultimately to 8.9 million cubic feet; the cost of the building, initially, was not to exceed $1.5 million; leading European archives were to be inspected before the completion of the plans; and, for preliminary plans, $5,000 was authorized for the "employment of technical and engineering services in the Office of the Supervising Architect."[9]

The bill was signed by President Taft on March 4, 1913, the last act of his administration.[10] To those interested in the archives, felicitations were in order. Among others, Chairman of the Public Archives Commission Herman V. Ames congratulated Jameson and acknowledged that he felt certain "that we are largely indebted to you for the bill going through."[11] Jameson congratulated Senator Poindexter "upon the passage of a public buildings bill containing substantial provisions for a National Archive Building." He declared feelingly that "all who are occupied with history should be grateful to you for what you have done toward bringing this about."[12] Poindexter replied that he would like to have Jameson help to "take up the question of proper selection of site" and enclosed a letter of introduction for Jameson's use in approaching the supervising architect, Oscar Wenderoth. Jameson thanked him for the introduction and said he would try to see Wenderoth before his, Jameson's, departure for Europe on March 18, where he planned to stay till mid-May.[13] Neither Jameson nor Poindexter, at that heady moment, imagined that a decade later they would still be battling for an appropriation for the building.

But Jameson was not entirely pleased with the apparently successful outcome. Although the provisions of S. 5179 were incorporated in the act of March 4, 1913, there was a watering down of the $5,000 item for preliminary plans. In S. 5179 an appropriation was posited for that sum. In the public buildings act it was merely authorized.[14] Jameson's attempt to get a direct appropriation for it was, to say the least, naive, as authorization bills and appropriation bills are handled by separate and independent committees of the Congress. Therefore, attempting to appropriate in a bill introduced by a functional committee, such as Public Buildings and Grounds, usurped the rights and prerogatives of the Appropriations Committee.

Nor was Jameson happy about the provision in the act for a Public Buildings Commission. The commission was to consist of the secretary of the Treasury, the postmaster general, the attorney general, two senators, and two representatives. It was to make recommendations to Congress concerning public buildings in the country at large as well as in the national capital. But as Jameson told the AHA in his year-end report, it was the intention of the commission in its first report to "confine itself to . . . local buildings"—that is, to post offices and the like —and no report could be expected for some time concerning buildings in Washington. Jameson, therefore, was "sorry to say" to the AHA that the "immediate prospects of a national archive building" were not bright. "The point of attack," he said, was not the Public Buildings Commission, but rather the House Appropriations Committee, which could appropriate for a specific item such as the preliminary plans for the archives. He therefore adjured AHA members to write to Appropriations Committee members for support.[15]

On March 18, 1913, Jameson embarked for Europe. The day before he had his conference with the supervising architect, Oscar Wenderoth, and left with him various archival materials: Leland and Van Tyne's *Guide to the Archives of the Federal Government* and a plan of the Public Record Office in London. He also advised that the report of the British Royal Commission on Public Records was available at the Library of Congress. Substantively, the conference was noncommittal, but at least the two principals got acquainted.[16]

APPROPRIATION FOR PRELIMINARY PLANNING

On the very threshold of Wilson's inauguration, Poindexter and Jameson had achieved their first great step—the statutory authorization of a national archives building. There was no actual money available to do anything, however, and Jameson was eager to get at least an appropriation of $5,000 for preliminary planning at the supervising architect's office. Once more he girded his loins for the fray.

Immediately upon his return from Europe, Jameson had Poindexter get in touch with the supervising architect. In answer to a telephone conversation between Poindexter's secretary and the supervising architect, Assistant Secretary Sherman Allen of the Treasury Department informed the senator that there were no new developments regarding the archives building, because the $5,000 authorized by the act of March 4, 1913, had not been appropriated.[17] Jameson thereupon wrote to William Gibbs McAdoo, secretary of the Treasury, asking to see him in "the next seven days," as he was leaving on June 18 for his customary summer retreat in Maine.[18] The upshot was that McAdoo's private secretary advised Jameson that McAdoo was too busy to see him but that Assistant Secretary Allen would be glad to talk over the matter with him.[19] The matter rested there until the fall of the year.

In the meantime, Senator Poindexter requested Rep. John J. Fitzgerald of New York to include the $5,000 "in the Urgent Deficiency Appropriation Bill," which Fitzgerald was preparing. The senator told him that work on the "designs and estimates for a National Archives Building" called for in the act of March 4 was being held up by the supervising architect, who was "awaiting the appropriation."[20] Several weeks later, Allen apprised the senator that the $5,000 had been included by the Treasury "in the estimates for the Urgent Deficiency Bill now before Congress."[21]

In September, after returning to Washington, Jameson turned again to the campaign. He got in touch with his friend Edward G. Lowry, managing editor of the New York *Evening Post,* asking for information about and a letter of introduction to Byron R. Newton, who, Jameson said, "has just been appointed Assistant Secretary of the Treasury with the public buildings as one portion of his charge." Newton, Jameson thought, would prepare the Treasury estimates for future buildings. "Therefore," he told Lowry, "I want to see him about the archive building."[22] Lowry responded that Newton had been a reporter on the New York *Herald* while he, Lowry, was in Washington as a correspondent. During the 1912 campaign Newton was with Democratic headquarters and had previously served as one of Woodrow Wilson's publicity agents. Lowry concluded by telling Jameson to get in touch with "Gavit, our [New York *Evening Post*] Washington correspondent," whom he had asked by telephone to make an appointment. Gavit, he said, would "take you to the Treasury Building and personally introduce you to Newton." Furthermore, Lowry declared, "When I come down [to Washington] I want to join you in the agitation for that archive building."[23]

Jameson now turned his attention to the members of the Public Buildings Commission, to each of whom he sent a letter about the archival problem. He hoped that the commission might "recommend warmly the decisive steps toward the erection of . . . a repository, and the immediate making of the necessary appropriations."[24] Senator Sutherland replied that he sympathized with Jameson's point of view "and shall do all I possibly can to bring about the recommendation and later an appropriation for the erection of this very necessary building."[25] Congressman Austin stated, "I have always . . . favored the construction of a national archives building . . . and will continue to . . . until a sufficient appropriation is made to complete the same."[26]

In December 1913, at the annual meeting of the American Historical Association at Charleston and Columbia, South Carolina, the status of the movement for a national archives building was the subject of discussion by Solon J. Buck of the Minnesota Historical Society and the custodians of archives in North and South Carolina, Alabama, and Mississippi: R. D. W. Connor, A. S. Salley, Jr., Thomas M. Owen, and Dunbar Rowland.[27]

The beginning of the new year, 1914, witnessed new initiatives. Gaillard Hunt, chief of the Manuscript Division of the Library of Congress, a long-time ally of Jameson, took a hand in the proselytizing work. In early March, he wrote to President Wilson suggesting that he direct the formation of an interdepartmental board to develop an archives proposal for submission to Congress. He appended a draft executive order that called for the creation of a board consisting of representatives of each department, plus the Library of Congress.[28] A few days later, Harry A. Garfield, president of Williams College, wrote to Wilson seconding Hunt's suggestion.[29]

In his reply to Garfield, Wilson promised to "pay attention to Mr. Gaillard Hunt's suggestions with regard to the archives."[30] But Wilson's intentions were better than his performance. The president's primary concerns with the important legislation implementing the New Order promised during his election campaign, the difficulties posed by the Mexican Revolution, the problems of neutrality and, later, participation in the First World War led him to place all thought of the archives on the back burner of his mind.

Whether or not in direct answer to Jameson's urgings, Secretary of the Treasury McAdoo did take cognizance of the archives problem. In April 1914, he wrote to Rep. Frank Clark of Florida, chairman of the House Committee on Public Buildings and Grounds, that he desired the amendment of section 21 of the act of March 4, 1913, so that it would conform to the suspension of civil service requirements as contained in section 17 of the same act, concerning the Patent Office project. In the Patent Office section of the act, the supervising architect could employ "technical and engineering services . . . without regard to Civil Service laws and regulations," but the national archives section did not contain the same proviso. This dichotomy, McAdoo explained, would force the supervising architect to employ two different sets of personnel, one within and one outside civil service rules. But if the Patent Office proviso was also contained in the national archives section of the act, the same set or types of personnel could be used for both projects. As "the sum authorized for technical and engineering services will barely prove sufficient," said McAdoo, it "must be used to the best advantage."[31]

Accordingly, on April 14, Clark introduced a bill, H.R. 15653, which amended section 21 as McAdoo had requested.[32] The Committee on Public Buildings and Grounds acted most expeditiously, reporting out the bill favorably two days later, and the bill was placed on the Union Calendar and submitted to the Committee of the Whole House.[33] There was no further action on the bill.

To cover the Senate front, Jameson had advised Senator Poindexter that the secretary of the Treasury had supplemented his estimates with a letter recommending the appropriation of $5,000 for plans for the archives building. Jameson expected that this item would come up in two or three days in the sundry civil bill. He therefore asked Poindexter to speak to Rep. Franklin W. Mondell of Wyoming, who was "on the subcommittee of the Committee of Appropriations for that bill," and to stress the "importance of the item." The next day, Poindexter replied that he would "be glad to speak to Mondell." However, he had tried earlier to get the item in the urgent deficiency appropriation bill and had spoken to both Fitzgerald and Mondell about it, "but apparently without effect."[34]

Early in June, Jameson again wrote to Poindexter, complaining that he was "sorry to see that the House committee on appropriations has reported out the Sundry Civil bill without the item of five thousand dollars, which the Treasury sent in, for planning a national archive building." He hoped that Poindexter could obtain the insertion of the item as a Senate amendment to the sundry civil bill. If the amendment were inserted, he thought, "it would be a pretty small thing to throw it out in conference" between the two houses.[35] A couple of days later, Jameson again wrote to Poindexter about the archives appropriation and informed him that the secretary of the Treasury would attempt to get an amendment in the Senate to the sundry civil bill; he asked the senator to see to it that it was referred to the Senate Appropriations Committee and incorporated in the bill. Here Jameson displayed his lobbying skill in the making of combinations:

The sub-committee on the Sundry Civil Bill consists, I learn, of Senators Martin, Overman, Chamberlain, Warren, and Perkins. I venture to suggest that, of this group, the senator from your region, Senator Chamberlain, is likely to be particularly willing to oblige the National Society of the Sons of the American Revolution, who have taken up this matter warmly; for that Society is to have its next annual convention in Portland [Oregon].[36]

As "a certain momentum has been gathered in this matter," Jameson concluded, "it would be a pity to lose it by not securing the initial appropriation." Such a frustration should be prevented, he thought, "if there is any ratchet by which the thing can be prevented from slipping back now that we have got it so far up the slope."[37]

Poindexter, in turn, informed Jameson that he had secured the passage by the Senate of the desired appropriation as an amendment to the urgent deficiency bill, only to have it dropped in conference. Poindexter thereupon protested the action on the floor of the Senate and was "assured that it would be taken care of in the Sundry Civil Bill," and he would "insist upon" this. Accordingly, he was "immediately preparing an amendment" and would at once introduce it.[38]

Early in July, Assistant Secretary of the Treasury Byron R. Newton informed Poindexter that the Treasury had addressed a letter to the president of the Senate on June 27, which called attention to matters that should be considered by the Appropriations Committee in connection with the sundry civil bill, and that the national archives item was one of these matters.[39] Poindexter, on his part, told Newton that although he was "glad to know your views on the matter," he had already introduced an amendment to the sundry civil bill covering this item and "will . . . do what I can to secure its passage."[40]

Poindexter was successful in pursuing the amendment route to legislation in the Senate. A week later he sent Jameson a marked copy of the *Congressional Record*[41] showing that the Senate had adopted his amendment to the sundry civil bill, which called for an appropriation for preliminary designs and estimates for the archives building. This, of course, meant that the matter would go to conference between the houses. He therefore urged Jameson to do what he could to help "impress on the conferees of the House and Senate the importance of the amendment."[42]

Jameson, of course, had not been idle while the legislative maneuverings were in progress. At critical junctures he always made an effort to bring to bear on his target the heavy artillery of outside citizen pressure. In May he had corresponded with R. C. Ballard Thruston, president general of the National Society of the Sons of the American Revolution, to drum up support in that quarter. Thruston, who lived in Louisville, Kentucky, assured Jameson that Bruce Haldeman, the president of the *Courier-Journal* Company, which he characterized as "the leading democratic newspaper of the south," promised "that he would write a letter to the Hon. Swager Sherley, urging his support of the appropriation of $5,000 for the architect's plans for the Archives Building," and that, furthermore, the "Filson Club of this city, passed a resolution to that effect." In addition, the following Monday night Thruston was scheduled to appear before another club in Louisville to address the archives topic and have appropriate resolutions passed. He wanted Congressman Sherley to receive letters "from prominent democrats in his own district, and from others, urging support of this appropriation."[43] Jameson was grateful for the president general's help, especially at that time. He told Thruston that "such letters as will come to Sherley at the present moment are particularly timely, since the Sundry Civil Bill is now under consideration, and he is a member of the sub-committee on it."[44]

Toward the end of May, the American Library Association held a national conference in Washington, D.C., and Jameson took the opportunity to address the organization on "The Need of a National Archive Building." He marshaled some excellent points in this address. After recounting the contrast between European and American attitudes toward archives, and the European centralized status versus the chaotic American bureau system of "archives management," he observed, "If this national archive building comes into existence, as surely it some time will, it will be brought into being, less by the clamor of historians, a feeble folk relatively, than by the steady and powerful pressure of administrators, worried beyond endurance by the increase of files and painfully conscious of the drag which primitive methods of storage impose." Jameson attacked the suggestion to transfer "dead files" to the Library of Congress. He characterized the idea as futile, asking, "Where should the Library of Congress find space?" As to the corollary idea of transferring only "historically important papers," he declared that it was "impossible to accept the underlying assumption that there is a small and perfectly distinguishable portion of the government archives which is historically important, while the rest is not."[45]

Jameson anticipated the position taken by the National Archives administration in later years when he declared that "library administration is one thing, and archive administration . . . is quite a different thing. . . . no national government combines the two." In concluding his message to the librarians, he commented that "the result of thirty-six years of agitation" is an item of $5,000 for making "provisional plans, now before the House Committee on Appropriations, as a part of the Sundry Civil Appropriation Bill." Then he recalled that Francis Bacon's similar idea of 1616, came to fruition 240 years later, in 1856, in the building of the Public Record Office. So, he exclaimed, "We have still some time."[46]

Gaillard Hunt, who followed Jameson at the rostrum, corroborated his statement that "none of the European countries have the archives and the library together." But he took issue with the supposed necessity of keeping the archives and the library apart. He thought that at least they should be in juxtaposition to each other. He deplored the London situation, where students must "play shuttlecock between the Public Record Office and the British Museum." Furthermore, they were not in the "fullest cooperation" with each other. But Hunt stated that the locus of administration was a detail, pleading, "Give us a government archive, and we will attend to the cooperation." He would leave to the future the decision "whether a government archive should absorb the Library of Congress, or the Library of Congress should absorb a government archive."[47]

Victor Paltsits of the New York Public Library, and chairman of the Public Archives Commission of the American Historical Association, closed the program with the presentation of a resolution backing the archives on behalf of the American Library Association. With the "unanimous approval" of the meeting, the resolution was referred to the council of the association.[48] The council promptly passed the resolution supporting the national archives concept and "urged upon Congress the passage of the appropriation . . . in the Sundry Civil Appropriation bill, for making plans for such a building."[49]

On the same day, Thomas M. Owen of Alabama moved the adoption of a similar resolution by the National Association of State Libraries:

Resolved, That we, the members of the National Association of State Libraries now assembled in Washington in our 17th annual conference, most respectfully . . . urge . . . the speedy construction and equipment of a suitable national archive building, lest our national archives meet with some such disaster as that which occurred at the New York state library.[50]

In adopting the resolution, it was also resolved that copies be sent to the president of the United States and "the appropriate official of Congress."[51]

Finally, Jameson sent separate letters to key members of Congress, invoking the prestige of the American Historical Association and its three thousand members, almost all of them, he said, "of standing and influence in their communities," who desire the erection of such a building. And he declared, "Every intelligent man in the United States is proud of the Library of Congress"; and "every one of them would be equally proud of a suitable national archive building and of its contents, and would regard with approval and gratitude any statesman who took the decisive step in bringing such an institution into existence."[52]

At last, this crescendo of effort for so insignificant an amount was successful. The chairman of the House Committee on Appropriations, Rep. John J. Fitzgerald, informed Jameson that the Senate amendment "is at hand . . . I beg to inform you that it has been agreed to."[53] As for the upper house, Sen. Lee S. Overman of North Carolina, chairman of the Senate Committee on Rules, told Jameson that he had supported the Poindexter amendment on the floor of the Senate, and "it was held in the Bill in Conference," except that the provision for exempting appointments for technical work from civil service rules was struck out.[54] Jameson, though naturally thankful for the primary result, could not refrain from telling the senator that he regretted that the act would "not permit the employment of outside architects," as the building was of a very special type and "the Supervising Architect's office is much congested."[55]

The recommendations of the conference committee were in due course agreed to by both houses, and the sundry civil appropriation bill was approved by President Wilson on August 1, 1914.[56] At long last Jameson had his $5,000!

Now came the cream of the jest!

Oscar Wenderoth, the supervising architect, would not proceed with preliminary plans, claiming that the amount appropriated was wholly insufficient. His superiors, Assistant Secretary Newton and Secretary McAdoo, supported this contention.

Poindexter, undoubtedly taken aback, pointed out that the request for $5,000 was based on reports of James Knox Taylor, in 1912, who was then the supervising architect. Taylor was succeeded by Wenderoth on July 16, 1912, who was thus in office more than seven months before the passage of the Public Buildings Act of 1913 yet had said nothing in contravention of the provisions of the act. In rejoinder, Newton asserted that Wenderoth "was not . . . interrogated by either Committee on Public Buildings and Grounds regarding the adequacy of an allowance of $5,000 for the preparation of plans." Newton denied that the Treasury Department had ever indicated that the sum was sufficient for the purpose. He enclosed excerpts of a letter from the secretary of the Treasury to the chairman of the House Committee on Public Buildings and Grounds, which referred to the archives project and indicated the need to amend section 21 of the act of March 4, 1913, recommending an increase to $25,000 for preliminary work. As to the suggestion that the Treasury proceed with the work under the appropriation provided in the act of August 1, 1914, Secretary McAdoo said,

. . . you are advised that this cannot be done. The Comptroller of the Treasury has ruled that the administrative officer charged with the expenditure of an appropriation may not undertake that expenditure unless he believes that all the objects for which it was intended may be accomplished within the limit of cost. If he deliberately undertakes the expenditure, knowing that the limit is insufficient, and knowing that he will create a deficiency, he commits a penal offense.[57]

Poindexter forwarded the correspondence on this unexpected controversy to Jameson. The latter took thought and answered in a very able eight-page letter, which recounted the history of the past efforts to estimate the space requirements for the archives, going back as far as Secretary of the Treasury John G. Carlisle in 1896, and President Theodore Roosevelt's executive order of 1907, and the information gathered as a result thereof. He pointed out that Secretary McAdoo's demand for $25,000 was based on a building cost of $3 million, whereas it was proposed, initially, to expend only half that sum. Presumably the cost of sketches likewise would be less. As to Assistant Secretary Newton's allusion to the "time and money which would have to be expended in an inspection of European archive buildings," Jameson observed that "circumstances have changed since 1911" when he "first embodied" the inspection provision in the bill. War conditions, he noted, "make it impossible to inspect the models, for an indefinite time to come. That requirement should be deleted in new legislation."[58]

The upshot of the contretemps was that nothing was done until, fortuitously, Wenderoth left office in the spring of 1915. Thereafter, a designer in the office undertook on his own to draft some preliminary sketches. But, more important, this development focused attention on a sleeper in the existing legislation, namely, the need for further legislation to get rid of the European inspection requirement in the act of March 4, 1913.

ELIMINATING THE EUROPEAN INSPECTION
REQUIREMENT

It has been written countless times that July 28, 1914, was an epochal day. On that day Austria-Hungary declared war on Serbia, because the Serbian government's reply to an ultimatum concerning the assassination on June 28 of Archduke Francis Ferdinand and his wife was deemed unsatisfactory. The interlocking alliances of the great powers of Europe now came into play. The European war that all dreaded was inexorably in full cry. With the later accession to the belligerent ranks of Italy, Japan, the United States, and lesser powers, it would become known as World War I.

In the microcosm of Jameson's personal world in Washington, the war would necessitate amending the archives legislation to eliminate the very clause he had originally introduced and insisted upon—the requirement to inspect leading European archives before final plans were drawn for the national archives in Washington. And as luck would have it, among the archives Jameson considered outstanding were those in Berlin, Dresden, and Vienna—all now behind the battle lines of the Central Powers.[59]

In the meantime, the making of preliminary plans or sketches, as distinguished from final working drawings, could be pursued usefully. After Wenderoth's departure from office, Jameson was fortunate on two counts: first, the new acting supervising architect, James A. Wetmore, a lawyer by profession, was less stern and more flexible in architectural matters; and, second, the chief designer of the office, Louis A. Simon, became an enthusiastic collaborator on the archives project. The fruitful cooperation of Jameson and Simon on the archives project was destined to last for the following two decades.

In late May 1915, Jameson reported to Poindexter, who was then in Spokane, Washington, "mending his fences," that Simon and he were making progress on the archives plans. The Supervising Architect's Office, by "means of the State Department," as Jameson put it, had gathered plans of European archives. With the use of this material and the personal knowledge of conditions abroad that Leland and he had, Jameson hoped to have suitable plans ready by the time of the next congressional session. He therefore asked Poindexter to "undertake to secure" the repeal of the European inspection clause by January 1916, when he expected to have the preliminary plans ready.[60]

Poindexter, in his turn, was gratified that Jameson was taking advantage of his "continued presence in Washington to press further . . . the Supervising Architect's Office" to comply with "the provisions of the law providing . . . plans for an Archives building," so that the plans would be ready when Congress convened in December. Furthermore, he agreed with Jameson that the "European inspection provisions of the law should be repealed."[61]

During most of the subsequent summer, Jameson removed himself from Washington's air-conditionless heat and humidity, as was his wont. In the late fall he reported to Poindexter that upon his return to Washington, D.C., he found that under Wetmore's supervision the preliminary plans for the national archives building had gone forward satisfactorily. Jameson was particularly taken with Louis Simon, declaring that "the chief designer has taken hold of the matter with great care and intelligence, has consulted Mr. Leland, Dr. Herbert Putnam, and others who know about archives, and has made plans which seem to me very admirable."[62]

Poindexter, of course, was "delighted to know that the work on the plans" was progressing. It showed the value, he said, of "having someone on the job" like Jameson, who was "really interested in the matter" and kept after it. He "regretted, exceedingly," that he had not been in Spokane when Jameson had made a visit there during the past summer, but he had been "busy all season, politically and otherwise." He had been "absent from the State almost continuously for several years" and had much fence mending to do in "getting in touch with matters at home."[63]

At this juncture, the senator thought the time ripe to consider two related points besides that of the European inspection requirement, namely, the question of site selection and an initial construction appropriation. Poindexter reiterated that he perceived no difficulty in obtaining an amendment to eliminate the inspection requirement. In any case he saw no need to delay the project on that account, as, he said, "eliminated or not . . . the provision would be regarded as directory and not mandatory, and inability to comply with that technicality would not in any way invalidate the remainder of the act and proceedings under it."[64]

The senator was more optimistic than the situation warranted. He had yet to learn the full extent of foot dragging possible within the legislative system. The commission established by the act of March 4, 1913, had the duty of selecting a site after it approved the proposed plans. Though the inspection matter would seem to be a nonsubstantive requirement, it was later pounced upon by the commission as an excuse to postpone action on a site until the inspection requirement was either complied with or statutorily rescinded.[65] At any rate, Poindexter, still in Spokane, urged Jameson to try to "persuade the Secretary of the Treasury to include at least a half a million dollars" for the archives building in his estimates. If the secretary would do so, the senator assured Jameson, he had no doubt that the appropriation could be secured, "in view of the fact that the building . . . has been authorized by law, and it is quite unusual to fail to make such appropriations, when they have been authorized, as fast as the appropriations are asked for by the construction department, in this case the Treasury."[66]

Jameson, as usual, had anticipated the moves suggested by the senator. In a letter that evidently crossed Poindexter's in the mails, he told the latter that "lately I have been endeavoring . . . to persuade the Secretary of the Treasury to include in the estimates, an item of $500,000 for the construction of the building." Jameson had also written to all members of the Sixty-fourth Congress with whom he was acquainted, and had asked friends to correspond with other concerned citizens. He remarked,

It is interesting and gratifying to see how much more appreciative and favorable are the replies which I now get to such letters than those which were received in similar cases six, four, and two years ago. Almost every member of Congress seems now to agree that something ought to be done in the matter.[67]

Other measures of support were again organized. In the spring of 1915, the program committee of the AHA arranged with its Public Archives Commission to hold a large meeting in Washington during the association's annual December meeting, to be held that year in the national capital. The affair was enlarged into a joint meeting with other societies interested in the archives problem. The cooperative nature of the event was emphasized by making the organizing committee representative of the three major social science associations: the American Historical Association, whose representative, Victor H. Paltsits, was chairman of the meeting; the American Economic Association, represented by George A. Plimpton; and the American Political Science Association, represented by Charles A. Beard.[68]

The organizing committee met in New York, November 3, 1915, with Waldo Leland acting as secretary. A program was agreed upon and entrusted to the chairman and secretary for execution. According to Paltsits the burden of the work fell most heavily on Leland:

He secured the capacious auditorium of Continental Memorial Hall and provided the numerous slides to be shown by those who had illustrated talks. He also took charge of the publicity features with good results.[69]

With his usual perceptive sense of the fitting, Leland saw to it that Senator Poindexter was invited to take part in the proceedings. "It would be singularly appropriate" he wrote "and would greatly honor the occasion if you would consent to preside. This is the earnest wish of those who are organizing the meeting." Poindexter graciously accepted.[70]

The meeting was held on the afternoon of December 28, 1915. It was well attended, with some four hundred persons present. Senator Poindexter, who presided, in his introductory remarks "spoke strongly of the great need for a proper building . . . to house the records of the Government." Prof. Frank W. Taussig, the Harvard University economist, spoke of the value of government records in the study of history, economics, and politics. Gaillard Hunt of the Library of Congress stressed the importance of proper arrangement, classification, and housing of the archives for the efficient operation of the government. Prof. Benjamin F. Shambaugh of the University of Iowa, gave many examples, with slides, of what American states, cities, and corporations had done for the preservation of their records. Waldo G. Leland followed, describing and illustrating with some thirty slides, various archival buildings in Europe, especially those in London, Paris, Belgium, the Netherlands, Germany, and Spain. He considered some of the best-administered archives to be those of the Dutch towns and provinces. Leo F. Stock, also of Jameson's staff at the Carnegie Institution, "exposed with [some two dozen] telling photographs the shocking conditions . . . prevailing in the various buildings in Washington."[71]

After it had been shown how far behind foreign countries, and some American states, the federal government lagged, Louis A. Simon of the Supervising Architect's Office closed the demonstration with an exhibition and explanation of the architectural studies prepared under his supervision for the proposed national archives building. In closing its description of the proceedings, the *American Historical Review* reported, "The movement for such a building . . . has now been for eight years pursued by the Association. Ultimate success is certain, and . . . without exaggeration, we are destined to have the finest national archive building in the world."[72] That was undoubtedly the work of the editorial pen of Jameson, peering into the future, but the statement was prescient indeed! Victor Paltsits, chairman of the Public Archives Commission, presented a resolution that was passed unanimously by the meeting:

Resolved, That we, members of the American Economic Association, of the American Historical Association, of the American Political Science Association, of the American Sociological Society, of the Naval History Society, and other societies in general meeting assembled under the auspices of the Public Archives Commission, do cordially approve of the efforts which have been made toward the erection of a national archive building in the city of Washington, and respectfully urge upon Congress the passage of appropriations for the speedy construction of a suitable building in which to concentrate and properly care for the muniments of the American people.[73]

This carefully prepared and significant meeting was duly noted by the metropolitan press. The *Washington Post* had an editorial on the topic in its issue of December 29, 1915. The New York *Evening Post,* Paltsits reported to Poindexter, "ran a good account of the meeting at Continental Hall," and he noted that "some cognizance was taken of the meeting in the news items generally." In January 1916, the *Outlook,* an influential periodical of opinion, published an editorial.[74] Using a recent fire in one of the government's rented buildings as a text, the Washington *Evening Star* ran an editorial on "The Government's Fire Risk."[75] The energetic Paltsits further assured Poindexter, as well as Leland and Jameson, that "when the psychological time arrives, we shall be pleased to prepare a circular of endorsements and editorials to use in a further campaign of enlightenment, and to secure the continued cooperation of the press."[76]

The preliminary plans were completed early in 1916. On April 4, the commission of five created by section 21 of the act of March 4, 1913, examined them. The commission, however, refused to take any official action on the choice of a site. As Assistant Secretary Newton reported it to Senator Poindexter, the commission held "that it was without authority to act until the provision . . . for an examination of modern European archive buildings had been observed or repealed."[77]

Toward the end of the month, Jameson urged Poindexter to introduce the necessary amendment very soon, as he hoped there might be a hearing before the appropriations subcommittee of the House before "the annual removal of this department to the Coast of Maine . . . in about six weeks."[78]

Anticipating the question of site selection, Jameson had already supplied Poindexter with a lengthy private memorandum respecting possible sites for an archives building, with a view to eventual submission of his ideas to the committee of five. Someone, apparently the Speaker of the House, caused it to be printed as a public document. The premature action embarrassed Jameson sufficiently to cause him to assure Poindexter that he was not aware that it was to be printed "and had no part in bringing this about."[79]

Poindexter was "strongly of the opinion . . . that the law has been substantially complied with in the preparation of the preliminary plans," he told Jameson, and that this was done "as completely and satisfactorily through an examination of the plans, drawings, pictures, etc." in Washington "as though one were on the ground" in Europe. But as a "practical matter . . . to meet the objections" of the commission, "it would necessitate amending the act, and unless the objection was withdrawn shortly," he would introduce an amending bill in the Senate.[80]

As the amendment desired would neither appropriate for nor authorize an expenditure, it had the least controversial and most rapid progress through the legislative mill of any of the bills that had been or were to be submitted with respect to the national archives building.

On May 3, 1916, Poindexter introduced a bill in the Senate to effect the repeal of the inspection clause. On May 9, acting for the Senate Committee on Public Buildings and Grounds, Poindexter reported the bill favorably and asked unanimous consent for its consideration. The vice president, presiding, asked if there were any objections. Sen. Robert Owen of Oklahoma inquired about the purpose of the bill. Poindexter explained that it was "to relieve the Treasury Department of the duty of sending a commission to Europe for the purpose of making an inspection of the archives buildings there." He emphasized its impracticability under wartime conditions and noted that it would "save the Government some ten or fifteen thousand dollars" and enable the work to go ahead as contemplated in the "law which was passed in 1913." Senator Owen cleared the way when he declared, "Mr. President, I raise no further question." The bill was thereupon "considered as in Committee of the Whole," ordered to be engrossed for a third reading, read the third time, and passed. On May 16, the bill was taken from the Speaker's table in the House and referred to the Committee on Public Buildings and Grounds.[81]

Jameson testified at the hearing held by the House committee and said, in part, "while we of the United States could give points, so to speak, to all the world in the matter of library buildings, archive buildings are a newer matter. . . . The best models of national archive buildings now in existence are those of Berlin, Dresden, and Vienna, not accessible to . . . inspection in war time." As the Treasury Department had secured the necessary data, Jameson continued, "the repeal of the paragraph is simply to remove obstruction to further action." In answer to committee questioning, Jameson further explained that in addition to the foreign plans secured through the State Department, one of his assistants, Mr. Leland, secretary of the American Historical Association, who had spent most of his time during the past seven years in Europe, had collected plans and data on archives buildings and relevant papers read at European congresses. "All of that information" was placed "at the disposal of Mr. Simon," and Jameson considered the plans made by the latter "to be very admirable . . . and in the light of European experience." After further questioning, Jameson reread the offending paragraph in the statute, and stated,

. . . after the plans had been made and they were laid before a session of this commission of five, that commission would take no action in approval or disapproval of the plans, or approval or disapproval of any site which the Secretary of the Treasury might lay before them until this provision had either been complied with or repealed.[82]

James A. Wetmore, the acting supervising architect, corroborated Jameson's statement, saying that he had been present at the meeting. In reply to a query as to whether his office recommended the repeal, Wetmore replied that "we are recommending it." The plans, he said, were prepared and were in the hands of the Fine Arts Commission for study.[83]

On May 24, the bill was favorably reported by the House Committee on Public Buildings and Grounds. The report went on to state that "war conditions . . . made it almost impossible to carry out . . . the procedure," and, anyway, the "best models were in Germany and Austria." The existing provisions, therefore, "merely obstruct progress toward the erection of the building."[84] On June 10, the bill came up for action on the Unanimous Consent Calendar of the House. This meant that it could be passed without a formal vote if there were no objections. The Speaker's call elicited none. The bill was therefore ordered engrossed and read a third time and passed. The president signed the measure on June 28.[85]

The devoted partnership of Jameson and Poindexter had thus brought to pass, in the brief period from 1913 to 1916, three successive legislative measures concerning the national archives project. They could rightfully expect quick results thereafter. Yet, exactly a decade of wearisome frustration lay ahead of them before Congress could be brought to act substantively.

6

Jameson and Poindexter: The War Years

PRESIDENT WILSON'S REBUFF

With the act of June 28, 1916, having successfully passed the Congress, there was now no question, or should not have been, that there was proper authorization for the selection of a site, for the drafting of a set of plans, and for the construction of the building. The catch was that there remained the arduous task of obtaining appropriations: first, for the purchase of a site; second, for the drafting of plans; and, third, for the construction of the building.

Before the year 1916 joined its barren predecessors, Jameson took his courage in hand and appealed to President Wilson. He asked the president to recommend in his next message to Congress the erection of a "suitable national archive building." To reinforce his appeal, he referred to their common graduate training at Johns Hopkins. "Beginning in 1878," he wrote, "when you and I were in college, bureau chiefs and heads of executive departments have made urgent representations to Congress upon the subject." He told Wilson, "Since 1908, several societies have cooperated with the American Historical Association in urging the matter." President Taft, Jameson reminded the incumbent, "made forcible recommendations . . . in his annual message of February 2, 1912." Furthermore, the Public Buildings Act of March 4, 1913, had authorized plans, and under a small appropriation made in 1914, "sketch plans of great excellence have been made in the Office of the Supervising Architect of the Treasury." These preliminary plans "received favorable consideration from the Fine Arts Commission, from the historical people, and from the Librarian of Congress. . . . What we

need now is an appropriation for the purchase of a site. . . . It would
. . . be a great help if you would make a strong recommendation in your
message to Congress."[1]

In conclusion, he assured Wilson that he had "abundant data on all
aspects of the proposal, and on all stages of the legislative progress of
the measure relating to it, and shall be happy to place these at the
disposal" of any person in the Executive Office "with whom I might
confer." Jameson felt that the recommendation to appropriate to the
$1.5 million limit authorized by Congress "would come with additional
force, from one who is not only Head of the Executive Department of
the Government, but is known to speak with authority from the point
of view of an historian. I hope that we may count upon your aid in both
capacities."[2]

The president, at this juncture, as was so often the case, was preoccupied with foreign affairs. Wilson was ever keeping a wary eye on the
progress of the European belligerents in the First World War, and in the
late fall of 1916 he was readying his offer of good offices for the initia-
tion of negotiations between the Allies and the Central Powers. His
reply to Jameson, however, rested on legislative grounds. "I wish it were
possible . . . but there is absolutely no use in proposing it at a short
session of Congress," he asserted. "I hope that we can turn to it at some
future Congress. . . . I know that you will understand."[3]

Jameson's letter of appeal to Wilson had ended with the sentiment
that "I hope I may be allowed to add a word expressing the pleasure
. . . I have felt on account of your re-election."[4] Yet just a few days later
Jameson, still rankled by the summary rejection of his suggestion by his
former Johns Hopkins colleague, unburdened his true feelings to Prof.
Andrew McLaughlin. "I do not mean to talk politics," he wrote, "while
a little inclined toward Wilson . . . I still have to reflect . . . upon the
languid interest taken by democratic officials in the great cause of the
National Archive Building." Jameson told McLaughlin he did not then
expect an appropriation for the purchase of a site, but he would feel
content if only he could get the commission of five, provided for in the
act of 1913, to select a site. He vented a somewhat unscholarly opinion
to his fellow scholar:

I think Republicans are a little more interested in things like good filing systems
than the Democrats are, because they come largely from Urban centres and less
largely from Squashville and Podunk.[5]

Undeterred by Jameson's feeling of pessimism, Secretary of the Treasury William G. McAdoo and Senator Miles Poindexter took steps to
push the archival cause in the Congress. On January 5, 1917, Secretary
McAdoo transmitted to the Speaker of the House a suggested draft of
"additional legislation deemed necessary in connection with the pro-

posed archives building," which was, in the usual course, referred to the House Committee on Public Buildings and Grounds. The draft called for amending paragraph 6 of section 21 of the act of March 4, 1913, to the effect that if the commission set up by the act did not select government-owned land as a site for the national archives building, authority was granted "for the closing of such portions of intersecting streets and alleys as may be necessary in order to combine the several parcels acquired for said site."[6]

Four days later, Poindexter introduced a bill in the Senate, amending the 1913 act in accordance with the McAdoo suggestion and authorizing the Treasury secretary to "contract for a building of not less than 3,000,000 cubic feet of interior space, at a cost limit of $1.5 million, exclusive of metal stacks and conveyors." An authorization of $35,000 for design and engineering services in the Office of the Supervising Architect was also requested.[7]

Although the legislative efforts of Poindexter and McAdoo were obviously necessary to further the project, the crux of the immediate problem was the selection of a site. Without a site the supervising architect was not able to proceed with more definitive planning. But the official responsibility for site selection was vested in the commission of five established by the act of 1913.[8] Only the vice president, as chairman of the commission, could call it into session.

Reflecting on these points, Jameson made a direct appeal to Vice President Thomas R. Marshall, asking him to call a meeting of the Public Buildings Commission. He pointed out that the act of 1916 amended that of 1913, so that an on-the-spot survey of European archives no longer had to be undertaken. On the other hand, the secretary of the Treasury did have tentative sketch plans ready, and before progress could be made it was imperative to select a site. Jameson concluded that if the vice president would call the commission into session he, Jameson, would place at its disposal all studies and materials relative to the national archives that he had in his possession.[9]

Marshall replied that he did not deem it possible to get through an appropriation in the current session, and this was the reason he had "not proceeded more expeditiously." Jameson tried another tack. He shifted from emphasis on the site appropriation to the necessity for preparing plans based upon a selected site. He told Marshall that he agreed with him on no site appropriation but, he said, "it is not impossible that an appropriation of $35,000 for the preparation of the drawings, specifications, and estimate, as provided in . . . Senator Poindexter's recent bill (S. 7778) might be secured." The preparation of the plans and selection of the site, Jameson argued, "will advance the object in view almost as much as securing a million dollars for a site," because the work in the supervising architect's office "would be a matter of eight or nine months" before any work could be done on the site itself. If the commission would only pass upon the sketch plans and choose a site, there would be "a real advancement of the main object without a serious amount of immediate expense."[10]

Several weeks later, Marshall flatly informed the secretary of the Treasury that there would be no appropriation act "at this session of Congress, for an archives building," as he and the Speaker of the House had been "devoting as many hours of the day to the public service as we feel we ought to." He did not altogether rule out the possibility of calling a meeting of the commission "after consultation with the Speaker."[11]

THE NATIONAL ARCHIVES MOVEMENT IN WORLD WAR I

The entry of the United States into the First World War did not halt the movement to establish a national archives. Poindexter and Jameson, of course, did their utmost to keep the ball rolling. Among others, Secretary of Commerce William C. Redfield, in his annual report for 1917, again called attention to the records of the Coast and Geodetic Survey, which, he said, "are of priceless value" and "it would be impossible to replace them if they were burned." He also adverted to the records of his other bureaus, which would "require 85,000 cubic feet of space in the proposed archives building." With some eloquence, he concluded with the following:

There is no argument in favor of the existence of the Library of Congress that does not apply to the establishment of our Government records in a building which shall serve for them the same purpose that the Library of Congress does. Not long ago, in a village of but a few hundred people, I saw a brick building, fireproof and separate from all the others, bearing the title above the door "Village Records." One could not but feel how much wiser the authorities of that hamlet were than the Government of the United States has been in the same connection.[12]

The fear of helter-skelter disposal of valuable records by federal agencies, by reason of the wartime pressure for space, triggered protests and proposals from both private persons and institutions. The Daughters of the American Revolution, other patriotic societies, the National Genealogical Society, and various historical societies passed resolutions of protest relating to the problem.

The president general of the DAR, Sarah E. Guernsey, wrote to Herbert Putnam, the librarian of Congress, expressing her concern and that of her society at the reported destruction of records by government departments and her desire to confer with him about the matter. Putnam told the president general that a hall of records was needed to solve the problem permanently, requested the help of the DAR in the movement, and stated that he would pass on the correspondence to Jameson.[13]

Jameson promptly wrote Mrs. Guernsey that "the Daughters . . . are in a position to . . . bring about the erection of a National Archive Building if they resolved to do so." He recalled his efforts in 1911, when he addressed the Continental Congress on the subject and followed this up with a circular to each chapter regent, requesting that each write her congressman; many did so. Also, "the National Board of Management passed some excellent resolutions appealing to Congress." Though some headway had been made, he told the president general, "progress toward actual appropriations for site and construction . . . halted at the point which we have now reached."[14]

Jameson's concentration on the archives project is again illustrated by the fact that though America was straining every nerve to create, train, and equip a vast army, and simultaneously build up giant new war industries, he had the fortitude to tell his newfound ally, "I do not think . . . that we ought to wait for the conclusion of the war before pressing upon Congress the immediate appropriation . . . needed for this important purpose. . . . I mean to press the matter upon Congress at its next session as urgently as I can."[15]

G. M. Brumbaugh, editor of the *National Genealogical Society Quarterly*, was among those who expressed their fears to Jameson that "the various Departments are submitting new annual disposal lists." He was gravely concerned that large amounts of materials which he characterized as "very important for general historical and also genealogical value," would be destroyed as waste paper. He told Jameson that he recently had gone to Harrisburg, Pennsylvania, to alert the governor and the state librarian, Thomas L. Montgomery, to the magnitude of the problem, and he claimed that both were ready "to influence the Pennsylvania [congressional] delegation to early action." He concluded that "a temporary fire proof storage place must be secured at once."[16]

Jameson told Brumbaugh that in "the attempt to secure a temporary building" the basement of the Lincoln Memorial had been suggested, but this "would be likely to delay or defeat the effort to secure a proper national archive building, which would be a great pity."[17] Again Jameson turned to Poindexter for advice and help. He asked the senator if anything could be done before the next session of Congress and referred to the committee of five. As Vice President Marshall was still chairman of that body, he wondered if Poindexter knew Marshall's current attitude. The senator replied that, alas, the vice president's attitude was still "one of indifference."[18]

Brumbaugh, disappointed by the lack of action on the part of public officials, vented his spleen in an editorial in the genealogical *Quarterly*, in which he stated that the demand for space in all government departments "has rendered imperative the speedy erection of a National Archives Building." He also called attention to section 21 of the act of

1913, which specifically authorized the construction of a large fireproof archives building for $1.5 million.[19]

The matter of "certain old papers" being removed and sold or destroyed in Washington because of wartime conditions was aired at the fourteenth annual Conference of Historical Societies. Resolutions were passed urging "temporary housing" and cooperation with the Public Archives Commission of the American Historical Association in urging the authorities to preserve these records. The secretary of the conference was requested to "bring these resolutions before the 500 historical societies of the country, urging them to take action on the subject." It was further suggested that the historical societies "communicate with their Congressmen and Senators . . . in seeing to the preservation in some way of these valuable records."[20]

Nor were the patriotic societies behindhand in responding to the issue. Prof. Robert M. Johnston of Harvard, speaking at the request of Waldo G. Leland on the "Archives of the Food Administration as Historical Sources," expressed his frustration. "I am boiling over with indignation on this question of a national building for archives," he said; "before the war began it seemed our hopes might be realized. . . . This matter should not be neglected, and I don't think that it is a difficult thing at the present time for the Government to undertake the erection of a national archive building. . . . It should be done as a war economy." Then he told his auditors about "a dinner . . . four weeks ago . . . at which almost all of the patriotic societies of Massachusetts were represented . . . and at which Mr. Worthington C. Ford, and Professor [Frederick Jackson] Turner, and myself were present." They "put forward the case for the public archives building." Johnston thought the meeting was "of a most hopeful character." He told them of the effort to organize the records of the current war, and he characterized the audience's response as excellent. He thought that while patriotic societies were "not making use of archivists and historians as they should," they were nevertheless deeply interested in the records of the past. "[W]e passed a resolution on this subject," he asserted, "and that resolution is being submitted to all the patriotic societies throughout the country, especially in the Southern States, and the support of these societies will be enlisted."[21]

The *Military Historian and Economist,* in a lead editorial of six pages dealing with the handling of records, their indiscriminate disposal under wartime conditions, and the need for an archives building, propounded an interesting theory as to why the United States lagged behind other advanced nations in the proper housing of records:

It is a peculiarity of the organization of our country that its capital should have been, so to speak, an after-thought. . . . Even after its foundation, [the city of] Washington . . . did not set standards for the national life . . . cultural influences were virtually non-existent. . . . this is doubtless in part the reason why we have lagged behind every civilized people in the matter of the housing of our national records. The sentiment which makes for the preservation of records was a sentiment impossible to find in Washington where everyone arrived with a carpetbag and lived in a hotel.[22]

On the other hand, for the preservation of local archives, the climate of opinion was better. "In the small New England towns and through all the older parts of the country, local patriotism was strong, and the records of the locality were cherished." The editorial writer noted that "we have today more local museums, more local stores of records and history, more local historians, than any country in the world." But our national records, he asserted, "are still wholly neglected; indeed . . . in many cases arbitrarily destroyed by indiscriminating agents for nothing better than reasons of immediate convenience."[23]

Having set the stage, the writer turned his attention to the current wartime situation, stating that the influx of war-related documents would make the congestion far worse and pose "very important problems of classification and utilization of documents." But, he added,

The question of the War Department records should be subordinated to that of national records as a whole. . . . It should not be difficult to evoke a wide sentiment in favor of the immediate handling of the problem. In fact, action is already being taken by important bodies. It is clear that the Patriotic Societies have the strongest standing in this question. Their very existence depends on the preservation of records; and they have at various times in the past exercised pressure at Washington in matters of this sort.[24]

The editorialist thought that if these societies collectively raised their voices for "suitable and scientific storage of our national records" they would be listened to. The American Historical Association, he admitted, had "long made efforts in the same direction," and "partly through the agency of the Association" legislation was pending in Congress for an archives building. But, he alleged, the "legislation has not been pushed actively."[25] The latter assertion must have been news to Jameson.

Turning again to the matter of records disposal as a means of solving the space problem, the writer declared, "There is doubtless much to be said in favor of some degree of destruction; but it is quite objectionable that destruction of this sort should be carried on by inexperienced hands." The experience of historians, he stated, "is overwhelming and unanimous . . . that often it is the apparently insignificant and trivial document that furnishes the invaluable item of information." He wished that he had "the pen of a Macaulay to stir the imagination of our readers, and to drive in . . . the essential virtue that lies for a nation in honoring and cherishing the records of its past."[26]

Nor was the writer thinking in small and simple terms, as he stated that "an archive building should undoubtedly be monumental in character." And he did not forget the archivist. "A dozen trained archivists could probably accomplish the work that is now imperfectly done by a hundred government clerks; and . . . more effectively." As a practical suggestion, he thought that the Council of National Defense should have a "decisive voice in this question . . . it harmonizes and coordinates the work of departments, just as a central archive building would harmonize and coordinate the documents of the different departments." Warming to this theme, he added:

The Council of National Defense must . . . realize . . . that it should be able to lay its finger on any document which it requires . . . and it must realize that we are accumulating . . . especially on the economic side, a wonderful record of our country's present situation . . . surely it is a matter of national concern that they should be housed in such a way that when those who come after us wish to ascertain the conditions under which we struggled they shall be able to compile our record.[27]

Waldo G. Leland was busily engaged on war-related work, but he did not forget the archival problem. In a report to the American Historical Association entitled "Archives of the War," he used the reorganization of the wartime General Staff as the point of departure:

It is earnestly to be hoped that in the reorganization of the General Staff, now being effected, some place may be found for an historical section . . . which shall insure the proper collection and organization of the military records . . . the military records alone will present a problem of unexampled magnitude . . . the accumulation of records for the war period . . . in the War Department, the cantonments, the American Expeditionary Forces, the draft boards, etc., will greatly exceed the previous accumulation of 120 years. The absolute necessity . . . for an archive building becomes more apparent than ever.[28]

During these times of alarms, patriotic fervor, and the crusade to make the world safe for democracy, neither Poindexter nor Jameson overlooked his primary personal commitment. Early in 1918, Jameson sent the senator a revised version of his 1916 memorandum on proposed sites for the archives building.[29] This was, apparently, in answer to Poindexter's request to "bring along . . . the diagram you had of available sites for an Archives Building. . . . Some senators would prefer to specify the site in law" instead of leaving it to a commission.[30] Jameson replied that his secretary would deliver a copy of the "private memorandum on available sites which I made for you and the members of the Commission of Fine Arts. . . . Selecting a site should rest on deliberate consideration. The site should be large enough to admit of adequate enlargement of the building."[31] Trying to hold to this principle was to give Poindexter many a troubled moment in the years that followed the war. Poindexter informed Jameson that he was writing "the Assistant Secretary of the Navy [Franklin Delano Roosevelt] and other officials" to canvass support for the coming legislative efforts, and he said he thought they could bring "our bill to a decision" during the summer session of Congress.[32] Gifted more with optimism than prescience, the senator might have been fatally discouraged had he realized by how many years and how much travail he missed the mark.

Jameson, too, was infected with a certain measure of optimism generated by the unexpected wartime boom in paper. He told his friend, David Parker, in the fall of 1918, "We really seem to have a prospect of progress this winter, due . . . to pressure on the official mind of the great masses of new papers . . . made by the new bureaus and boards connected with the war." He observed further, that "armies of female children, 18, 19, and 20 have been imported by these boards to cover . . . papers with typewritten matter, supposed to be of value, but the question where they shall be preserved (the papers, not the children) immediately arises with pressing insistence." But with a degree of cynicism born of long experience, Jameson commented that the "official mind can see the importance of check-stubs relating to the war when it can not see the value of similar documents of 1818."[33]

In this letter, Jameson also offers a vignette of the behind-the-scenes influence of the librarian of Congress in the archives building efforts. He noted that Putnam had appointed Charles Moore acting chief of the Manuscript Division, "with a special view to building it up on the side of war materials . . . with an eye to the collecting and preservation of the records of the mushroom boards and thereby to the securing of an archive building." Jameson also told Parker that "the Librarian of Congress has now taken hold of the matter and brought it along a further stage. The site has been decided upon, diagonally southwestward from the big building of the Post Office Department, and agents of the Treasury are securing options on the property." However, he was not expecting much toward the actual construction, remarking that "in the present state of the building trades, and under the present prices, no more than the essentials will be erected, without stone facings . . . and without . . . work rooms."[34] Jameson naturally welcomed the help of the distinguished librarian of Congress, and the record amply attests that he and Putnam worked hand-in-glove for the attainment of the great objective.

THE POSTWAR PAPER INUNDATION

On the eleventh hour of the eleventh day of the eleventh month of 1918, the guns fell silent on the Western front. The news of the armistice swept the entire world with a feeling of exhilaration and relief that is indescribable to those who did not live through it.

As far as is known, no entry in a diary or other document attests to Jameson's personal reactions to the momentous tidings. Though a sympathizer with the cause of the Allies, more particularly with the fortunes of Britain, he had not taken an active part in the war. He continued to be immersed in his historical, archival, and cultural interests throughout that period.

Within weeks after the termination of hostilities, Jameson was rejuvenating the American Historical Association's Committee on the National Archives. He wrote Prof. Henry Jones Ford of Princeton that his AHA committee of three (himself, John Bach McMaster, and Rear Adm. Alfred Thayer Mahan) had tried for nine years to advance the cause of the national archives. Actually, of course, Jameson was the sole working member. He now proposed to change the committee of three into one that would "really act." He declared that "the interests of scholars are not insignificant, and there is need of some authorized body to represent them."[35]

Charles Moore, Jameson noted, had been active in helping to push the matter of a site, so he intended to reconstitute the committee with Moore, Frederic L. Paxson, and himself. But in addition to historians, Jameson felt there were also the "interests of political economy and political science." Accordingly, he requested Ford and Henry B. Gardner, presidents of the American Political Science Association and the American Economic Association, respectively, to appoint representatives on his committee.[36] The two association heads complied, Ford by appointing William F. Willoughby, and Gardner by naming Victor S. Clark.[37] Twenty-four months later, Paxson was replaced by Col. Oliver Lyman Spaulding, Jr., of the Historical branch of the War Department General Staff.[38]

In the meantime the irrepressible Poindexter had again tried his luck in the Congress. In May 1918, he had introduced a bill in the Senate that authorized the secretary of the Treasury to erect "a fireproof national archive building of modern library-stack type of architecture . . . in the city of Washington . . . bounded on the north by B Street Northwest [now Constitution Avenue], on the east by Twelfth Street, on the west by Fourteenth Street, and on the south by a line extending westward from the south line of the new National Museum Building." Plans were to be in accordance with designs already prepared in the Office of the Supervising Architect, and the plans were to provide for a building of not less than 4 million cubic feet and capable of being expanded to 9 million cubic feet. The building was to cost "a sum not exceeding $3,000,000." This was double the previous figure requested but, as it included heating, lighting, and ventilating equipment, elevators, hoists, plumbing fixtures, metal stacks, and approaches,[39] it is likely that it was not really larger than previous requests, which did not include metal stacks and some of the other mechanical equipment. Since Poindexter's bill followed the usual route to oblivion, he tried again in early 1919, submitting an amendment to the sundry civil appropriation bill "to appropriate $486,000 for a site for a national archives building."[40]

Seeking support in every possible quarter, Senator Poindexter canvassed the heads of emergency war agencies as to their need for an archives building. For example, he carried on a considerable correspondence with Harry A. Garfield, the wartime fuel administrator. After the armistice, Poindexter wrote Garfield, "We are endeavoring to bring to a conclusion our long campaign to secure a government archives building," and he would like to know "the situation of the Fuel Administration as to the need for a fireproof storage of papers . . . properly protected, indexed, and made accessible and available."[41]

Poindexter got the reply he wanted. A week later, Garfield wrote, "I hasten to assure you that I look upon a Hall of Records, or whatever such a building will be called, as a very vital need of our government. The winding-up of many war administrations emphasizes the need . . . [to have the records] not only stored, but made available." Garfield added the information that he had been discussing the matter with Gaillard Hunt, "now a historian of the State Department." The senator, evidently gratified in finding a new ally, asked the fuel administrator to make a statement to the Senate Appropriations Committee.[42] Garfield obliged with a succinct statement of the problem:

One of the duties connected with the closing . . . of the Fuel Administration will be to collect the records that are scattered through the various states of the Union. These records are to be sent . . . to Washington. . . . If the Archives Building were now in condition to receive these records . . . they would be safe, and accessible to persons or officials . . . authorized to consult them.[43]

Then he hit upon the very essence of the cross-sectional data value of a central archival agency. "If such a building contained . . . records of other administrations, it would make it much easier for future historians to gather material on various war problems in which . . . the work of several administrations might . . . overlap."[44]

Members of the cabinet, as usual, lodged their requests for archival space. Two department heads who were especially concerned with the archives problem as members of the Public Buildings Commission, Secretary of the Treasury Carter Glass and Secretary of Commerce William C. Redfield, alluded to the matter in their annual reports. "Under authority conferred by the act of March 4, 1913," said Glass, "an examination has been made of the plans of a number of archives buildings of Europe, outline plans have been prepared and approved, a site selected, and estimates submitted for an appropriation for the land and the construction of the stack portion of the building. . . . The attention of the Congress is respectfully drawn to the very urgent need for . . . funds . . . for this important purpose."[45] Redfield "earnestly . . . hoped that the archives building . . . may be promptly constructed," as the Commerce Department would need "not less than 85,000 cubic feet therein."[46]

Indeed, Secretary Glass addressed a letter to the Speaker of the House of Representatives early in 1919, requesting appropriations of $486,000 for a site and $1.5 million for a building, which was to include mechanical equipment and approaches but exclude metal stacks and conveyors. He reminded the Speaker that the site was authorized by the act of March 4, 1913, and that the building was authorized by both the 1913 act and the act of June 28, 1916. He reiterated the government-wide anxiety about the war records, stating that "papers and records which are the defense of the Government in claims arising from war activities are now stored in wooden buildings of the most temporary character, or in private buildings for which high rents are paid." Furthermore, Glass advised, "As the special war commissions complete their work there is no place to store their papers, and no one is authorized to take charge of them." He also informed the Speaker that "the location, plans, and estimates have been approved by a commission" which consisted of the president of the Senate, the Speaker of the House, and the secretaries of the Treasury, of War, and of the Interior. "The need for the building," said Glass, "is imperative."[47]

In midsummer 1919, the acting secretary of the Treasury, J. H. Moyle, again drew congressional attention to the Treasury's request. He noted that the appropriation was not included in "the sundry civil bill which . . . was finally enacted on July 19, 1919." He hoped that the recommendation would be included in "an appropriation . . . which shall receive the favorable consideration of Congress during this present session."[48]

In an article entitled "Cellars and Attics for Archives," the *New York Times* commented on the crowded records storage conditions in Washington, noting that "the files of the War Department, one of the best cared for . . . occupy nearly one hundred rooms in the State, War, and Navy Building." In the Treasury Department, "there are 100 miles of shelves devoted to archives" which, the paper said, "would fill the Library of Congress twice." The *Times* estimated that the war would double all the records that had been accumulated by the country up to 1917 and specifically mentioned the records of the Food Administration, the Fuel Administration, the Railroad Administration, the War Industries Board, as well as those of the regular departments; it was noted that "the Draft Board records were shipped in some weeks ago; truck load after truck load of them have been stored in a building at the War College. . . . Officials are at their wits' end where to place all these papers, and yet the greatest volume of records of all, those of the A.E.F., have hardly begun to arrive in Washington." The *Times* alluded to historical values in these records, as well as the need for the protection of the government and of individuals in lawsuits and claims for years to come. "In order to give them some fireproof protection pending . . . action by Congress, it is proposed to set aside as large a space as possible in the semi-fireproof Munitions Building," the paper concluded.[49]

In the first postwar year—1919—the Navy Department brought up the rear of the parade of government testimony on the records problem.

The congressional Public Buildings Commission held a hearing on October 13, 1919, at which Assistant Secretary of the Navy Franklin Delano Roosevelt testified and presented a written statement from Secretary of the Navy Josephus Daniels. In his comments Roosevelt said, "I do not know that there is anything . . . that I want to add, except that we are trying to consolidate this record proposition. . . . As a result of starting the historical section, we are going to save a great deal of space of all of the navy yards and navy districts." Then he added, "For instance . . . the historical section dug out the two basements in the Washington Navy Yard that were filled with Civil War records. Those basements were very much needed in the Yard. Those records have to go somewhere. We hope to concentrate them . . . in the Navy Department."[50]

Secretary Daniels's communication to Sen. Reed Smoot, chairman of the commission, was triggered by a request from the Shipping Board that the Navy release 65,000 square feet of contiguous space for the use of the board. With the navy's own space problems in mind, this Shipping Board request disturbed the secretary. He pointed out that in the continental United States and its territorial possessions there were sixteen naval district headquarters during the war. The records at these various headquarters would be brought to Washington. Also, Daniels stated, "the historical section of the Office of Naval Intelligence . . . needs considerable additional space."[51]

The secretary also told the senators that floor load limitations greatly reduced the space that could be utilized in the Navy Building:

In view of the heavy weights involved by these records this office can only be located on the first floor of the Navy Building. . . . the second and third floors . . . are designed with an allowance of 75 pounds superimposed load per square foot. The storage space for heavyweight material is, therefore, limited to the first floor.[52]

In addition, the Marine Corps needed some three thousand square feet for storage of records. Daniels concluded that some space could be released in the Navy Building, but this space would not be contiguous, since giving up 65,000 feet at that time "would place the Navy personnel in a more congested condition than during the war period."[53]

As far as government archives were concerned, the first postwar year saw the problem relegated into the traditional limbo of archival frustration. Cabinet officers, in their annual reports for 1920,[54] almost as a reflex action dutifully referred to the problem, but their hearts were not in it. As though despairing of any forward movement, Secretary of State Bainbridge Colby asked for funds to convert a large room in the State, War, and Navy Building, into a "fireproof room" at a cost of between $20,000 and $25,000. In addition, the secretary intended to get a fireproof safe for the room and place therein the Declaration of Independence and the Constitution of the United States. Colby did not hide his chagrin; he stated that these documents are stored in a way "that is really quite indefensible" and explained that

The Declaration of Independence and the Constitution are in an antiquated little metal safe. It is very old and it is hardly a protection against a prying meddler, to say nothing . . . of fire, and it seems appalling to think that it is up there, in a little office chest, unsecurely locked, with no protection whatever. The original treaties of the United States and the original statutes . . . are stored in a sub-basement. It seems to me that it is wrong.[55]

Colby further stated that the recommendation for a special fireproof room was submitted to him by an "informal committee of three very distinguished gentlemen," historians and librarians whom he had designated to consider the question and make recommendations. The subcommittee did not seem much impressed with the idea. It objected that the building still would not be fireproof and that the money would be wasted when the new archives building was constructed.[56]

In April of 1920, writing to Graham Botha, the archivist of the Union of South Africa, Jameson was very pessimistic:

. . . I am delighted to learn . . . that I may have the pleasure of seeing you in Washington next month. . . . I shall be ashamed of the situation [as I shall not be] able to show you anything helpful. I have been struggling for a dozen years to obtain the erection here of a suitable national archive building, and a site has been selected and sketch plans prepared, but I am not likely, even in this present session of Congress, to get the necessary appropriations.[57]

The second postwar year, 1920, passed as fruitlessly as the first. At the end of 1919, Jameson had reported to the American Historical Association that he had "labored individually with various Members of Congress" and had had informal consultations with members of his archives committee, but he confessed that "all efforts to secure appropriations in last summer's sundry civil appropriations act were unsuccessful. The . . . majority members of the House subcommittee concentrated on the necessity of cutting from the estimates everything not deemed vitally necessary, in order to reduce six billions of estimates to four billions of appropriations." He therefore saw little hope of securing "any appropriation for the purchase of the site or beginning of construction." In fact, the only forward movement, if it could be called that, came from the nonlegislative side. In February of 1919, the proposed site was at last selected by the Supervising Architect's Office, approved by the secretary of the Treasury and the members of the commission constituted by the act of 1913. This site was "the square . . . bounded by Twelfth and Thirteenth and B and C streets, NW." Jameson considered the lot suitable and inexpensive. The Treasury, he said, had secured options on all the property and was awaiting appropriations.[58]

"At the same time," Jameson reported, "the pressure for space for the storage of documents is being heightened by the return from France of archives of the American Expeditionary Force." Thus, he thought, "the needful appropriation may be obtained by means of the Senate."[59] He was evidently thinking of Poindexter's favorite gambit, tacking on an amendment to an appropriation bill. This was repeatedly tried over the next several years, only to encounter stonewall resistance from a House of Representatives jealous of its power over the purse.

The year 1920 sped by with comparatively less effort toward his goal than Jameson had hitherto invested. He was both tired and discouraged, telling Colonel Spaulding, his recent committee recruit, that he did not call a committee meeting during the year as he felt there was nothing for the committee to do in view of "pronouncements on economy" from the House Committee on Appropriations.[60] And at the end of the year he reported to the American Historical Association that "in the last session of Congress it was found impossible to persuade the House Committee on Appropriations to make any appropriation for the national archive building." In the meantime, his other committee member, Charles Moore, was active in lobbying with individual congressmen to create, as Jameson expressed it, "a more hopeful situation." He thought that ultimately Congress would "institute a regular program of building operations in Washington," and it would probably follow the "recommendations of the building commission." If that should happen, Jameson felt that his project would have a better chance, as Senator Smoot, chairman of the commission, had declared that it would accord "a foremost place to the national archive building" in its recommendations.[61]

Thus closed the year 1920. Jameson, after his rebuff in late 1916, apparently never again appealed to President Wilson. The president, during 1917 and 1918, was completely absorbed in the war effort. Afterward, his labors at the Paris peace conference and his unsuccessful struggle with the Senate for approval of the peace treaty and the League of Nations left Wilson physically and morally drained. But political help on the highest levels was on the way. If, as Jameson felt, the Republicans were more approachable on the archives problem than the Democrats, he had not long to wait to test his belief. The major event of 1920 was the defeat of the Democratic candidates, James M. Cox and Franklin D. Roosevelt, for president and vice president and the landslide victory of Republicans Warren G. Harding and Calvin Coolidge. As fate would have it, the two vice presidential candidates in the election of 1920, when each in his turn became chief executive, were to have a profound influence on the realization of Jameson's dream.

7

The Battle of the Amendments, 1921

RESUMPTION OF THE NATIONAL ARCHIVES MOVEMENT

Forward movement on the archives problem, as so often in the past, was once again sparked by a dramatic fire. As the *New York Times* reported, the "priceless" census records of 1890 were destroyed by a fire in the Commerce Department Building in Washington, on January 10, 1921. The blaze originated in the basement and was largely confined there by the exertions of the firemen who responded to a five-alarm fire call. The *Times* reported that the 1920 census records on an upper floor were not damaged; but the census records of 1860, 1870, 1880, 1900, and 1910 "were partly damaged by water." Enumeration records from before 1860 were left practically intact. Nevertheless, the census of 1890 was gone, and Chief Clerk T. J. Fitzgerald of the Census Bureau estimated that "at least one-third of the records from 1790 to 1910 would have to be copied." The *Washington Post* reported that many of the records were saved, though somewhat "wetted-down," because they were in a fireproof vault, located in the southeast corner of the building. In this vault, measuring about one hundred by forty-five feet, were stored the oldest volumes of the Census Bureau, "dating back 130 years to the first census made in 1790." The *Post* further recalled that "Senator William J. Harris of Georgia, who was director of the census at the time the census records were moved to the Commerce building, protested, declaring that they were of too incalculable a value to be risked in any location not absolutely guaranteed against fire. Other written protests were filed at the time, but the records were sent to the Commerce building." According to the *Times,* "Officials said that it was probably the most disastrous loss of records the Government has ever sustained."[1]

Jameson made instant use of the unfortunate event. He immediately composed and within forty-eight hours despatched letters to various United States senators calling attention to the "historic importance" of the records destroyed in the fire. He expressed the hope that the Senate Committee on Appropriations would "insert in the Sundry Civil Bill" a provision for the purchase of the lot "designated by the Public Buildings Commission . . . authorized by the Act of June 28, 1916."[2] He also informed Senator Poindexter that he was writing to the senators, and especially cautioned him that it was imperative to convert to the cause Sen. Francis E. Warren of Wyoming, chairman of the Appropriations Committee of the Senate.[3]

The *New York Times,* always faithfully watching the Washington scene, in an editorial entitled "Economy Can Be Costly," called attention to the requests of department officials "for years and years" for relief in the matter of proper records preservation and berated the "habitual reluctance and frequent refusals of legislators" to do anything about it:

It would be harsh, and probably unjust, to say that this reluctance and these refusals are due to the fact that money spent for vaults in which to store old papers and documents brings in little or no return in the way of political strength or repute; the explanation probably is mere negligence, based on ignorance . . . or forgetfulness of the value which such records have. . . . It is a familiar story, and probably will remain familiar till the millennium comes and common sense ceases to be the most uncommon sense there is.[4]

Nor did Secretary of Commerce Herbert Hoover pass over the incident without remark. In his annual report for 1921, he observed, "The growing need for a national archives building was forcibly emphasized on January 10, 1921, when a fire of unknown origin in the basement of the Commerce Building destroyed a large quantity of valuable records of several bureaus of the Department."[5]

The *Washington Post,* not to be outdone in commentary, noted that "a short time ago a fire burned up 50 years of lighthouse records" and that the records of various departments "are being hustled about from one temporary building to another." It observed that if "Congress really wants an archives building, an archives building can be had in the shortest possible time." The *Post* noted that "the Secretary of the Treasury . . . repeatedly recommended to the appropriations committee the inclusion in the sundry civil bill of an item covering the cost of the site and working drawings" and asserted that "the sources of United States history as well as the documents on which the government relies as defense against all sorts . . . of claims continue to be destroyed from time to time. Such 'economy' is sheer waste." The paper concluded that "Congress seems wedded to the theory 'Happy is the country that has no history.' "[6]

THE POINDEXTER AMENDMENT

Within a week after the Commerce Department fire, Senator Poindexter submitted an amendment to the sundry civil appropriations bill "proposing to appropriate $496,000, for the purchase of a site and for working drawings for an archives building in the District of Columbia."[7] Jameson had not been sitting by idly. While the bill was still being considered in the Senate committee, he had asked friends in the academic world to write or wire Sen. Francis E. Warren, chairman of the Appropriations Committee, to include a site purchase provision in the bill. For example, he asked Prof. Wilfred Munro to wire Senator Warren that the Rhode Island Historical Society wanted an appropriation for the national archives. Jameson noted that Senators Smoot and Poindexter "are going to work upon" Warren and that he hoped to "get into action as many other influences as possible." If the Senate inserted the amendment in the bill, Jameson thought it "would go through the House with a whoop."[8]

In his remarks relating to the reason for the amendment, Poindexter called the Senate's attention to an advertisement which showed that "the public records of the Government are being hawked about the country and sold to libraries and collectors." The senator supposed that the papers had been "abandoned in times past and picked up by collectors." In the present case the documents included a "collection of port papers," Revenue-Cutter Service letters to and from Secretary of the Treasury Samuel D. Ingham, and "other papers covering the years 1830 to 1831." Also for sale were "shipping papers of John Lasher, surveyor of the port of New York . . ." and others "covering the years 1781 to 1905." Senator Poindexter, in reading the lesson of purloined, misappropriated, wrongfully disposed of, or otherwise abandoned records, highlighted yet another great danger to unprotected documents. These papers, he concluded, "cover about a century of Federal history" and are of high value especially to students of American economic history. To buttress his argument, Poindexter quoted from the recent editorial in the *Washington Post,* which pointed out "that this traffic in Government documents is going on continually" and that many libraries bid against each other "for documents which should be in a Government archives building" in Washington, "accessible to all students" as well as to government officials.[9]

In concluding his argument for the proposed amendment, Senator Poindexter again called attention to the fact that the building had been authorized as far back as 1913, that preliminary plans had been made, and that the secretary of the Treasury was directed to acquire the site when the selection was approved by the relevant commission. The senator then noted that the commission had performed the functions devolving upon it under the acts of 1913 and 1916—it had approved the plans, and it had approved the site selected by the secretary of the Treasury. The government now had the obligation to complete the procedure by making the necessary appropriations. In reply to a query from Senator Warren, Poindexter stated that the site had not been actually purchased; it had been selected and an option had been taken, but the actual purchase could be effected only by an appropriation, and that was the purpose of his amendment.[10]

THE UNDERWOOD PROVISO

On February 4, 1921, Senator Warren reported out the sundry civil appropriations bill. As reported to the Senate, the measure carried a total of $410,921,107. This was $28,437,415 more than was provided in the measure passed by the House. If adopted, the Poindexter amendment would add slightly less than half a million dollars to the foregoing figure.[11]

On February 7, the Poindexter amendment was debated on the floor of the Senate. Sen. Joseph T. Robinson of Arkansas led off by introducing a constituent's letter, from one R. R. Williams, who suggested that the Navy Building and the Munitions Building be used for the storage of the government's records. Senator Poindexter commented that these buildings were not intended for storing large masses of records and, moreover, they were wartime emergency structures intended to be demolished eventually.[12] Poindexter's negative reaction to the suggestion again confirmed the point that he was not to be diverted from his goal of creating an archives building. Referring to the Williams letter, he added, "So far as the statement made by the writer of the letter that this building will ultimately cost $15,000,000 is concerned, that is contrary to the facts and contrary to the law. The law under which this appropriation is being made fixes a limit of $1,500,000 for the building." Senator Robinson's Arkansas constituent was indeed a seer. In quoting $15 million as the ultimate cost of the archival project he anticipated the truth by some fifteen years. Senator Poindexter pointed out that the appropriation desired in his amendment was only for the purchase of a site. He explained that a part of the site, consisting of Ohio Avenue, which it was proposed to condemn, was already owned by the government. "The land to be acquired," he said, "consists of a lot on one side of that avenue and a lot on the other side of it, the entire tract lying between B and C Streets NW, and Thirteenth and Twelfth Streets."[13]

Then Poindexter referred to other archives locations considered in the past. One suggested site was the land that had been cleared of temporary wartime and other buildings between the Senate Office building and Union Station. Another site was near the Library of Congress, which he thought was preferable. The question of cost was the reason for choosing the Ohio Avenue site. That site, the senator said, could be acquired for three dollars a square foot, whereas the site near the Library of Congress would cost in the neighborhood of five dollars a square foot. To buttress his case, Senator Poindexter called attention to a letter from former Secretary of the Treasury McAdoo to the Speaker of the House, dated November 13, 1918, in which McAdoo declared that

In order to care for the great increase in Government records created by the war it is necessary to act immediately . . . to acquire a site and erect an archives building. . . . The site is the one suggested in the Congressional Public Buildings Commission's report, between B and C, Twelfth and Thirteenth Streets NW. One-third of the land is now owned by the Government—the easterly end of Ohio Avenue. . . . The full legal value on the assessor's books is $475,805 . . . [and it] may be purchased for less than that figure.[14]

Sen. Oscar Underwood of Alabama rose to state that he had understood that the plan contemplated in the Poindexter amendment was not intended to close any of the streets south of Pennsylvania Avenue. Now, he understood that it was proposed to close Ohio Avenue. "Is that correct?" he asked. Senator Warren, the committee chairman, replied, "that is correct."[15]

There ensued a lengthy debate, mainly between Underwood and Poindexter, but joined in by some fellow solons. Senator Underwood objected to the proposed closing of Ohio Avenue. To Poindexter's point that the avenue, by legislation, was already theoretically closed between Fourteenth and Fifteenth streets, the Alabamian replied that he had heard that asserted before, but that instead of closing it the government had recently paved a part of Ohio Avenue as an outlet for the thousands of government clerks who worked in the area below Pennsylvania Avenue.[16]

Underwood admitted, answering Poindexter's query, that people could get out by going north several blocks, or by going south of the Treasury Building, but he considered that traffic there "is now congested and . . . dangerous" for pedestrians as well as drivers. He did not believe it was necessary to take a convenient thoroughfare away from the people to erect an archives building.[17]

In Underwood's words, his stand was not against the archives project itself.

So far as the erection of the archives building is concerned, I am as heartily in favor of it as the Senator from Washington. I think that such a building . . . is necessary for the preservation of the documents and records of the Government; but I had a great deal rather see Congress take the block which the Government now owns between B and C and Fourteenth and Fifteenth Street, which was originally purchased for the erection of a State Department building. That land will . . . not be utilized for that purpose for 15 or 20 years to come. Since the War and Navy Departments have moved into their new buildings on B Street there is ample room for the State Department in the old State, War, and Navy Building. We could take the other block without any cost to the Government . . . and could thereby save half a million dollars and it would be a better block on which to erect an archives building . . . and its utilization would not close any street.[18]

Poindexter professed to remain unmoved by Underwood's argument, but he had motives as yet undisclosed. Certainly, on the face of it, Underwood's stand and that of those who supported him was not unreasonable. The senator from Washington replied that the Alabamian's proposal would still close Ohio Avenue, but Underwood denied this. Senator Robinson asked, "Which block does the Senator from Alabama propose to use?" Underwood stated that he wanted to use the block between B and C and Fourteenth and Fifteenth streets, which already belonged to the government. "It is," he asserted, "just as big" as the "original block that the Government had bought" for an archives building, "where the Interior Department is now located." He added that it was "the wise thing to do" to take the block which the government now owns "and erect the archives building on it, and not spend $500,000 for the purchase of more land."[19]

To effect his twin objectives of leaving the way open for the Senate to include an archives appropriation item in the bill yet concurrently deny to Poindexter the site he wanted, Underwood proposed an amendment "to insert a proviso at the end of the paragraph [concerning the archives site appropriation] which will read"

Provided, That no streets or avenues shall be closed or utilized for the purpose of the erection of the archives building.[20]

Before the Underwood amendment came to a vote some further debating ensued. Robinson thought "it would . . . be much better to locate this building . . . by the Library [of Congress] where persons . . . using the records and books there may have easy access to the records in the archives building." Sen. Marcus Aurelius Smith of Arizona favored a location on Pennsylvania Avenue opposite the Willard Hotel, a site already owned by the government and very convenient to the Treasury and State departments.[21]

Sen. William H. King of Utah attempted to knock out the Poindexter amendment by making a point of order against it. Chairman Warren, at this point, parried the blow, stating that "the point of order would hardly lie against this amendment. It is estimated for. It is provided for by legislation heretofore. It has come in from a regular standing committee, and the appropriation has been recommended. I know of no point of order that can be made against it that would defeat the amendment in that way." Senator Warren conceded, however, that though not subject to a point of order, the amendment "is open to amendment." Senator King, realizing he was checkmated, addressed the chair. "In view of the statement of the Senator from Wyoming, Mr. President, I withdraw my point of order."[22] But Senator King was by no means through. On another day he utilized to the full the gambit inadvertently underlined by Warren, namely that "the amendment is open to amendment."

The presiding officer then put the question, and the Underwood proviso to the Poindexter amendment was passed by the Senate. Senator King must have been in an unpleasant mood. As the debate for the day terminated, he ominously served notice on Chairman Warren "that before the bill leaves the Senate I shall offer an amendment along the lines which I have indicated."[23]

THE KING AMENDMENT

Two days later, the debate was resumed when Senator King rose to introduce a substitute amendment to take the place of the Poindexter amendment as modified by the Underwood proviso. The presiding officer, ascertaining that the Senate had no objection to reconsidering the vote previously taken, permitted the offering of the King substitute amendment:

To enable the Secretary of the Treasury to carry out the provisions of section 21 of the public buildings act approved March 4, 1913, authorizing him to secure a site for an archives building, he is hereby authorized and directed to take over and appropriate for the uses of said archives building the block of land now owned by the Government, No. 230, according to the map and survey of the District of Columbia, and located between B and C Streets NW, and to erect said building on said property. For the working drawings in accordance with the plans prepared by the Supervising Architect and approved as by law provided for said building, $10,000.[24]

Senator Underwood immediately rose to the support of the King amendment, on the basis that the location was excellent and that the government already possessed the real estate. He also urged its economy, as the block contemplated would otherwise probably remain unoccupied for twenty years, and at 5 percent interest on the capital investment saved, the property would be 100 percent amortized within the twenty years.[25]

Senator Poindexter observed that the proposed site had been acquired for the Commerce Department building. Senator King contradicted this assertion, stating that the land had been acquired for the State Department, but that as the War and Navy departments had relinquished the old State, War, and Navy building to the State Department, the latter would not need additional space for many years to come. Poindexter demurred at the idea that the War and Navy department offices were permanently domiciled in the Munitions building complex on B Street, as these buildings were intended to be temporary structures. He also wanted to know where the thousands of employees housed in buildings on the site recommended by Underwood and King would go if those structures, temporary or otherwise, were removed to make way for the proposed archives building.[26]

King, speaking for the Democrats, riposted the Washington State Republican:

May I say to the Senator that I hope our Republican friends in the coming Congress will materially reduce the personnel in the Government service in Washington. It was charged by Republicans during the campaign . . . that there were more than 40,000 clerks in Washington who were unnecessary, and the Republican Party pledged itself not only to a material reduction in the number of Federal employees, but also promised . . . efficiency and economy in the administration of public affairs.[27]

If these Republican promises were carried out, thought King, the remaining personnel from the Fourteenth and B streets area could be concentrated in the "large building for the Internal Revenue Bureau opposite the Treasury" which houses "hundreds of employees."[28] Poindexter rejoined that after the Republican party executed the reforms "there will still be lack of space for the housing of Government activities," and he reiterated his demand that the lot covered by his amendment be chosen. Sen. Knute Nelson of Minnesota joined the fray, wanting to know why the government could not use some of the "property now owned by the Government . . . in the neighborhood . . . instead of buying more." He declared, "There has been too much buying of dead property in this city to help out real estate men. I am utterly opposed to it."[29]

At this juncture, Senator Overman asserted that the true reason Poindexter and others stubbornly insisted on buying more land was to help carry out a comprehensive scheme for the beautification of the city. Said Overman:

I remember very well the . . . reason why we bought the lots. . . . To beautify the city we began to buy on the south side of the Avenue, and we bought this square to get rid of the old buildings down there. We ought to look at it with that purpose . . . in mind. We ought to buy all the land on the south side of the Avenue and erect Government buildings there, so as to make Pennsylvania Avenue one of the greatest streets in any city in the world.[30]

Senator Poindexter acknowledged that his colleague's words did express "the general policy." He further claimed that Senator Nelson had been in accord with the policy of acquiring all the property south of Pennsylvania Avenue. The Minnesota senator strenuously denied he favored the policy, stating that the whole area south of Pennsylvania Avenue was "formerly nothing but a swamp." The Tiber Creek flowed through that section, and the Post Office Building should not have been located there. Nelson declared, "I am informed that it was located there . . . to placate the owners of certain big newspapers in the city . . . who desired the building" to be "convenient to them."[31]

There then ensued another lengthy exchange between the two original adversaries, Poindexter and Underwood. The latter said he did not doubt that the archives building would be ornamental, but thought it would be more "properly placed at the end of Fourteenth Street just above the entrance to the Mall." Poindexter insisted that his site between Twelfth and Thirteenth streets would be more economical in the long run, if the policy prevailed of improving that section of the city, as there were only some old "tumble-down buildings" on the site at that time, and the property could be obtained for the cost of the land alone. Sen. Wesley L. Jones of Washington asserted that if they followed Poindexter's course they "could get nowhere toward providing an archives building," because the Underwood proviso would effectually block use of the site Poindexter favored.[32]

Then the root motive in Poindexter's insistence on his own way was disclosed, for he responded:

I think the Senator is entirely right. We can take the property subject to the contingency of securing future action by Congress . . . closing . . . Ohio Avenue; and if we do not secure that action, we can not erect an archives building on the site . . . but we will have a property which . . . is in line with the policy which has been generally recognized as a proper policy in the development of the city of Washington.[33]

In short, despite his dedication to the concept of a national archives, Poindexter was willing to subject it to risk for another objective—the improvement of the area soon to be known as the Federal Triangle.

Senator King, in moving the question for his amendment, closed the debate with the following remarks:

. . . a casual examination of the map showing the two lots proposed to be purchased and their relation to Ohio Avenue . . . will convince Senators . . . that the two little strips on either side of it [Ohio Avenue] for which we are asked to pay nearly half a million dollars, would be utterly unsuitable for an archives building. . . . Doubtless the purchase for $490,000 of this property would be advantageous to the owners of the same . . . they would rejoice to get this large amount for two little strips of land. Mr. President, it seems to me there can be no argument against . . . [my] amendment.[34]

The presiding officer then put the question. The King amendment carried the day. Poindexter lost, yet he had also won. Although he did not get the site he wanted, the Senate had now approved a site for the archives building.

The American Historical Association's Committee on the National Archives anxiously followed the legislative action. Jameson and his principal committee colleague, Charles Moore, now chairman of the Fine Arts Commission, did what they could in the proceedings. Jameson was in frequent touch with Poindexter. On February 5, he congratulated Poindexter and assured the senator that he would try to see every member of the House of Representatives whom he knew personally, to get acceptance of the amendment by the House. And, he concluded, "we are then sure to have the building. . . . If so, it will be your work, and all the historical folk will be duly grateful to you."[35] A few days later, as the debate unfolded, he again wrote Poindexter that he had "read yesterday's [*Congressional*] *Record* . . . with admiration of the detailed knowledge with which you handled the matter of the Archive building." Upon the Senate's approval of the King amendment, Jameson told Poindexter that "Dr. Fess and Mr. Wetmore both agree that it is best to let the measure go through in its present form."[36]

When interviewed by the press after the Senate passed the King amendment, Charles Moore displayed a skillful ambivalence in his remarks. He felt that if the House accepted the Senate's position "in locating the long-talked-about archives building at the corner of B and 15th streets, a long step will be taken in the improvement of the area south of Pennsylvania Avenue." After completing his obeisances as a tactful official, Moore launched into an exposition of his real views. The site, he said, was selected by the Senate because the government "already owns the ground." The argument for it, he said, was "based on economy." But the site, he continued, "is now occupied by a building that would last for ten or more years." He believed that "the wrecking of this building will cause a loss equal to about half the cost of the land" originally proposed to be purchased. "The new site," Moore stated, "also involves a much more elaborate structure than the one proposed for the site recommended. So that in the end the cost to the government will be increased beyond the first proposal." Yet, if the south side of Pennsylvania Avenue was ever to be cleared up, the government would still have "two more blocks to buy."[37]

Moore need not have worried over the various facets of the problem. The House refused to accept the Senate amendment. Once again, an important legislative battle for an archives building was lost.

POSTLEGISLATIVE DIGRESSIONS AND EXCURSIONS

A writer in the *Daughters of the American Revolution Magazine,* undismayed by the lack of progress to date, was buoyed up by the prospect of the incoming national administration, declaiming:

After forty years of varying activities carried on by organizations and individual patriots, the movement to establish a National Archives Hall at Washington . . . is about to reach its fruition. The new Congress convening in March for its first session under the Warren G. Harding Administration is expected to complete the legislative details, so frequently begun in the past, for a suitable archives depository.[38]

She concluded with the comforting thought that "the present growing recognition of the need to make adequate arrangements for the Federal archives is a distinct sign of national maturity."[39]

Other self-appointed keepers of the records had, in the meantime, informed Poindexter about alleged destruction of records by the secretary of Commerce. Replying to the senator's inquiry as to the truth of the matter, Herbert Hoover assured him that there "are some misimpressions" about this report, "as I have no notion of destroying any records." Alluding to the other side of the coin, the secretary observed, "What appeals to me though is that these records are in constant jeopardy." Pointedly referring to the events in January, he noted that "they have already been partially destroyed by fire. . . . The actual cost of providing a watchman and extra fire service probably amounts to more, if we take the Government as a whole, than it would cost to put up a proper fireproof Archives Building."[40]

As the summer legislative doldrums approached, Jameson, weary of his labors in behalf of archives and history, decided to refresh the muse by attending the Anglo-American historical conference in London and doing some sightseeing on the Continent. He informed Poindexter of his plans. Poindexter wished him an enjoyable vacation in Europe, but he couldn't refrain from unburdening himself, confessing that he was "disappointed in the obstacles put in the way of execution of the law which we secured way back in 1913 . . . but we will keep trying until we obtain the desired object." The senator considered it unlikely that anything further could be done "until the general appropriation bills come up next winter." In the meantime, he hoped "we will be able to find some desirable site which is not subject to the objections and personal interests . . . we . . . encountered in regard to the other proposed sites."[41]

When Jameson returned from his holiday in Europe, he found new accessions of strength for the national archives movement. For one thing, Sen. Reed Smoot was now chairman of the Senate Committee on Public Buildings and Grounds, and, as one enthusiast saw it, that "almost insures the bill's passage during the new Congress," because "Smoot sees in the removal of these historic papers a timely opportunity to get more desk room out of the present quarters, both rented and owned."[42]

But by far the most important development was the acquisition of a vital new force in support of the movement. Despite the long-continued efforts of Jameson, Leland, and their adherents in the Senate and the House, and of some of the state and local historical fraternity, the fact remained that hitherto the movement had lacked the most essential ingredient for promoting congressional action—powerful grass-roots political support. This hiatus was about to be filled.

8

New Allies

THE AMERICAN LEGION

While officers and men of the American Expeditionary Forces were still in France after the armistice, certain of the officers, including Col. Theodore Roosevelt, Jr., remembering the political power of the old Grand Army of the Republic, organized a meeting in Paris in 1919 and founded the veterans' organization of World War I, the American Legion.[1] Jameson probably did not dream of the importance of this development for the archival cause.

Within a couple of years, several hundred thousand former servicemen had joined the Legion and established posts in every state and territory. The primary purpose, of course, was to aid the new veterans in resuming civilian life and to help the disabled, the widows, and the orphans of the war. And just as the Grand Army had promoted monuments throughout the land, memorializing the dead and the victors, so the Legion was intent on a similar course after the First World War.

The national commander of the Legion, F. W. Galbraith, Jr., appointed a National Memorials Committee to consider and advise on the form and nature of war memorials to be erected in the national capital and elsewhere in the country.[2] An additional function of the committee was to oversee the care and handling of the service records of the veterans of the war. Concurrently, a Massachusetts officer, Eben Putnam, was appointed national historian of the Legion.

Putnam was born October 10, 1868, in Salem, Massachusetts, son of an old Bay State family. In 1890, he assumed the management of the Salem, Massachusetts, *Press* and founded the *Historical and Genealogical*

Record, which later became *Putnam's Historical Magazine* and the *Genealogical Magazine.* In the meantime, he had successfully managed various business ventures connected with Putnam family investments. Foreseeing America's entry into the great war then engulfing Europe, Putnam joined the Citizens Military Training Camp at Plattsburg, New York. In 1917 he was commissioned in the army and served in France as a captain in the Quartermaster Corps. After the war, Putnam became a charter member of American Legion Post 72, in Wellesley, Massachusetts, and served as department (state) historian.[3]

The emergence of Putnam was one of those fortuitous events which cannot be anticipated. Jameson immediately recognized his potential usefulness to the archival cause. At the annual meeting of the American Historical Association in December 1920, a Committee on Military History was established, and Putnam was appointed a member of this committee.[4] He now had a post of a similar nature in both the Legion and the AHA. This conjuncture of man, organizations, and function was to have an important influence on the archival movement.

The first meeting of the Legion's National Memorials Committee was held at the National Headquarters in Indianapolis, Indiana, on April 2, 1921. Among the various proposals before it was one referred to as "America's Memorial Church." The committee recommended that the Legion take no part in its promotion, as it "might tend to open up a question of religion which would do more to disrupt this organization than politics." The National Executive Committee concurred and rejected the idea. Another proposal was the establishment of a "National Memorial University." Although the Memorials Committee deemed this project worthy, the committee nevertheless felt that it was "not universal enough in its benefits to warrant endorsement by the American Legion" and therefore recommended its refusal. And so it went with a variety of proposed projects, all of them found wanting for one reason or another.[5]

It was at this point that Eben Putnam's appointment, earlier in the year, to the Military History Committee of the American Historical Association proved of decided advantage to the archival cause. Two months before the Memorials Committee met, the AHA Military History Committee held its first meeting.[6] Although Jameson, Moore, and Leland were not members of this committee, at least two members, Allen R. Boyd of the Library of Congress and Oliver L. Spaulding of the Army War College, were familiar with both the leading personalities and the problems involved in the promotion of a national archives. Putnam must have received a good briefing on this problem because he proceeded to sell the chairman of the Legion Memorials Committee, T. Semmes Walmsley, on the idea.

When the Memorials Committee learned of the idea of establishing a national archives, the project struck its fancy at once, and for very practical reasons. In its report to the third convention, the committee stated that its chairman had "investigated conditions in Washington relative to a proposed National Memorial" and found that "there is an imperative and immediate need of an archives building." Since this building would "house all the records of the service men and women of this War," the committee thought that the Legion should "urge Congress to include in its next appropriation an amount for the archives building." The committee also agreed that the proposed archives building should be of a type approved by the American Historical Association and "should be located on Pennsylvania Avenue, and as close to the Library [of Congress] as possible."[7]

Putnam followed up his successful effort with the Memorials Committee with further representations to the national adjutant, Lemuel Bolles, requesting Bolles to take up the matter of the national archives building with the Legion authorities. Putnam referred to the failure of the effort in the Senate at the last session, when a promising attempt "struck out" in the House-Senate conference committee, and he hoped Bolles would do some hard work to "help along this excellent project" in the next session.[8]

In anticipation of the meeting in Washington on April 28–30, 1921, of the Organization of War History Commissions, Putnam wrote the Legion's assistant national adjutant, R. G. Creviston, expressing the hope that the Memorials Committee would take some action concerning the archives building which he, Putnam, could report to the war history organization as the official position of the Legion. He knew, of course, that the Memorials Committee had taken the project under advisement, but he wanted to be sure that they understood what was at issue, and he cautioned that "an Archives building can hardly be used as a social gathering place. It could be part of a museum; but Washington has no lack of museums. It could contain an auditorium."[9] It is interesting that this sagacious New Englander had such a good grasp of the problem. Even though the archives might have to be promoted in the guise of a memorial, he wanted to avoid a multifunctional structure. As far as it was attainable he wanted an archives structure per se, standing clear and uncluttered by other functions.

Continuing his thought, Putnam pointed out to Creviston that "for nearly twenty years the historical people have been vainly seeking the erection of a safe storage place for records. . . . If the Legion . . . insists there be erected such a building, whether as a Memorial building or not, it will be erected." This was expressive of the power of the Legion! Then he cleverly wove it in with the Legion's own interest, the desire to improve its image as an organization, saying, "the Legion will get the credit for it—another point scored against those who claim we are after only the loaves and fishes." Then again, exhibiting a knowledge of his subject that commands the respect of a professional archivist, he commented on the idea of segregating war records from all other records in a separate depository:

It would be a mistake . . . to urge the segregation of records relating to this War. What is needed is a place of deposit for all dead files of all Government Departments and Bureaus. . . . It will require a very large building, for not only must there be the stacks and storage spaces, but repair rooms, research and reading rooms, and rooms where certain records can be exhibited, to say nothing of work rooms for the office force. Such a building . . . should be perfectly protected, conveniently situated, and . . . one of the show places of the City.[10]

After the war history meetings in Washington in late April, Putnam communicated further views to T. Semmes Walmsley, chairman of the Memorials Committee. He stated that he had conferred recently with Waldo Leland and with Colonel Spaulding of the AHA committee, and he noted with concern that "Col. Spalding [*sic*] . . . in charge of a portion of the records of the A.E.F. [American Expeditionary Forces] is working for a consolidation of all war records in a proposed War Department Archives." This was neither the first nor the last time that the thought of a ministerial archives beclouded the issue. Putnam reiterated that it seemed proper to him that the projected memorial should take the form of a national archives. As the Legion's Memorials Committee was to consider the question of the care and preservation of the service records of the war, formal action by the committee, thought Putnam, would "exert favorable effect on Congress."[11]

Putnam observed that, although the Memorials Committee had met, it had left "open for future discussion the character which the proposed Memorial Building at Washington was to take." His solution of the difficulty was that all interests, asking severally for the erection of an archives building, of a large auditorium, and of a memorial, should unite and work toward one end, "the establishment of a Memorial group of buildings, two of which might be designed for archives [a military archives and a civil archives], and one for an auditorium."[12] The leverage for this solution—for accommodation of disparate elements—though supported with reluctance by Putnam, lay in a grandiose private project about which he had been closely briefed by Charles Moore and Waldo Leland.

In June of 1921, Putnam wrote Walmsley what he had learned about a gigantic memorial project dreamed up by a Mrs. Henry F. Dimock. This project was to be a "George Washington Memorial" to be erected on the Mall, for which a public subscription of $10 million was to be made. The lady had started the idea rolling before the First World War; by 1921, Putnam stated, she had amassed $400,000, and *mirabile dictu*, Congress "had set aside a block on the Mall." Furthermore, continued Putnam, within the past month Mrs. Dimock had "obtained from both President Harding and Mr. Coolidge public recognition of her plan." He thought that neither the president nor the vice president were "fully informed of all the angles" of what Putnam judged to be an "absurd proposition."[13]

"The lady was smart enough to tie it in with the late war," the Legion historian wrote. She modified her original plan "so as to make her building a Memorial to all soldiers in all Wars." She had a scheme to place on the dome of the memorial as many stars as there were men enlisted in the First World War, with the initials of a man on each star. Mrs. Dimock also planned to "make her building the headquarters of various organizations, patriotic and also historical," one of the organizations "being a 'fake' historical society now operating from New York as a publishing concern." The building was to include an auditorium.[14]

The Legion historian, naturally, was not happy with the thought that the Dimock project would get somewhere. He was therefore pleased to observe that there were fissures in the lady's support. She was, he said, "so thoroughly tied up with every sort of scheme to raise money that she is tied up in many ways." Moreover, her plan no longer had the support of some of the persons she had originally interested in it. However, she was "procuring endorsements of her scheme from many organizations, as for instance the Veterans of Foreign Wars." Yet, "among those interested in Congress," some were becoming restive and were considering not extending their option to use the land set aside for the project. Nevertheless, Putnam told Walmsley, there was a resolution pending in Congress "that on the receipt of subscriptions aggregating half a million dollars, which will cover the architect's fees," she should "be allowed to commence the foundations" of the building. Being a practical man, Putnam admitted that he was at first inclined to think that the Dimock project "might be utilized in whatever general plan of a memorial was advanced by the Legion," but he was now convinced that "her whole Memorial scheme should be sidetracked." He told Walmsley that any project that involved a memorial to "the men of this War" should first be submitted to and approved by the Legion.[15]

Putnam then reminded Walmsley that he had earlier suggested that "our Memorial should take the form of a group, and should be of great extent." He thought that a number of ideas could be combined, stating that "perhaps we could utilize the demand for an archives building . . . and the local demand for an auditorium," and even, possibly, include the Dimock scheme, "in such a grand memorial group." Putnam feared, however, that such a scheme "would require the condemnation by Congress of a large tract of land which probably could not be done."[16]

This line of thought brought him to an alternative idea. He would get a large tract of land on the Mall nearest the area of the Capitol. This tract could include the "block already set aside for Mrs. Dimock." A large building could be erected there "at a cost of say seven or eight million dollars." The building would have two wings: one wing would be devoted to military and naval archives; the other would house archives of other departments of the government. The two wings would be joined by a "great rotunda" which would be an exhibition hall "with previous historical documents, battle flags of past wars, and our own standards" of the First World War. "It would serve to house and protect the records of the soldiers of all wars, as well as all memorials of the nation as expressed by its records. It would not include any offices or meeting rooms of any sort, except the offices of the Archives officials and the search rooms. It would provide a grand building which everyone reaching Washington would see and visit, and would occupy the most conspicuous position on the Mall."[17]

Here one perceives the germ of the concept for the great Pantheonlike exhibition hall in the future National Archives Building. "If the Legion will get behind this proposal," Putnam asserted, "the chances are that it can be put through." But he advised Walmsley that "it will be necessary for you to personally meet with the men who are interested to learn all the details, the difficulties, and the possibilities of success." Foremost among them was Charles Moore of the Fine Arts Commission, with whom he would arrange a meeting for Walmsley.[18]

Indeed, eight weeks later, Putnam and Walmsley met in Washington. On August 22 they had what the former characterized as "a most satisfactory conference . . . with Dr. Moore and Mr. Leland" and, later, with Senator Smoot. "Walmsley studied the matter from various viewpoints and is heartily in accord," Putnam jubilantly reported to the Legion's assistant national adjutant, R. G. Creviston. The two Legion officials were "working together to bring about the erection of a properly designed and sufficiently large archive building," said the national historian, which would be "situated in a proper location" and with memorial features "embraced in the design."[19]

The conference in Washington was thus a rather significant meeting. The upshot was that the Memorials Committee of the Legion would support the movement for an archives building and push the idea in its report to the annual convention of the Legion. Putnam wrote Creviston that he was "satisfied with progress so far" and believed that the Legion would "have the opportunity to score again in the estimation of people who look to it to take a stand in all matters of national interest, aside from politics." Internal evidence of his correspondence indicates that the Legion's national historian was both a sensitive man and one who stubbornly held to the course he believed to be right. Certainly he did not relish the gibes that the Legion was interested solely in the material welfare of its members. He repeatedly referred to an upgrading of the Legion's image as an organization devoted to the general public interest. In concluding his report to Creviston, Putnam cautioned him not to release any news item on the matter as the time was not yet right. At the right time, he said, Walmsley would "give out something to stimulate interest."[20]

In the meantime, in his correspondence with the department (state) historians of the Legion, Putnam lost no opportunity to push the archival idea. For example, writing to the historian of the department of Virginia, he noted with pleasure that "the minutes of the second convention of the Department of Virginia . . . contain two resolutions concerning the Memorial Library and the Preservation of War Records."[21] And he wrote to Leland, "It occurred to me that in my report this fall [to the Legion national convention] I might summarize what has been done . . . by the various states. If you have anything to suggest I would be glad to have your views."[22]

THE FIRST LEGION RESOLUTION

The testing ground for all this preliminary activity within the Legion was the third annual convention at Kansas City, Missouri, October 31–November 2, 1921. Here, at the annual conventions, resolutions were passed which not infrequently reverberated through the halls of Congress. Chairman Walmsley, in presenting the report of the National Memorials Committee, declared that he had "investigated conditions in Washington relative to a proposed National Memorial" and found "an imperative need of an archives building." The Legion, he said, "should urge Congress to include in its next appropriation an amount for the archives building."[23]

The Memorials Committee report included several pages of data detailing the location, nature, and housing of "the National records in Washington" concerning America's participation in the World War.

The records of the G.H.Q., A.E.F. [General Headquarters, American Expeditionary Forces] were made up at Chaumont and shipped home, and with the records made up in this country by the Historical Branch, War Plans Division, Chief of Staff, are of primary importance for the history of unit operations . . . many important records of the S.O.S. [Services of Supply] are also in the Historical Branch. The records of The Adjutant General's Office, pertaining to organization, administration, and personnel, together with the previously mentioned series are stored . . . in Building E, at 6th and B Streets, which is a building with concrete walls and wooden floors . . . poorly adapted for protection against fire originating within the building. The files occupy about 140,000 square feet of floor space . . . in steel filing cases, four drawers deep, and weigh nearly 2000 tons.[24]

The report, which was probably indebted to source material gathered by Leland, went on to state that the individual records of men serving in the army were also in Building E and that in the State, War, and Navy Building were the records of the judge advocate general and the inspector general. The Munitions Building on B Street contained the records of a number of branches: the Office of the Chief of Engineers and the Engineer Corps; the Graves Registration Service of the Office of the Quartermaster General; the Construction Division, relating to camps, cantonments, and the like; the Air Service, including unit histories; the Signal Corps; the Historical branch of the Quartermaster Corps (other quartermaster records were at Fort Myer, Virginia); the Ordnance Division; and the Army Medical Corps and the Nurses Training Corps, which were partly in the Munitions Building and partly in the Army Medical College, where a medical and surgical history of the war was being prepared.[25]

After noting that the records of the Coast Artillery and Field Artillery were mostly in the files of the adjutant general, the report drew attention to the point that "important records of troop units" were to be found at every military post in the country, mostly housed in buildings that afford little or no protection against fire, "the custodians of which were often ignorant of their contents."[26]

As to the navy, the report stated that "the Historical Section of the Office of Naval Intelligence and the Bureau of Navigation contain the most important naval records of the War," and they were housed in the new Navy Building at Seventeenth and B streets, where the records of the Marine Corps and the U.S. Shipping Board were also.[27]

The truly comprehensive report dealt also with the records of the various war-related agencies: the Selective Service records were in the Washington Barracks and included the records of 51 state and territorial headquarters, 155 district boards, 4,568 local boards, and the records of 23,908,576 registrants, all of which weighed a total of 8,000 tons; records of the War Risk Bureau occupied 90,000 square feet in the Arlington Building; records of the Council of National Defense, the War Industries Board, and the Committee on Public Information had been removed to the Munitions Building; records of the Food Administration, the Fuel Administration, and the War Trade Board were in temporary buildings; and records of the War Finance Corporation and of the several Liberty Loans were in the Treasury Building and at Federal Reserve Banks.[28]

Finally, the report stated, "many other important files . . . are to be found in the files of the Departments . . . in the files of the House and Senate Committees, and in the Library of Congress." In view of these specifically adduced facts, the American Legion's National Memorial Committee significantly concluded the following:

This very brief summary of the character of our latest War records and their places of deposit, made during the past summer at the request of the National Historian, serves . . . to indicate . . . the woefully inadequate method of storing the records and protecting them. . . . Unquestionably the mass of useful national archives has more than doubled since 1917, at which time there were no adequate housing provisions for their preservation and protection. The memorials of a nation . . . of incalculable value, which if destroyed can never be restored, are in no other progressive civilized country so poorly protected, the menaces to their safety so lightly regarded by the nation's legislators, as in our own country.[29]

The value of a report, no matter how well researched and well written, ultimately depends upon the objective results. This report had two significant consequences: first, it aborted the nascent idea of erecting a huge National Victory Memorial Building on the Mall in the national capital; and, second and more important, it caused the American Legion to enlist actively in the movement to erect a national archives building as a prime element of its memorials program.

Responding to the joint representations of the National Memorials Committee and the national historian, the Committee on Resolutions introduced, and persuaded the delegates to pass, the following resolution:

Whereas, the American Legion is vitally interested in the securing and preservation of the archives of our national government, now
Be it Therefore Resolved, by the American Legion in convention assembled that the American Legion urges the proper legislation for the erection of a suitable repository for all national archives where they may be safe from any future possibility of fire, vermin, or other causes for their destruction.[30]

A few weeks later, Putnam felt that the time had come for a major publicity effort. In a letter to Waldo Leland, he declared that

There is no doubt in my mind that during the next fortnight there should be whatever publicity can be had through the press and Legion sources concerning the fact that the Legion has come to know the disgraceful conditions attaching to the matter of preservation of our national records, and of the long and almost futile fight those who are best qualified to know, have made for the safety of the records, a matter of concern to the nation . . . realizing this condition, the Legion has demanded that the records, the memorials of the nation, be made safe and also accessible, and that no picayune methods be used either. . . . The Legion has asked Congress to provide the means. It of course steps aside to let those men who are trained in archives, determine how those means should be used.[31]

Jameson, realizing the value of the Legion's resolution, and always on the lookout for useful allies, lost no time in adding Putnam to his team. Late in 1921, he had the New Englander appointed a member of the Committee on the National Archives of the American Historical Association. By past association and personal experience, Putnam was well endowed to assist Jameson in furthering the movement.

OTHER VOICES

As the congressional session of the winter of 1921–1922 opened, others besides the American Legion voiced their support of the national archives concept. Foremost, of course, was the American Historical Association. At the AHA annual meeting in December, Jameson asked its council to dispatch another memorial to the national legislature. The council agreed and instructed him to draft the document and subscribe to it the names of all the council members. Reviewing the past failures to act, the memorial stated, in part,

For Thirteen years, beginning in 1908, a committee of the American Historical Association has annually urged upon Congress the erection of a suitable national archive building in Washington, in which the records . . . of the Government, now kept in a hundred different repositories, mostly unfit and unsafe, may be preserved in safety, arranged in good order, found rapidly, and consulted with ease.[32]

What had happened during those thirteen years? As Jameson noted, "Congress authorized the erection of a building [acts of 1913 and 1916], and provided for preliminary plans" in 1914, the Public Buildings Commission selected a site in 1918, but "the recommendations and estimates annually submitted by the Treasury have not . . . been followed by any appropriations" for the purchase of a site or the beginning of construction. The memorial concluded that since the war "the situation has grown far worse and calls more loudly for remedy." Specifically cited were the records of the American Expeditionary Forces, and others "representing many millions in tax claims," as well as records in American embassies and consulates abroad "needing better and safer care."[33]

The seventeenth annual Conference of Historical Societies also met in December. It appointed a committee consisting of Victor H. Paltsits of the New York Public Library, Solon J. Buck of the Minnesota Historical Society, and Morgan P. Robinson of the Virginia State Archives to draft an appropriate resolution expressing the sentiments of the gathering. On December 29, the conference approved the resolution, which stated that the national archives in Washington were "now scattered and disorganized," that in the "aid of historical research and for administrative efficiency," the records should be "concentrated in an adequate national archives building." The resolution also urged Congress to provide a site without delay and declared that, pending the construction of a building, the government should prepare regulations with adequate oversight "to prevent further ravages among the public records."[34]

Paltsits, who for years was the principal historical society figure agitating for a national archives building, did not rest content with merely forwarding conference resolutions to key senators. He personally wrote to senators Smoot and Underwood and sorrowfully reported to Jameson that the senators' answers "showed that Smoot and Underwood were in a deadlock . . . over the site for the building, Underwood stating the suspicion of a real estate game." In addition, Paltsits said, "I wrote to forty-five of the 'statesmen' from New York," and he saw to it that other historians wrote their congressmen. He specifically mentioned the efforts of Solon J. Buck in Minnesota, George S. Godard in Connecticut, John C. Parish in Iowa, and Morgan P. Robinson in Virginia. Robinson, in particular, was successful with the Virginia legislators. He reported that he had received satisfactory answers from both senators and five of the ten members of the Virginia delegation in the House. Both Sen. Claude A. Swanson and Sen. Carter Glass promised that they would do all they could to further the cause.[35]

The American Library Association passed a resolution, which, in addition to the usual call for a national archives building, was unlike the others in making the request that the federal authorities manifest a "sense of responsibility . . . in the preservation and . . . administration of . . . archives located outside of Washington."[36]

The Washington, D.C., Board of Trade's Committee on Public and Private Buildings also added its voice. In his recommendation to the board, William A. Rawlings, the chairman, said, "Your Committee believes there is an urgent need for a Hall of Records, and recommends that the Board of Trade go on record as favoring the immediate erection of such a building, the design and location to be approved by the Fine Arts Commission." The resolution was adopted by the board of directors on March 6, 1922.[37]

The ever-hopeful stewards of the federal government added their prayers to Congress. Secretary of the Treasury Andrew W. Mellon sent a letter to the Speaker of the House requesting funds for the construction of an archives building.[38] Secretary of the Navy Edwin Denby told the legislators that the navy's historical section "is continuing the work of collection, arrangement and filing of documents" of the "late war, with a view to building up a historical archives," and this, of course, would require safe quarters.[39] Secretary of Commerce Herbert Hoover, referring to the census records fire early in 1921, described the great research values of the records in his custody:

The state governments of New York, Pennsylvania, and Arkansas, as well as . . . important cities, have at different times maintained corps of clerks in the Bureau [of the Census] to copy special material from these records. . . . The Bureau of Internal Revenue, the Bureau of Pensions, and other Federal offices . . . and individuals and societies interested in genealogical and other research work are frequently requesting information contained in the returns.[40]

Hoover concluded that, in accordance with the reports of his predecessors in office, "it should require no argument to justify the wisdom of erecting an archives building."[41]

The National Commission of Fine Arts, after noting that the Poindexter amendment to the sundry civil appropriation bill for fiscal year 1922 was deleted in the conference committee, pointedly observed that "an archives building is urgently needed. . . . The need is admitted on all hands, but no action results."[42]

The last phrase neatly summarizes the story. And why no action? The reasons are quite evident: congressional inertia and congressional ignorance of the values at stake, compounded by suspicion of motives, and, as will be seen hereafter, congressional insistence on the time-honored pork barrel.

9

Renewed Legislative Efforts

TWO CONTRETEMPS

The abortive attempts for archives legislation at the 1922 session of the Congress, in Jameson's opinion, were due to two errors based on faulty information: one was perpetrated by Acting Supervising Architect James A. Wetmore; the other was due to the unfortunate interposition of Rep. Thomas L. Blanton of Texas, who killed a promising amendment to the Treasury Department appropriation bill.

Before the opening of the congressional session, the director of the budget approved the Treasury's request for the inclusion of an item of $500,000 for the acquisition of a site for an archives building. At the hearing before the House Appropriations Subcommittee, an unfortunate error occurred. Jameson, informing Victor Paltsits on developments, told him that "on misinformation supplied by the wrong-headed Acting Supervising Architect" the subcommittee expunged the item from the appropriation bill.[1] Writing to Senator Smoot to obtain his help, Jameson explained how the matter went. When the Treasury item for $500,000 was considered by the subcommittee, the chairman asked the witness, the acting supervising architect, "when was this [item] authorized?" Wetmore, perhaps not properly briefed on the background of the case, replied, "The building itself, in my opinion, has never been authorized."[2]

Jameson surmised that the chairman thereupon expunged the archives item, thinking that "if no building was authorized, it would not be good business to buy a site," and, perhaps indefinitely, "take it out of the taxable property of the District of Columbia." Yet, of course, the truth was that the archives building was already statutorily authorized. As Jameson pointed out to Senator Smoot, the act of June 28, 1916, though concerned mainly with the repeal of existing legislation requiring that European archives be inspected prior to planning, stated explicitly that "the construction of the said building according to the terms of the said Act of March fourth, 1913, is hereby authorized without such inspection . . . in Europe." Jameson further advised Smoot, "the acquisition of the site could be immediately followed by the erection of the building, without further legislation than a suitable appropriation."[3]

One can imagine Jameson's chagrin at this turn of affairs. His correspondence does not hide his bitterness. The New England granite in him determined his rejoinder. When the appropriation bill came to the House floor, he had Rep. Frederick W. Dallinger of Massachusetts primed to move an amendment restoring the item to the bill. He informed Prof. Andrew McLaughlin, "I provided the materials for his speech."[4]

At this juncture Representative Blanton of Texas made a point of order against the amendment on the ground that section 21 of the act of March 4, 1913, "had not been complied with," because the site selected by the Treasury and the plans based on the site had not been approved by the special commission consisting of "the Vice President, the Speaker, and the Secretaries of the Treasury, War, and Interior." Jameson was furious. In letters to various correspondents he excoriated Blanton who, "as usual, said what came into his head."[5] But the maneuver was successful. "The confounded chairman of the Committee of the Whole," Jameson told McLaughlin, "sustained the point of order so the amendment was lost."[6]

Jameson reiterated to Senator Smoot that "the successful point of order was based on wrong information." As Poindexter was absent from the city, Jameson was depending on Smoot's help, so he reminded the senator that "all persons . . . concerned with the National Archive Building know, that the commission *did* act in November 1918." Furthermore, Jameson said, he saw "yesterday at the Treasury Department, the letters of Secretary McAdoo to the other four members of the commission, dated November 13, 1918, submitting . . . the Treasury's choice of site and plans," and he saw the "document dated November 29, bearing the signatures of all five members of the commission" signifying their approval. Therefore, Jameson concluded, "All the action taken in this session by the House and its Committee on Appropriations has been based on misinformation."[7]

Then, recalling the Senate debate of the previous year, Jameson observed to the senator from Utah, that "objection is likely to be raised against buying any land" as the "government owns plenty of sites." Yet, the fact remained, and the Senate must take it into account, that none of the sites was large enough for a building of 9 million cubic feet, "as required by the Act of March 4, 1913, except locations on the Mall or in Potomac Park." But the objections to these locations were that such a structure would ostensibly spoil the appearance of the Mall and that Potomac Park was too far from other department buildings.[8]

Harking back to the Underwood-King amendments in 1921, Jameson observed that the Senate-approved amendment transferred the site of the proposed building "to a square . . . at Fourteenth and Fifteenth and B and C Streets," in the belief that only temporary buildings, "with some Treasury clerks in them," were on the square. The King amendment, however, was lost in the conference committee when it was discovered that the square had on it a large building which had cost the government "half a million dollars and was at that very time occupied by 3,615 Treasury clerks." Yet, in Jameson's view, there was no validity to the objection to the Ohio Avenue location since Ohio Avenue was only three squares long and the western third of the street had already been closed by legislative enactment. Also, Jameson said, "it is about the worst looking street in town, and leads nowhere in particular."[9]

Reminding Smoot that Senator Poindexter's aid could be counted on "if he returns in season," Jameson appealed for action on securing an appropriation during the current session "which will make a beginning of remedying the present deplorable conditions." He assured Smoot that "all the historians of the country will be very grateful to you."[10] The senator heeded the appeal and brought in an amendment to the appropriation bill which was then before the Senate Committee on Appropriations. If successful in weathering the further congressional gales, the amendment would restore the half-million-dollar item expunged by the House.

SENATE APPROVAL

Toward the latter half of January, the Senate debated the archives site amendment brought in by its Appropriations Committee. Senators King of Utah and Duncan U. Fletcher of Florida attacked the amendment; senators Smoot of Utah and Warren of Wyoming defended it.[11]

Predictably, Senator King objected to the purchase of more land and again upheld Senator Underwood's objection to closing Ohio Avenue. Buttressing his argument, he read to the Senate a lengthy communication from one J. H. Lord, identified as an engineer interested in city planning:

It appears that 15 or 20 years ago the triangle area between Pennsylvania Avenue and the Mall was planned out in detail for future Government buildings by a commission [the Macmillan Commission] and in 1908 a start was made by the purchase of the blocks on Fifteenth Street to be used under the plan for the State, Justice, and Commerce Departments, Squares Nos. 226 to 230, together with the inclosed streets. In 1913, an archives building being needed, a commission reported the designation by the Secretary of the Treasury of the blocks between Twelfth and Thirteenth, B and C Streets, consisting of squares 294, 295, and the portion of Ohio Avenue between them. . . . The purchase of this site is now contemplated.[12]

Before 1913, Mr. Lord thought, "there was no doubt little objection to this site," for the reason that Ohio Avenue was then "paved with grass-grown cobbles," and had little traffic. But by 1922, it was paved, and "traffic congestion on Pennsylvania Avenue vastly increased." Alternative routes were needed, thought the city planner, and he favored "a general restudy of the problem." He concluded with the opinion that "for the Government's own convenience" the "facility of ingress to this triangular area," when it is ultimately filled with federal government buildings, "will be highly important, and the closing of the only broad thoroughfare in the area," in his view, appeared to be a "very short-sighted policy."[13]

Senator Smoot countered the negative attitude of his colleagues with the statement that the archives building "must be centrally located or there would be no gain owing to the time and expense necessary for long trips to a building not located near the departments." He closed his address with a notable peroration:

I wish to assure the Senate that your commission wants to save every single dollar that it is possible to save. . . . The only question to decide is whether we are going to have an archives building. I say now without a moment's hesitation that if I had the power of the Government of the United States I would construct an archives building just as quickly as it would be possible to do it. . . . I do not ask for any elaborate building. I do not ask for marble and carved statues, and all the pillars of ancient Greece and Rome to be duplicated in this building. I want a large building, a fireproof building, a substantial building, that will serve the purpose of the Government of the United States for 100 years at least.[14]

The senator further advised the upper house that if an archives building were not erected in the near future, "the commission will have to go out and rent space wherever we can." He observed that records of the "recent war piled up in New York," they were "piled up in Philadelphia," and they "were scattered all over the United States." The records could not be brought to the District of Columbia, he asserted, because "we have not any place in which to put them. The only way to solve the difficulty," he concluded, "is to construct an archives building."[15]

Smoot's adversary, Senator King, agreed to the necessity for the building but warned him that if the commission did not select a site then owned by the government, "it could expect to be criticised." Nevertheless, when it came to a vote, the Senate adopted the amendment supported by Smoot.

HOUSE OPPOSITION

On February 2, 1922, the House of Representatives debated the archives amendment. Representatives Frederick W. Dallinger of Massachusetts and Simeon D. Fess of Ohio fought for approval of the amendment. Rep. Martin B. Madden of Illinois, chairman of the House Committee on Appropriations, led the opposition.[16]

Chairman Madden opposed the purchase of a site for the archives building, contending, as the *Evening Star* put it, "that an ideal location would be at 6th and B Streets, where the George Washington Memorial building is under construction." Rep. Joseph Walsh of Massachusetts reinforced Madden's contention with the argument that the time limit had expired "during which Congress had given the land to the memorial association and that . . . the building is being erected on land to which the association has no right."[17]

John W. Langley of Kentucky, chairman of the Public Buildings and Grounds Committee of the House, also strongly opposed the archives item, as well as the George Washington memorial, stating that the "representatives of the American Legion . . . are opposed to erecting any monument or memorial building for the World War veterans until the sick and disabled are properly cared for and a just compensation law has been enacted." He conceded that there was a need for an archives building, but, he said, "we also need other buildings in this country, hundreds of them." He continued,

. . . if we permit another body to stick in here and there a provision authorizing the construction of buildings that existing law . . . has not authorized, the first thing we know we country dirt-road farmer Congressmen will be knocked out of any public buildings at all, and I am opposed to any such procedure as this.[18]

In its customary dry style, the *Congressional Record* observed that this statement received applause. No doubt it did. It was an authentic expression of the pork barrel, certainly one of the most potent obstacles in the path of archives legislation. Chairman Langley again repeated the erroneous assertion that the archives building was not authorized. He should have known better.[19]

Langley continued with an explanation of the George Washington memorial building matter. It was then under consideration by his committee, and a hearing had been held. It appeared that Lt. Col. C. O. Sherrill, in charge of public buildings and grounds in the national capital, had represented the president at the laying of the cornerstone. At the House committee hearing he had admitted that the cornerstone was laid without legal authorization. Apparently the judge advocate general, having given an initial opinion that the laying was lawful, later discovered a law indicating that his previous ruling had been incorrect. As a practical matter, however, Colonel Sherrill decided that his programmed presence at the ceremony was the lesser of two evils. Langley went on to say that his committee certainly did not intend to authorize the beginning of a memorial project that would take a decade to complete, unless the government was willing to expend 7 or 8 million dollars in order to build it. "We have had some experience along that line," Langley remarked, "as, for instance, the Washington Monument."[20]

At this point, Congressman Dallinger reminded members of the House that the national archives building was authorized "almost eight years ago in the last omnibus public buildings bill passed by Congress." He then read the act of March 4, 1913, with its authorizing clause, and moved that "the House recede and concur in the Senate amendment." In subsequent altercation between him and Representatives Langley and James T. Begg of Ohio, the debate once again hinged on the advisability of using government-owned sites versus newly purchased sites. Langley asked whether "the Congress ought to go ahead and purchase property when the Government already owns enough property in the District . . . to build five times as many buildings as the Government needs." Dallinger replied, "I certainly do," because "upon every one of the sites now owned by the Government" other buildings were to be erected, in accordance with the general plan for the Mall and adjacent areas made by the Fine Arts Commission. Langley responded that he had "very little respect for its plans."[21]

Representative Fess came to his colleague's aid, stating that he did sympathize with the chairman of the Appropriations Committee and those interested "in not allowing the Budget System to be broken down by additional amendments in another body," meaning the Senate, which, if offered in the House, "would be subject to a point of order." On the other hand, Fess lamented, "the movement for an archives building is more than 40 years old, and every time the suggestion is made it meets with just such objections as we now hear." Langley replied, "And if it goes on this way, it will soon be 40 years since we had a public buildings bill," alluding to the real concern of the House members.[22]

Rep. Louis C. Cramton of Michigan, joining the debate, suggested that the Patent Office Building would be ideal for the use of an archives, because, he said, "it has walls 4 feet thick of masonry and limestone . . . and is thoroughly fireproof." Moreover, its central location at Seventh and F streets, N.W., made it "available for all branches of the Government," and he considered it "unsuitable for patent work. . . . I submit," he said, that "we ought to take into consideration such alternatives . . . before we enter upon any such real estate speculation as this amendment provides for."[23]

But Langley would not be budged from his stand for a general public buildings bill. With some bitterness he declaimed, "You gentlemen who have all the buildings you need in the large populated centers do not care so much about it; but when you talk about erecting a public building . . . here in the District of Columbia you call it patriotism." Then turning directly toward Fess, Langley continued, "When we talk about some public building that we absolutely need in our own sections of the country, the gentleman from Ohio refers to it as 'Podunk.'" Proceeding from the particular to the general, he protested that "the people generally, and some of the elite press, call it graft and 'pork barrel.' I am sick and tired of it, and I think the entire country is . . . we ought to go ahead and get all these necessary buildings together in one omnibus bill and take decent care of all sections of the country."[24] This outburst by Chairman Langley was met by the applause of his colleagues. The House was indeed overripe for an omnibus bill but, on the part of the administration, economy was the watchword of the day. Men such as Harding, Coolidge, and, above all, Secretary of the Treasury Andrew Mellon were genuinely appalled at the size of the wartime national debt, until then unparalleled in American history.

With respect to the efforts to obtain archives legislation by the amendment route, another speaker, William E. Andrews of Nebraska, adverted to one of the cardinal legislative points about which congressmen seemed to be irritated, namely, the bypassing of the orderly budgetary process. Professing to "deeply sympathize" with the need for an archives building, as well as for other buildings "where the Government needs are clearly defined," Andrews nevertheless felt that there "ought to be a very orderly . . . procedure. We have had much discussion," he said, of "the usurpation of power by appropriation committees, thereby depriving legislative committees of the duties assigned to them under the rules of the House." Then commenting on the archives amendment, he stated his view that "this proposition makes a direct encroachment upon the prerogatives of legislative committees." Therefore, the House owed it to its Committee on Appropriations "to insist upon the regular legislative course in making authorizations for this purpose."[25]

The result of the debate was predictable. The following day, February 3, the *Washington Post* summed up the matter:

Two Senate amendments, one carrying $1,000,000 for the construction of a vault for the Treasury and the other $500,000 for a site and other preparations for erecting a national archives building . . . were disagreed to, and the bill was sent back with the expectation that the Senate would agree to elimination of the two items.[26]

In an editorial the same day, entitled "Housing the Archives," the *Post* thought there was "a hint of an impending policy on the part of leaders of Congress" for "a definite program" for public buildings, "to be carried out through the orderly processes of legislation." The new policy would favor the "use of property already owned by the Government." The *Post* especially seized on the possibility of "remodeling the old Interior Department buildings, at Seventh and F Streets [the Patent Office] into structures capable of housing the public archives." The

House committee, the newspaper confided to its readers, "believes that these historic old buildings, dating back to a past generation, are especially suited to the object in view," as "they were built before the age of the cheap skyscrapers or the hollow tile shell. . . . they are indestructible and absolutely fireproof . . . their walls are of masonry as solid as those of the Capitol itself." The *Post* estimated the cost of converting the old buildings for the "storage of valuable government papers" at $500,000. Congress was "in a mood to discuss this question academically," but the editorialist demanded, "Let us have action."[27]

At this juncture other ideas emerged. Sen. John Sharp Williams of Mississippi wondered why the Union Station Plaza could not be used for an archives building. He thought a fine building erected in the center of the square would enhance its beauty. He believed the Senate was too rigid in insisting on the purchase of a new site. The senator felt that the House would go along with appropriating for a building, even though it refused to do so for a site.[28]

The conference committee met on February 7, 1922, to compose the differing versions of the bill as passed by the two houses. The Senate conferees recommended to their colleagues "that the Senate recede from its amendments, numbered 20 and 21" to H.R. 9724, "for Treasury Department appropriations for the fiscal year ending June 30, 1923." These amendments were, respectively, for the archives site and the Treasury vault.[29]

Senators Smoot and Poindexter were both keenly disappointed, as was natural for the two foremost congressional protagonists of a national archives. Smoot, a later convert to the archives movement, was impatient for results. Poindexter, a tested veteran of many defeats and some victories, figuratively dug in his cleats for another try. Although Smoot did not formally object to the conference report when put to the vote in the Senate, he did say it was "an awful mistake . . . when the House insisted upon striking that particular item out of the appropriation bill." He emphatically declared, "So far as I am concerned, as Chairman of the Public Buildings Commission . . . I shall assume no further responsibility for the safekeeping of the Government records." Senator Poindexter, in venting his disappointment, stated:

I merely wish to call attention . . . to the fact that . . . on three separate occasions the Senate has attached amendments to . . . appropriations bills providing for an archives building, and I sincerely trust that it will continue to do so, and that at some time when the appropriation bills come back here from the House of Representatives the Senate will make a stand for an appropriation . . . for . . . an archives building . . . and that the proper care of these invaluable records . . . be taken by a Government which is wealthy and perfectly able to do so.[30]

On this note the legislative effort of 1922 ended.

THE AFTERMATH

The reaction of Jameson to the frustrating events may be clearly seen in his correspondence with Victor H. Paltsits, whose function was to lobby state and local historical societies in behalf of the national archives concept and to bring their influence to bear on the congressional scene.

The repetition in congressional debates of the allegation that no archives appropriation could be made because no previously authorizing statute had been passed seared the soul of the New England scholar. Following the end of the 1922 legislative effort, he told Paltsits, "I have spent many hours on Capitol Hill . . . during the critical period" of the debate in the House. After witnessing the valiant but fruitless fight of Dallinger and Fess that ended in a crushing defeat by a vote of 131 to 8, Jameson pessimistically forecast the immediate future. "I watched this scene from the gallery," he said, "and was perfectly convinced that, for the next few years at least, no appropriation that involves the purchase of a site has the slightest chance of getting through the House."[31]

Jameson, of course, was aware that the fight over a site was really a smoke screen to obscure the real problem—the desire of a large number of members of the House that the post offices in their districts should be built first. In addition, there was "the animus against the purchase of any more real estate in the District of Columbia." Nevertheless, he felt that, "in spite of a great many difficulties" with existing sites, "the fight has to be kept up."[32]

Paltsits, replying to Jameson's sad news, confessed that he had been so certain of the passage of the archives item in the appropriation bill (after the representations of the American Historical Association, the American Legion, the historical societies, and others) that the "hurricane" that hit "that $500,000 in the House and blew it to 'kingdom come'" stunned him. "I have been 'knocked out,'" he mourned.[33]

Jameson tried to comfort his field general. "Do not let us be discouraged," he wrote, "I am sure that the plowing which you and your associates did in the hard Congressional soil of New York, Minnesota, Connecticut, Iowa, and Virginia will add appreciably to the fertility of that soil next year."[34]

If Jameson and his cohorts were downcast at this latest defeat, one important official did not propose to take it lying down: Colonel Sherrill was stung! An officer of the Army Corps of Engineers, he was in charge of public buildings and grounds in the national capital. In that capacity, he was also a member of the Public Buildings Commission whose chairman was Senator Smoot. To set the record straight once and for all, he forthwith compiled a report on the subject of sites and their relation to the national archives movement which was succinct, complete, and clear. In a letter to Smoot, he recommended that "this report be transmitted by the Public Buildings Commission to the President of the

Senate and to the Speaker of the House . . . for reference to the proper committees."[35]

Beginning his statement with the provisions of the act of March 4, 1913, Colonel Sherrill noted that the act provided that, as soon as the designs and estimates for an archives building had been approved by the commission, "the Secretary of the Treasury was authorized . . . in his discretion, to purchase or condemn the site approved by the Commission." The secretary of the Treasury had submitted a plan for the proposed site, and the commission had approved. The requirements for an appropriation were therefore met. In the meantime, Sherrill pointed out, "On December 18, 1917, the Public Buildings Commission . . . submitted a comprehensive report to Congress analyzing the needs of the Government departments . . . in the District of Columbia," and in this report "certain important principles, which should be followed in the construction of new buildings" were enunciated:

First: Public Buildings, other than those of the executive departments should face the grounds of the Capitol.
Second: New executive departmental buildings may . . . be located to face Lafayette Square . . . and south of Pennsylvania Avenue along Fifteenth Street to B Street [Constitution Avenue], on the land already purchased and awaiting such occupation.
Third: Both sides of the Mall, with the exception of the space needed by the Department of Agriculture . . . should be occupied by museums and other buildings containing collections . . . but not by departmental buildings.
Fourth: The space east of Fourteenth Street, between Pennsylvania Avenue and the Mall should be occupied by public buildings.[36]

It is interesting to note that this prescription for the use of sites in the national capital has been generally followed in the nearly half-century that has elapsed. In fact, Sherrill's fourth point was meticulously followed in the later Triangle development, fostered by Secretary of the Treasury Andrew Mellon.

The Public Buildings Commission, in its 1917 report, remarked Colonel Sherrill, "specifically urged the immediate construction of an archives building." Furthermore, squares 294 and 295 [the Ohio Avenue site] were considered as "the best suited for such a building." The site was sufficient to provide the space required, he continued, and "98 per cent of the material to be stored therein is in departments located . . . immediately adjacent to or west of this location."[37]

Turning to the financial aspects of the matter, Sherrill observed that since the commission's report, the secretary of the Treasury had three times submitted estimates to the Congress for approximately $500,000 for purchase of the site and $1.5 million for construction of the building.[38]

Taking note of the number of times the charge had been made on the floor of the House that the government owned land of sufficient area and adaptability for an archives building, and that it was therefore "wasteful and uneconomical to purchase additional land" for that purpose, Colonel Sherrill referred the legislators to a "detailed investigation" of government-owned land in the District of Columbia. The investigation had been made to ascertain the availability of a site for an archives building.[39]

Sherrill listed some thirty sites which had been acquired by the government for purposes other than the erection of a specific building and a half dozen sites which were purchased with specific buildings in mind. The thirty sites included the Potomac Park area, the Mall, the Capitol Grounds, Rock Creek Park, the Navy Yard, Anacostia Park, Lafayette Square, Union Station Plaza, Meridian Hill Park, and others. All these areas were rejected for archives use for various reasons, such as being too remote from other government department buildings, being too expensive to build on because of fronting on the Mall, requiring new land fill for which an archives building would be too heavy, or encroaching on park land in a densely populated area.[40]

As to sites purchased for specific building purposes, Colonel Sherrill considered that the most important were those located between Fourteenth and Fifteenth streets and Pennsylvania Avenue and B Street. This area, he admitted, furnished several tracts of "sufficient size for the archives building," but, he thought, "they are entirely unsuited to a building of this warehouse type." Moreover, these areas had been purchased and were being held for the future construction of buildings for the departments of State, Commerce, Justice, and Labor. "Under no circumstances," Sherrill believed, "should these areas be used . . . for any building whatever, except for . . . the departments above enumerated."[41] Evidently, the colonel had not been adequately briefed by either Jameson or Leland when he referred to the archives building as of the "warehouse type," and he was far wide of the mark as to the monumentality of the building ultimately erected.

In concluding his exposition, Sherrill once again reverted to the disputed tracts, squares 294 and 295. He affirmed that not only should these two squares be acquired for the archives building, but that "every piece of land from 14th Street to the Capitol, between Pennsylvania Avenue and the Mall should be at once purchased for future Government building." Furthermore, he declared,

There is no area of land in the whole of Washington, which so urgently requires cleaning up and renovation as that south of Pennsylvania Avenue between the Capitol and the Treasury. The present condition of buildings in this area is a disgrace to the National Capital, and a source of humiliation to every true American who has an iota of national pride. The most important avenue in the city is an eyesore instead of being the beauty spot it is capable of being made.[42]

Sherrill was equally and courageously emphatic in noting that "the claim has been made by members of Congress that real estate interests are trying to force the purchase of these squares. This claim has not the slightest foundation in fact." He was indignant that anyone "could accuse the distinguished Commission" which recommended these sites, namely, the vice president of the United States, the Speaker of the House, the secretaries of the Treasury, of War, and of the Interior. Nor could the "distinguished members of the Fine Arts Commission" who approved the selection "be accused of petty graft in recommending the purchase of this land." From the facts adduced, he stated, "it is absolutely essential . . . to buy . . . Squares 294 and 295" for an archives building.[43]

PREPARATIONS FOR NEW EFFORTS

Several days before the Sherrill report was publicly issued, fate, as if to underscore once again the urgent need for action in the preservation of the nation's documentary heritage, essayed a bit of propaganda. A fire in the roof housing of the Treasury Building, on February 8, 1922, alarmed responsible persons and the news media without actually doing much damage. The *New York Times* ran a lead editorial entitled "Imperiled Archives":

Every once in a while Americans are reminded by some striking . . . loss of precious historical documents of the necessity of housing them in buildings absolutely safe from fire. In 1911, the burning of the New York State Library made a monstrous gap in the materials . . . of our Colonial history. The Dutch records for seventy-five years of the seventeenth century, the English Colonial records, a priceless collection of Indian manuscripts, disappeared forever.[44]

After referring to the census records fire of the year before, the *Times* told its readers that the previous Wednesday "a fire in the Treasury Building came within a ticklish distance of the old records," which themselves were "not continuous or perfect, for the fire of 1833 gutted some of them."[45]

The *Evening Star* in Washington also editorialized on the fire, saying that "by great good fortune the United States was spared an irreparable loss yesterday when the fire in the Treasury building was confined to the structure on the roof. . . . But this fire," the *Star* thought, "should be . . . a definite warning, to be heeded in terms of prompt legislation."[46]

Jameson, ever alert for a propaganda gambit, very likely inspired the editorials, but in any case, he told Senator Smoot that in accordance with Smoot's "suggestion of February 17," he had written to the chairmen of the Senate and House committees on Appropriations and on Public Buildings and Grounds, Senators Warren and Bert M. Fernald of

Maine, and Representatives Madden and Langley, respectively. He avoided, he said, duplicating "Colonel Sherrill's very thorough letter respecting sites and the recent history of the movement for a National Archive building." Rather, he attempted "the removal of misunderstandings evinced in the House debates." Jameson reiterated what was certainly, by this time, common knowledge: "They all want an omnibus Public Buildings Act."[47]

Nevertheless, although losing hope for any forward movement at that session of Congress, Jameson, Smoot, and their supporters tried to think of other possible ways to advance their cause. In May, Jameson wrote Leland of one questionable scheme. On the basis that, legally, the secretary of the Treasury had the authority to purchase a site, Jameson said, "It appears that Smoot and his public buildings commission mean to persuade Secretary Mellon to buy the designated square . . . and so compel Congress to make the necessary appropriation." Jameson was not enamored with the idea of using that kind of force. Anyway, he had his doubts that Mellon would agree to do it. Jameson and Charles Moore concurred in the view that "to fly in the face of the House in that way would be a mistake." The tactic could very well result in "bad feeling for the whole project" and delay its fruition by at least a year.[48]

In searching for other means to advance the archives cause, Jameson turned to Eben Putnam. He had observed that the Legion was uncommonly successful in obtaining congressional appropriations for various veterans programs, and he asked Putnam for advice on how to do likewise in behalf of the archives. Putnam telegraphed Waldo Leland to "see a Mr. Raege at once." As Leland had left Washington and was about to sail for Europe, Jameson personally conferred with the Legion agent, H. H. Raege, who was in the comparatively new business of fund raising. Raege, Jameson wrote Leland, "is confident that he can get an archive building right off the bat, from Langley's committee or Madden's, or anybody's." The man's confidence, Jameson thought, was "based on the success of his organization in getting rapidly . . . quite outside of any consideration of the budget, an appropriation of $17,000,000 for additional hospitals for the soldiers of the late war." In view of this intelligence, Jameson initially thought he would have a conference with Senator Smoot, and thereafter call a meeting of the American Historical Association's Committee on the National Archives. To this meeting he would also summon Putnam and try to determine what was "best to do."[49]

Despite his willingness to fight hard and long for what he wanted, Jameson was too well reared in the straitlaced old New England traditions of scholarship to be comfortable with methods that violated his sense of the fitness of things. He always played the game of influence within the accepted rules of the legislative and budgetary processes of the American government. After several weeks of further consideration, and on hearing of Raege's probable connection with the proposal to have Secretary Mellon force the congressional hand by purchasing the site before appropriation, Jameson changed his mind. He told Leland, "unless I get further light, I shall not fall in with Raege's plan of having the meeting of our committee and then jamming the appropriation through the House by the power of the American Legion."[50]

Besides personal scruples, Jameson doubted that Raege's analogy with respect to his "$17,000,000 success is perfect." He shrewdly observed, "Seventeen hospitals in seventeen different congressional districts would be much more useful in the period preceding election than anything connected with a National Archive Building." Furthermore, he wrote, "I apprehend that members of Congress will ask themselves whether the voters belonging to the American Legion will be as mad at not getting a National Archive Building as at not getting the bonus or the hospitals."[51]

It is evident from Jameson's casual remarks in his correspondence that his informal alliance with the American Legion in the archives matter was disconcerting to him, yet he could hardly feel other than friendly toward the national historian, Eben Putnam, who so eagerly and unselfishly gave of his time, his substance, and his experience to promote the success of the cause.

Putnam was in frequent touch with Jameson, advising him of favorable actions taken by various Legion departments and other veterans organizations. Early in September he sent Jameson a copy of the resolution adopted at the convention of the Massachusetts department of the Legion. After referring to the action taken at the national convention in Kansas City, in October 1921, the resolution continued as follows:

Whereas, since the adoption of the above resolution no steps have been taken by Congress looking toward the erection of an archives building. . . . Be it Resolved by the Department of Massachusetts in Convention assembled, that we do protest the failure of Congress to provide a suitable building for the storing of our national records . . . and we call upon our representatives in Congress to use all proper means to obtain legislation which will provide adequate protection to our national archives.[52]

Putnam also urged Jameson to draft a resolution for presentation at the annual convention of the Military Order of the World War. The convention was to be held in Atlanta, Georgia, September 18–20, and the president of the United States was expected to attend.[53] Jameson obliged. Within a couple of days he sent Putnam a suggested resolution which neatly summarized the problem and the actions required. He also advised Putnam that there had been "some hopeful elements in the situation" with respect to prospects for an appropriation:

The Secretary of the Treasury has repeated his estimate and request of last year. It is now in the hands of the Director of the Budget, and I have been working upon him, and I hope making an impression. Senator Smoot as chairman of the Public Buildings Commission . . . seems also to be putting in good work upon him.[54]

Toward the end of September, Putnam reported to Jameson that the convention of the Military Order of the World War adopted the resolution on the archives "with a very slight change." As Putnam was a member of the Resolutions Committee, he had been in a strategic position to see the thing through.[55]

Other military-related organizations also raised their voices, using Armistice Day as a focal point. Among those who presented memorials to Congress as of November 11, 1922, were the Sons of Veterans, U.S.A., Maryland Division;[56] and the Army and Navy Union, U.S.A.[57]

In the meantime, at the fourth annual convention of the American Legion, October 16–20, at New Orleans, the National Legislative Committee of the Legion again submitted for action the resolution of the third annual convention. It was unanimously approved, and an appropriation of $2 million was requested for the archives. Putnam was optimistic about the immediate future, and this was reflected in the report of the National Legislative Committee, which stated, "Upon the reconvening of Congress on December 5, it seems to be the intention of the Committee on Public Buildings and Grounds of the House . . . to prepare a general omnibus public buildings law." The committee asserted that it had received assurances that "an Archives Building appropriation will be included therein."[58]

Despite the acknowledged aid for the archives cause rendered by the Legion, neither Jameson nor Leland ever seemed to be entirely comfortable about the most powerful veterans organization in the country. Especially in its younger days it was an exceedingly lusty aggregation, far removed from the placid, conventional, rules-following scholarly milieu. So we find Leland, then in France, writing rather agitatedly to Jameson in mid-November of 1922: "The reports reaching here of the recent convention of the American Legion are not very encouraging. Dr. Gros, who attended from here . . . says that it was a case of mob rule, with great disorder, drunkenness, gaming and even rioting on a small scale."[59]

Jameson replied a fortnight later that "our accounts here are to the same effect. The truth is, that organization has rushed into the baser kind of politics more rapidly than the G.A.R. did, and . . . the country will . . . be largely run for the next twenty years by the ex-soldiers." But Jameson was far more concerned with the overall political situation. The biennial congressional elections occurred in November 1922, and the national archives movement lost one of its most ardent supporters. "As a collection of individuals I do not see that Congress has been improved by the election," he wrote, "There were some bad losses (I count Poindexter one), and some . . . gains. . . . Both in the Senate and the House there will be new leaders." He hoped, however, that on the whole the new leaders would "represent more liberal tendencies."[60]

10

Poindexter's Last Stand

HEARST TO THE RESCUE

In January 1923, the Public Buildings Commission presented a report to the U.S. Senate, which included the following recommendation: "The erection of 15 stories of steel filing stacks in the interior court of the Pension Office Building at an estimated cost of $1,000,000. . . . That building is fireproof and is isolated from other buildings." This became the basis of the Smoot amendment to the independent offices appropriation bill.[1] It was Smoot's offer for an immediate solution of the records preservation problem.

The commission's argument for the use of the Pension Office Building may be summarized as follows: that the building was "admirably adapted for the purpose"; that the ongoing use of the building "could continue without interference"; that its court, to be used for stacks, contained 4 million cubic feet of space "going to waste"; and that the proposed stacks "would use 2,894,008 cubic feet" of the wasted space and "would provide 729,929 linear feet of shelving . . . with a net filing capacity of 948,900 cubic feet." The commission estimated that the cost "of erecting an archives building to accommodate an equal amount of shelving, including . . . stairways, elevators, corridors, toilets, etc., would be $1,680,000." In addition, however, the cost of shelving for the archives building was placed at $500,000 and the outlay for land at $200,000 more. The total cost of approximately $2.38 million for the archives building was then contrasted with the approximately $1 million cost of the Pension Building project. Furthermore, at the Pension Building, the existing guard and maintenance force would be sufficient, whereas these men would have to be provided for a new archives building.[2]

Through the providential interposition of the *Washington Herald*, Jameson promptly counterattacked the commission's position. Apparently Jameson knew in advance the purport of the report because on the very day it was publicly unveiled, January 4, a reporter from the *Herald* came to his office "to get ammunition on the matter of a National Archive Building." The reporter stated that "the Hearst papers were instructed, directly from Mr. Hearst, to push that matter." The following day, Jameson told his American Legion ally, Eben Putnam, "Senator Smoot has brought forward his plan for stacks in the old Pension Building, but I judge that these papers will oppose that solution in the interest of a better ultimate one."[3]

With the gusto characteristic of the Hearst era in American journalism, his mouthpiece in the national capital, the *Washington Herald*, mounted a propaganda barrage in favor of a national archives building that lasted throughout January and part of February, the entire period that the relevant measure was under consideration in Congress. The *Herald* ran several columns of stories each day, illustrated with photographs of storage conditions for old records.

The Pension Building proposal, which was considered a gambit for sidetracking an archives building, was vehemently attacked:

A temporary expedient such as recommended by the commission would delay a permanent one ten to twenty years in the opinion of Dr. J. Franklin Jameson, who pointed out that utilization of the Old Pension Building for a temporary archives building would be like constructing a $1,000,000 furnace in which to burn up the priceless records of the greatest nation on earth.[4]

Reporter Cloyd Gill repeated what Jameson told him about the danger that the "erection of steel stacks in the immense interior court of the building . . . would provide numerous flues with a sixty foot draught leading to an inflammable roof" which was of wood "and protected only by a thin covering of tin." As the larger part of the material to be stored in the building would be combustible, it "could not possibly be protected by the 'makeshift' plan of the commission."[5]

If nothing else, this passage in the *Herald* again illustrated the remarkably detailed knowledge Jameson had of all aspects of the problem. As a professional historian, he naturally knew thoroughly the history of the concept; as a promoter, he knew the needs of the project; as a lobbyist, he knew the strengths, weaknesses, foibles, and preferences of senators and representatives; but, in addition, he revealed himself as knowledgeable in the technical details of structure and materials of construction.

The point in the Smoot commission's project that particularly alarmed Jameson was that any temporary expedient, no matter how well intentioned, would only delay the day when a suitable national archives building became a reality. Jameson's heart was unalterably set on the shining goal of an archives edifice of which the nation could be proud. Thus, one finds Gill quoting Jameson: "The only wise course open for Congress is the erection of a modern fireproof building, spacious and imposing, in which to house the testimonials to the nation's progress." The use of temporary steel stacks he characterized as a "penny wise and pound foolish policy."[6]

Senator Smoot, of course, was known to be in favor of an adequate, permanent fireproof structure, but even more than Jameson he was horrified at the complete lack of protection for so many old and valuable records. Smoot's commission declared that "unless immediate steps are taken to house the records in safe storage . . . the original sources of a great part of the history of this country will be wiped out."[7]

Jameson, to whom these conditions were an old story, told the *Herald* reporter that the "obstacle to an archives building was not opposition" but rather "negligence and inertia." Then, warming to his thesis, he continued, "England, Scotland, Ireland, France, Belgium, in fact every country of any consequence in the world, has a national archive in which . . . most of the older records are stored." He then launched into a discourse on the natural history of archives:

The evolution of national archives is in most cases a definite and regular natural history. At first each government office preserves its own papers. By and by the space available for such documents becomes crowded. The oldest of them . . . are sent away to attics, cellars, or vacant rooms, it makes little difference where, to make room for the transaction of current business. Later the historians arise. They insist that these dead files are full of historical information, that they are a valuable national asset, that it is shameful to neglect them.[8]

Then practical administrative needs begin to underscore the problem. "[A]dministrators discover that, whenever administration depends upon the careful study of previous experience, it is inconvenient to have the papers recording that experience scattered through many unsuitable repositories, neglected and unarranged." The end result of the interaction of historians and administrators, as Jameson described it, was the beginning of "a movement for a national archive, a determination to erect a structure ideally adapted to the storage of documents and their preservation in accessible order."[9]

The day following, Waldo Leland continued the counterattack on the Pension Office proposal. He observed that "no government has expended larger sums of money for the purchase of historical papers, or made more lavish appropriations for the historical papers than the United States," yet no government had "more signally failed" in preserving and "rendering accessible to the student the first and foremost of all the resources of the nation's history, the national archives." Leland then went on to explain what was meant by *archives* and to how small an extent they were used in the United States, citing the lack of use of State Department and War Department records as examples. Leland complained also of the lack of guides or finding aids. He digressed on the records of the Revolutionary War, the records of the regular army and the volunteer armies, the captured archives of the Confederate government, the records of the Freedmen's Bureau, and the like. Then he reverted to his and Jameson's pet theme: "Archives . . . cannot be properly preserved and made accessible without a place to keep them, but as yet that place has not been provided. This failure is not due to the fact that the matter has not been called to the attention of Congress."[10]

Leland concluded his remarks by giving his reasons for the deplorable state of noncurrent records, blaming it on "the growth of Government business and the expansion of departments" which made the quarters then occupied "almost uninhabitable." Besides the other dangers to archives, the greatest danger of substandard quarters was fire. He cited the loss of records of the Geological Survey, the Land Office, the Patent Office, the Post Office, and those of other government offices, and the War and Treasury departments fires all the way back to 1800.[11]

Day after day the *Herald* maintained its barrage of accusatory items to shame Congress. Several days after the initial Jameson interview, under a banner headline, "Flimsy Boxes Hold Billions in 'Dry' Bonds," the Hearst paper recounted how securities stored behind thin, dry, and inflammable partitions in the Prohibition Bureau hourly faced destruction by fire. These were more than $3 billion worth of bonds written by surety companies to cover permits issued to doctors, druggists, manufacturers, and private individuals. The law provided that no one could handle alcoholic liquors without giving a collateral bond.[12]

Most damagingly, the *Herald* attacked Congress for the way it stored its own records. Claiming that "several Capitol employees learned yesterday for the first time" what the Capitol attic held, the newspaper featured the scare headline: "Entire Legislative History of U.S. Rotting Away in Attic of Capitol." "One of the worst conditions surrounding the archives of the nation" affected the hundreds of thousands of bills and resolutions, "the product of sixty-seven Congresses," covering some 140 years of American history, which "are piled in heaps or tied in rude bundles beneath the dome of the Capitol building." Numerous bundles had burst the cord with which they were tied, and the documents lay scattered over the floor. Other bundles "cracked with the excessive heat of summer days," and in winter were damaged by the heat of steam pipes along the ceilings of the rooms. The natural conclusion of the newspaper was that "the situation is one which can be remedied only by an archives building."[13]

The Hearst paper's campaign succeeded in drawing first blood in the imminent legislative struggle. Within a few days after the commencement of the series, Rep. John W. Langley, chairman of the House Committee on Public Buildings and Grounds, was quoted as stating that "this Congress would not acquiesce in this recommendation of the Public Buildings Commission." The congressman was of the opinion that the suggestion would not only destroy "the beautiful court of the Pension Office, but would in no sense meet the need for a repository befitting the dignity of the nation." Although this attitude of the powerful House leader was a reassuring gain, the corollary statement of Langley was ominous, namely, that "the House leaders would oppose passage of any public buildings measure" at that time.[14]

With the characteristic dauntlessness of Hearst journals bent on a mission, the *Herald* now brought into play the powerful weapon of the veterans. With another banner headline spread across the page, "United States Is Only Nation of World Lacking Archives Building," the paper quoted liberally from a letter from H. H. Raege, head of the Disabled American Veterans and money raiser for the American Legion, in which he protested the danger to war records on which the disabled veterans depended for the adjudication of their claims. Raege flatly asserted that "the United States of America is the only great power of the world today which has not erected a national archives building." He declared that "the disabled American veterans have but one plea . . . that Congress immediately adjust the difference between the two houses so that this national need can be met." Raege concluded his remarks with a reminder that the "almost undreamed of expansion" of the executive departments, and the addition of numerous independent agencies, had caused an employee crowding in the departmental buildings never contemplated by those who planned them, with concomitant harm to the records. Borrowing a thought from Jameson, he noted that aside from their usefulness to the government, "these records are the only original sources from which the future historians will be able to gather data essential to the writing of histories of the United States."[15]

During the succeeding week, as no action had yet occurred in Congress, the *Herald* continued to deploy its reserve artillery. Toward mid-January, another streamer announced "Many Rally to Support Washington Herald in Archives Building Fight." The Washington Board of Trade, it appeared, would "boost the cause" and name a committee to gather facts to present to Congress. W. L. Beale, chairman of the Board's Public Buildings Committee, commended the efforts of the *Herald* and declared the Board's intention to "join efforts with other organizations which have enlisted in the fight. For years past," Beale pointed out, "the Board of Trade . . . consistently advocated an archives building." Its recommendations were incorporated in its annual reports and in letters written to "leaders in Congress," but, he lamented, "without getting favorable action."[16]

The chairman of the Fine Arts Commission, Charles Moore, added his piece, and told the interviewer that the secretary of the Treasury had the power to acquire an archives site by the terms of the act of 1913 and asserted that "in order to care for the great increase in Government records created by the war" it was necessary to act immediately. "The proposal," he said, was "to build at once a portion of the interior or storage section of the building with a cubical content of 3,000,000 feet" and to leave the remainder of the building and its architectural treatment "to be dealt with when times become normal." The construction, Moore noted, was to be of reinforced concrete, and the building was to be so designed "that the regular Government filing cases can be transferred to it, together with their contents." Furthermore, he said, each department would control its own records.[17]

The drumfire of the newspaper campaign now caused some of the concerned congressional leaders to espouse the cause publicly. Sen. Morris Sheppard of Texas declared that "the time is ripe for pushing such a measure. . . . If the proper leaders in either house should take an interest in a bill . . . for an archives building . . . it would have no difficulty in passing." Rep. Simeon D. Fess, citing statistics on the various fires of the past, asserted that "every civilized country has provided a national archive for the documents marking its history. This is true even of such countries as Cuba, Mexico, Colombia, Canada, Rumania, Russia, Norway, Sweden, Hungary, and Portugal." Finally, Fess asked, "Is it good business for a government to spend vast sums for rental of bad quarters, when the same money could provide magnificent quarters with much greater capacity? Is it good business for a government that can borrow at 3 per cent to pay rent at 10 per cent?"[18]

The powerful Speaker of the House of Representatives, Frederick H. Gillett of Massachusetts, now contributed his voice, emphatically endorsing "the movement for a national archives building" and declaring it "one of the outstanding unsolved problems before Congress." Although he said he appreciated the "conditions under which the very important historical papers of this nation are stored," he favored the erection of steel stacks in the Pension Office Building, provided they "should not be intended as a substitute for a permanent archives building."[19]

Just before the matter was scheduled for consideration in Congress during the later part of January, President Harding and his cabinet discussed the proposed building program of the federal government, which was to include "a commodious, fireproof archives building." It was thought that with "department heads and historical organizations pleading for speedy action in providing an Archives Building . . . quick provision" would be made for such a structure. The *Herald* reported that "the discussion in the Cabinet meeting . . . centered about" a site on Pennsylvania Avenue, between Fourteenth and Fifteenth streets, occupied by Poli's Theater and the Oxford Hotel.[20]

At this juncture the stage was set for fateful debates on the Pension

Office and the archives amendments in the Senate and House of Representatives.

THE POINDEXTER AND SMOOT AMENDMENTS

After weeks of softening up enemy defenses with a journalistic drumfire barrage, the moment of truth had come. In January 1923, Senator Poindexter launched his final effort to achieve the objective he had fought for so valiantly and so persistently for ten long years—an archives appropriation. It was his last chance. In the congressional election of 1922, the citizens of the state of Washington had denied him a third term in the Senate. His Senate service would therefore terminate with the expiration of the current session of Congress, in March 1923.

Once again, Poindexter attached an amendment to an existing appropriation bill. It was necessary to go the amendment route because the time factor, if nothing else, made a separate bill out of the question. The year's effort started with a handicap that Jameson himself termed "almost fatal." The Treasury Department, as it had done the previous year, submitted to the director of the budget an estimate of $484,000 for the purchase of a site. The budget director cut it out. Jameson went to see him and tried to persuade him to change his mind but could not budge him. Director Charles G. Dawes told Jameson that he had direct orders from President Harding "to make both ends meet and this was a thing which could be deferred, and therefore must be."[21] This situation made it impossible for the House Committee on Appropriations to include the item in the Treasury appropriation bill, for the committee was determined to cut even below the budget director's figures.[22]

Thus on January 19, Senator Poindexter submitted his amendment to the Senate Appropriations Committee. As the committee was also considering Smoot's Public Buildings Commission amendment for fifteen stories of steel stacks in the Pension Office Building, some discussion ensued as to which should have precedence.

Poindexter asked Smoot whether the $1 million expenditure for Smoot's pet project couldn't be shifted to aid in the erection of a modern, fireproof archives building. Smoot replied, "I have stood upon this floor for two years pleading that an appropriation be made for starting the construction of an archives building." But, he contended, the space was needed immediately, and he continued to maintain that "everyone of those stacks could be used" in the future archives building. Then he enthusiastically rendered a brief description of the stack plans:

Here are the plans, showing where every bolt goes; and the other $50,000 will be used to build a foundation in the court . . . [to] sustain the weight of the stacks and the weight of the papers that will go into them . . . each story of the stack will be about 9 feet high. There are 15 stories of these stacks . . . placed upon one another, and fit exactly, just the same as the steel frame of a window is made.[23]

Smoot objected to the characterization of his stacks as firetraps, asserting that "no fire can start among the papers in any of these stacks. . . . I think Mr. Jameson is making a mistake when he makes the statements attributed to him, and he should not be fearful that I am trying to interfere with what he is so deeply interested in: that is, building an archives building."[24]

As Jameson told Leland later, it was at this point that "Poindexter rather skillfully got Smoot committed to saying that he would accept" the Poindexter amendment, after Smoot's amendment was approved by the Appropriations Committee.[25] Although Smoot's measure was promptly adopted by the Appropriations Committee that day, Poindexter's was delayed until the next because Senator King rose to "ask the Senator from Washington not to press his amendment today," as Senator Underwood was "profoundly interested" but not then present. Poindexter, taken aback at this minor monkey wrench, started to object that he saw no reason to postpone the matter. But, at this point, Senator Kenneth McKellar of Tennessee asked Poindexter "to let it go over until tomorrow." Poindexter acquiesced.[26]

The following day, January 20, Poindexter resubmitted his amendment, drafted by Jameson and so worded as to omit mention of a new site acquisition. Instead, it asked only for a construction appropriation with the hope that such action would be more palatable to the members of the House of Representatives:

For the construction of a National Archives Building in Washington, District of Columbia, on square east 88, including mechanical equipment, and the drafting of plans and specifications, which plans and specifications shall provide for a building not to exceed $2,500,000 in total cost, $500,000, said sum to be disbursed and the building to be erected under the direction and supervision of the Supervising Architect of the Treasury.[27]

The *Washington Herald* gave the measure front-page prominence, with the heading "Archives Bill Is Introduced by Poindexter." The paper asserted that "the movement for a national archive building neared its goal yesterday when Senator Miles Poindexter introduced an amendment to the independent offices appropriation bill." The *Herald* was sure that "favorable action on the amendment was indicated," because "Senator Warren, chairman of the appropriations committee, declared from the floor of the Senate that the immediate erection of a national archive was acceptable to him" and that "Senator Smoot, one of the strongest leaders in the Archives fight, and also a member of the Appropriations Committee . . . came out in support of the amendment." The paper added the information that the site chosen was between Twentieth and Twenty-first and B and C streets, N.W., "just three blocks from the D.A.R. Continental Hall." Rather as an aside, it also mentioned that "it was agreed to leave Smoot's one million dollar item in the bill and to pass both measures if possible."[28]

SENATE DEBATE AND APPROVAL

During the debates on January 19 and 20, the principal participants besides Smoot and Poindexter were Senators Joseph S. Frelinghuysen of New Jersey, George W. Norris of Nebraska, and Oscar Underwood of Alabama. Smoot's amendment was questioned on two main counts: that the result envisaged would not be truly firesafe and that it was a wasteful temporary expedient. The intention of Poindexter's amendment was not called into question, but there were demurrers on the grounds of the need for government economy and for procedural regularity.

Senator McKellar, on January 19, had asked Smoot whether he thought the Pension Building was really fireproof. Replying on the floor of the Senate, Smoot said, "Absolutely," and that a statement to the contrary "furnished to a good many of the Senators is not correct." He said he had a statement from Colonel Sherrill "and the engineers of the different departments that there is no building more fireproof." And then, whether he intended it as a personal reflection or not, he gave the direct lie to Jameson, saying, "The roof is of tile and cement . . . and the statement that it is made of wood covered with tin is an absolute falsehood."[29]

Continuing the debate, Senator Frelinghuysen contended that the open nature of the building rendered it a potential furnace. He said it was unsafe not because the building itself would burn, but because the combustibles within it, once a fire started, would roar upward under forced draft due to its open nature. Prompted by Senator Norris who repeatedly queried Frelinghuysen as to his views on the Pension Building, the New Jersey senator said that although he "did not pose as an expert," for thirty years he had been "in the business of insuring buildings of the character under discussion." He then gave a classic statement on the meaning of "fireproof," or in today's usage, "fire-resisting" buildings:

In the consideration of insurance, area always has a great deal to do with the question of risk in a building which contains inflammable material. The Pension Building is a structure of tremendous area. In the event of a fire the fire would spread rapidly and could not be extinguished . . . the elevator shafts are open. In a really fireproof building there are no light shafts, every floor being cut off separately without any such shaft; and wherever the spaces occupied by elevators or chimneys have to be carried through a floor such spaces are inclosed in brick. Furthermore, fire-resisting doors and fireproof glass is used upon all outlets to and from the shafts, which are then inclosed in an areaway. All openings are covered, not only with fireproof glass but with kalomine material covering the frame of the building. Every floor is separated with fire brick and a fireproofing material. In such buildings, no matter how inflammable the material may be . . . each floor is a separate risk. That is the modern standard of construction which governs the fire rules of every city . . . and no one connected with the National Board of Fire Underwriters, or with an up-to-date fire department, or a well-informed department of public buildings . . . would consider allowing a building to be constructed for the safeguarding of valuables or public records unless those modern methods and specifications were followed in the construction of the building.[30]

Having thus expertly delineated the problem, Frelinghuysen said, "A great building of that character can not be made fireproof and safe under any circumstances whatever unless it be torn down and reconstructed." Therefore he advised the Senate that if it considered the public records valuable it should erect a fireproof building and not try to rebuild the Pension Office.[31]

It is a measure of the powerful influence that an able, dedicated, and esteemed public servant, such as Senator Smoot, has with his colleagues —even when he is palpably wrong—that the Senate adopted the Pension Office amendment and was loath to reverse itself. As Senator Norris observed, "We have already adopted a provision to squander a million dollars" on Senator Smoot's idea, "it is in the bill now. That was done yesterday." Then referring to the Poindexter amendment, about to be debated, the Nebraskan observed, "It is perfectly foolish for the Senate to spend $1,000,000 to build stacks in one building . . . and then the very next day provide $2,500,000 more to build some more stacks in another building."[32]

The Senate then proceeded to a consideration of the Poindexter amendment. Norris at once flung down the gage of battle, stating that he took issue with the senator from Washington and "with the chairman of the [Appropriations] Committee on this proposition." He felt that a full investigation had not been made by the committee. Poindexter quietly replied that it had been before the committee "a number of different years, and has been approved by the committee a number of different times," and furthermore, "such an amendment has been agreed to by the Senate several times." He reminded Norris that it was "in pursuance of existing law," that it had been considered for nine long years, and that it was in the interest of economy.[33]

The Nebraskan pounced on the latter assertion, "I know," he said, "all such expenditures always are. That is always given as a reason for every appropriation I have ever known to be made." He then wanted to know whether the measure was "in accordance with existing law." It was,

Poindexter replied, and went on to cite the act of 1913. Norris raised the question of whether the government had title to the property where the proposed building was to be built. Poindexter stated, "It already has title to it." Norris conceded that that fact removed to a great extent the objection he was going to urge. Nevertheless, he continued his hazing on details about the site.[34]

At this point, an effort was made to throw out the amendment on a point of order. According to the rules of the Senate and the House, if the object of a proposed amendment to an appropriation bill has not been previously authorized by law, the amendment can be excluded on a point of order raised by any member. So Sen. Charles L. McNary of Oregon interposed that unless the amendment came "within the rule," he intended "to invoke a point of order against it."[35]

Once again, Poindexter had to go patiently over this contested ground. Again he cited relevant parts of the act of 1913. But Norris objected, "That is not an authorization in my judgment." Poindexter had a tested riposte ready. "I will call the Senator's attention," he said, "to a supplement and amendment to that act, entitled 'An act to repeal paragraph 4 of Section 21 of the public buildings act'" of March 4, 1913, which provided for the construction of a national archives building. Poindexter then read the clause in the act of June 28, 1916, which expressly stated, "the acquisition of a site for . . . and the construction of the said building according to the terms of the act of March 4, 1913, is hereby authorized."[36]

"It seems to me," concluded Poindexter, "that is quite an authorization." Norris admitted that he was "inclined to think that is right." But he wanted to know whether "this particular real estate is purchased?" Poindexter replied that "the land was not acquired under that act" and that the amendment he submitted provided for "the construction of a building upon land . . . already owned by the Government." Norris chose to interpret this statement to mean that land would still have to be purchased. "If no land has been acquired," he said, "I was right in my belief . . . that this Senator's amendment would require the purchase of real estate."[37]

"Oh, no," Poindexter rejoined, "that lot is already owned by the Government." Norris wanted to know, "How did the Government get title to it?" The senator from Washington surmised "it was probably purchased along with a large . . . tract owned by the Government in that vicinity." Norris was not yet satisfied; he wanted to know where the lot was located. Poindexter told him, "It is located near the Pan American Building. The lot is surrounded by Twentyfirst and Twentieth Streets and B and C Streets NW. . . . The number of the lot . . . is E-88 on the city plat."[38]

At that point Senator Norris conceded that the information provided by Poindexter "cleared up to a great extent one of the objections" he had in mind. But he still felt that his other objection was valid, namely, "the matter of economy . . . when," he said, "we are straining every effort to find something to tax in order to pay our debts and keep the Government running." Although not unwilling to admit that an archives building was "perhaps a worthy object," he still thought that "the idea of building an archives building is propaganda mostly originating in the newspapers of the city of Washington."[39]

Poindexter rejected the imputation that he was concerned with newspaper propaganda, stating that "my interest in the proposition goes back away beyond the newspaper advocacy of it. . . . I introduced the bill and it was enacted into law in 1913." And he reiterated, "I have been interested in the matter ever since." Furthermore, he resented the persistent insinuation that it was a real estate deal. Because the Senate had objected to the purchase of land, he had "abandoned that feature entirely," and the proponents of the measure proposed "to erect a building on land which the Government already owns."[40]

Though parried at every point, Norris continued to hector Poindexter. Now he wanted to know whether the Senate Committee on Public Buildings and Grounds had ever considered the matter. Poindexter responded, "It was referred to that committee, acted on by that committee, reported to the Senate, and passed the Senate and the House of Representatives. It is the law." "If there is a law in every way perfected and complete," Norris asserted, "we do not now need to authorize construction of the building." This appears to have been a deliberate misunderstanding of what was at issue, or an effort at stalling, and Poindexter replied, "That is true, but the pending amendment is not an authorization. It is an appropriation."[41]

At this point in the debate, Senator McKellar gained the floor. The Tennesseean thought that, as the building was already authorized, "the proposition of the Senator from Washington is the correct way of dealing with it." Placing stacks in the Pension Building would cause a work stoppage there, and moreover, they would not be safe. Nor did he believe that the stacks would ever be transferred to a future archives building. So, McKellar said, "My own judgment is that they can not and never will be so used . . . they will be found not in accord with the new building . . . and we will have to appropriate another million dollars or more for other stacks at that time, and the stacks which are to be purchased now will be thrown away." McKellar therefore felt that one or the other proposition "ought not to be agreed to." He was for the archives building rather than the stacks.[42]

Regaining the floor, Norris returned to his favorite theme, disparaging the great hue and cry for an archives building:

Mr. President, 20 years ago I came to the House of Representatives. I was put on the Committee on Public Buildings and Grounds. One of the first things . . . I ever did officially was to listen for several days to gentlemen talking in favor of an archives building. They showed that we had all kinds of documents that were in danger every day; that we might have a fire before night and make the Government absolutely bankrupt; and therefore we had to have an archives building, and have it at once. There was a great propaganda in favor of it. . . . For days and . . . months that went on; and these people came before the committee, [which was] composed of some good men and some suckers like me, and they poured that kind of argument into us until we were frightened. We thought the Government was going to fall. I did not sleep nights for fear a fire might take place and the whole thing might go up in smoke. . . . I could not hurry fast enough to get that bill out of committee. We reported it; we provided for the purchase of a square of real estate; and the propaganda for an archives building died the very minute we passed the bill and appropriated the money to buy the land. We never heard anything about it until about 20 years had elapsed.[43]

This was a revealing commentary on Norris's motivation. He was suspicious of the current effort. Referring to the happenings of 1903, he thought that behind the movement of that day was "a coterie of fellows who owned a whole block of land that they wanted to sell to the Government . . . at a good price, and when they put it across they forgot all about the safety of those sacred documents." In a more mellow vein, the Nebraskan thought that "probably we made a good deal, because the land has become very valuable." Nevertheless, he said, economy dictated the wisdom of waiting a while longer.[44]

Underwood summarized the feelings of a substantial number of senators, when he said toward the close of the debate that "in the beginning he was disposed to accept the viewpoint" of Smoot, but "after hearing what Senator Freylinghuysen of New Jersey had said," he realized that the inflammable element was not the building but the materials within the building. "We are going to prepare to build a bonfire," he said, "and we must prepare to stop it." He therefore switched to Senator Poindexter's position, preferring to spend the $2.5 million for the new building, and drop the $1 million for the Pension Building stacks. Then with a courtly bow to Senator Norris, the Alabamian continued, "I listened with much interest to what my friend from Nebraska said about the agitation for an archives building twenty years ago. I was in the same crowd with the Senator that thought we had to buy this land." Although several years ago "I was opposed to an appropriation for an archives," Underwood continued, "because they were going to stop up one of the streets," he now thought "we do need an archives building. . . . We owe something to those who come after us," and there should be "a proper place to store the records."[45]

Sensing that the debate was veering toward a positive rather than a negative conclusion, Senator McNary made one last effort to block the Poindexter amendment by invoking rule 16. The rule called for an item first being considered by the budget director, then duly submitted in the chief executive's budget to the Appropriations committees of the two houses. Otherwise an amendment could be knocked out on a point of order. McNary said,

I understand this amendment has not been estimated for by the Bureau of the Budget, and has not been reported by the Committee on Appropriations. Indeed, if it is an item as important as we are told it is, certainly the Director of the Bureau of the Budget would have had some estimate made . . . and . . . the committee would have made some report to the Senate on the item. This item being entirely overlooked, I suggest it comes within Rule XVI, and invoke that rule at this time.[46]

Senator Poindexter instantly replied that "the Senator from Oregon is mistaken as to the . . . Budget." The item was estimated for on "page 458 of the Budget." Whether Poindexter made this statement without realizing that it was in error is a matter of conjecture. In any case, Sen. Irvine L. Lenroot of Wisconsin at once pointed out that "the Senator from Washington has the budget for the wrong year." Caught in an error, Poindexter rather lamely asserted, "It is probably repeated in this year's estimate." But he had sufficient presence of mind to protect his flank by stating that there was an ameliorating factor; "I do not understand that the . . . rule . . . is applicable . . . where the appropriation is to carry out an existing law."[47]

The presiding officer reinforced the beleaguered Poindexter's contention by reading two applicable paragraphs: one from rule 16, the other from the act of June 28, 1916. Clause 1 of rule 16 stated that "no amendment shall be received to any general appropriation bill the effect of which will be to increase an appropriation already contained in the bill, or to add a new item of appropriation unless it be made to carry out the provisions of some existing law." Then quoting the 1916 act, the chair read, "the acquisition of a site for a national archives building and the construction of such building, according to the terms of said act of March 4, 1913, is hereby authorized."[48]

McNary was visibly discomfited but did not yield gracefully. He wanted to know if anyone had appeared before the committee and asked for the appropriation. Chairman Warren of the Appropriations Committee answered that "it was not considered by the Committee . . . because it had been so many times figured upon." But the members of the committee had talked together when the bill was brought to the floor "and decided . . . to let it go in and see what could be done with it in the House." Warren conceded that "a point of order would lie against the proposition except for the fact that it carries out existing law, as the Senator from Washington said."[49]

The presiding officer, Sen. Frank B. Willis of Ohio, then announced, "The Chair is ready to rule." He stated that without a doubt the Poindexter amendment did add a new item of appropriation, but the heart of the question was whether the item was previously authorized by law.

He concluded that the act of June 28, 1916, "seems to the present occupant of the chair to be an authorization. The Chair is therefore compelled to overrule the point of order." Willis then concluded the proceedings by putting the question: "The question is on agreeing to the amendment offered by the Senator from Washington." The *Congressional Record* laconically noted, "The amendment was agreed to."[50]

Eben Putnam, in Massachusetts, hastened to write to Jameson that he had just seen a news despatch that the Senate had passed a bill appropriating for an archives building and that he would like to "receive details of the victory." He hinted that if the proposal were carried to a successful conclusion, Jameson should let it be known that "the Legion was a factor in this matter." He further told Jameson that he had reported on "the Archives matter" to the Legion's National Executive Committee at Indianapolis the week before, stating that progress was being made and that the Legion "would accept no makeshift." He had been heartily applauded.[51]

RESULTS OF THE HOUSE-SENATE CONFERENCE

The spotlight now shifted to the House and the House-Senate conference. Jameson had anxiously watched the Senate debate from the gallery and was relieved and proud of Poindexter's skillful handling of the archives measure. Now, with the issue apparently so close to ultimate success, he steeled himself to see the struggle through. Putnam saw to it that American Legion lobbyists assisted Jameson, who spent the entire following week on Capitol Hill trying to influence congressional leaders.[52]

The *Washington Herald,* optimistic as ever, ran a double-column spread headed "Expect House to Pass Bill for Archives," the burden of which was that there was little opposition to the measure in the lower chamber, that Speaker Gillett favored the building, and that Congressman Langley had found President Harding agreeable to the measure. The newspaper quoted Jameson as being of the opinion that "there is little doubt of the bill's passage by the House" and that "it came before the House some years ago and failed only because the bill proposed to buy a new site for the building. Under the Poindexter amendment the archives building will be erected on land now owned by the Government, which will remove that objection."[53]

Days passed without action, however, and the paper reported, rather ominously, that Chairman Martin Madden of the House Appropriations Committee had "not decided whether he is favorable to an immediate appropriation for a national archives building." After a week went by, it became evident that certain House leaders were opposing the amendment. Jameson and others saw to it that historical societies throughout the country were alerted to the danger. The *Herald* reported the following:

Aroused by the reported opposition of House leaders to the Poindexter amendment . . . a hurry call sent out to organizations in all parts of the United States
has been answered in an overwhelming demand that Congress provide immediately for the preservation of the nation's records. . . . Under no conditions should
this building be sacrificed because it is not possible to provide every hamlet in
the country with a new post office, citizens are insisting.[54]

The *Herald* published extracts from the letters pouring in: from Russell
Duane, president of the Descendants of the Signers of the Declaration
of Independence; Earl N. Manchester, director of libraries of the University of Kansas; J. W. Crabtree, secretary of the National Education
Association, who wrote to all state directors of the association to get
behind the movement; H. H. McIlwaine, state librarian of Virginia, who
wrote to each of Virginia's representatives in Congress, and to various
state historical societies, asking for suitable resolutions; George N. Fuller, secretary of the Michigan Historical Commission; and M. L. Bon-
ham, Jr., of the history department of Hamilton College, who wrote to
all the senators and representatives from New York State. The New
York City Federation of Women's Clubs sent word that "so keen is the
sentiment in favor of the archives building that the Federation . . . will
meet in special session on February 2, to urge Congress to pass the
Poindexter amendment"; and the Historical Society of Pennsylvania,
one of the oldest and most prestigious in the nation, passed resolutions
urging Congress "to provide the necessary appropriation commensurate
with the dignity and wealth of the nation for the erection of an archives
building without further delay."[55]

Toward the end of January another of the principal newspapers in the
nation's capital, the *Evening Star,* sounded the alarm, with the headline
"Archives Building Faces New Peril." The *Star* recounted that although
Rep. William R. Wood of Indiana, chairman of the House conferees,
favored prompt action, the heavies of the scenario, Chairman Madden
of the Appropriations Committee and Chairman Langley of the Committee on Public Buildings and Grounds, were against any amendment
to an appropriation bill as a sin against the budgetary process.[56]

Although sentiment in favor of the archives measure was said to be
very strong among members of the House, as well as members of the
conference committee, it was possible for a small group of House leaders
to enforce its will. As the *Herald* pointed out, "Under the rules governing
amendments to appropriation bills conferees are authorized to adjust
differences between the two houses by striking out items added by the
Senate."[57] Thus a few representatives were able to defeat the wishes of
a majority of the House because the archives amendment was attached
by the Senate after the independent offices appropriation bill had passed
the House. So it was enough that Madden, Langley, Rep. Bertrand H.
Snell of New York, and several others opposed the measure. Their

contention was that they were adamant for an orderly appropriation process. Langley, however, revealed the true reason: "that any large amount of money, like $500,000 should not be appropriated . . . until hundreds of small cities throughout the country are included in a general public buildings program."[58]

Jameson, with sad forebodings, sat down and wrote Leland, then abroad, "It is now the afternoon of January 30. I presume that by this hour the conferees have done their deadly work and my amendment is dead and buried and damned."[59] His foreboding was entirely justified. Three days later, the conference committee made its report to the House, stating that both the Poindexter amendment and the Smoot amendment were stricken out.[60]

When Representative Wood moved the adoption of the conference report, Congressman Dallinger rose to say

Mr. Speaker, I would like to ask the Congressman from Indiana why the amendment in regard to the archives building was not kept in; whether that building authorized in 1913 is ever going to be built; whether the Committee on Appropriations is ever going to make an appropriation to start it; and whether we have got to wait until the records of the war are destroyed?[61]

The answer was by this time well known to all who followed the matter. "I am heartily in favor of an archives building," said Wood, but "I think it would be a mistake to agree to it in this bill." Proposals of this type, he thought, "would be absolutely destructive of the Budget system." He did not believe in appropriating a large sum merely to start a project without having an accurate idea of the ultimate cost. Representative Snell added, "no one knows whether it will cost two and a half million dollars or five million dollars . . . on a proposition of this kind we should start in a logical and sensible way." Congressman William E. Andrews of Nebraska also bore down hard on the budgetary aspect of the matter, and ably presented the opposition viewpoint:

Mr. Speaker . . . the recognition of this proposition would strike at the very foundation of the Budget system. . . . Take, for instance, the claim that this building was authorized by the act of 1913. . . . If you examine the act of 1913 you will find over a hundred other buildings were authorized by it . . . making the necessary allowances because of increased cost . . . we would have to appropriate about $50,000,000 to level that act up to the conditions of today. . . . We ought to have a hearing that will disclose . . . the actual measure of cost for the building, and we ought to do that in the regular way . . . the committee is correct on this proposition.[62]

The House accepted the report of the conference committee, and that ended the matter.

Jameson's views, of course, could hardly coincide with those of the budget system regulars. He found satisfaction, however, in the failure of the Smoot amendment. Later in February, in writing Eben Putnam about events, he said that Smoot's scheme "seemed an unsafe and dangerous thing, and also likely to defer indefinitely the real remedy, the erection of the building." So he was pleased that after the fate of the Poindexter amendment was sealed, Smoot's amendment "was quickly dropped in conference. There was not a voice raised in its behalf in the House."[63]

It will be noted that the site selected to help the archives proposal through the congressional session of 1923 was comparatively far removed from the site pushed a year earlier. Commenting on this to Leland, Jameson told him, "You will remember that last February our little patriots negatived the scheme on the ground that it would be a wicked shame for the government to buy any more land in the District of Columbia." It was therefore interesting to observe that "later in the session they bought seven squares in the region west of the Pan-American [Building], paying a million and a half for the same. One of the seven, bounded by B and C and 20th and 21st, was big enough for the Archive Building, and otherwise suitable except that it was a little too far west."[64]

He also told Leland that when the bill came to conference, he saw all of the House conferees, and afterward "I made up my mind that we would fail."[65] Nevertheless, with characteristic resilience, Jameson preferred to dwell on the silver lining rather than on the disappointingly dark cloud. "I am able to think," he wrote Putnam, "that the week which I spent . . . at the Capitol lobbying, and the efforts of the Legion authorities and others, did some good."[66]

In his letters to Leland and Putnam, he summarized the gains. "All the House members influential in the matter, and a number of others, have had it proved to them that the building is authorized," he wrote, and "the president of the Senate overruled on that ground a point of order made there, and the Speaker said he would do the same." The fact that a vote was taken in the Senate "for an appropriation for actual construction is an advance over last year."[67] He would now be able to get the Treasury to make its estimates "on the basis of construction on land now owned by the government," and with such an estimate he hoped to get the director of the budget to allow it. These procedures being complied with, he hoped to get "the House Committee on Appropriations to put it in the Treasury Bill where it more properly belongs."[68]

To both Leland and Putnam, Jameson reiterated that the "almost fatal handicap" was that the "Director of the Budget turned the thing down." He hoped the director would not turn it down again next year; but as one who had taken more than his share of buffeting, Jameson cautioned his loyal allies, "I fear that the thing will now have to take its chances with a raft of public buildings, so large and loosely constructed that it will sink."[69]

THE AFTERMATH

The House-Senate battle over the archives and stack amendments left a bitter taste in the mouths of some of the senators, especially Smoot and Claude A. Swanson of Virginia. Smoot, in fact, although a Senate conferee, had refused to sign the conference report.[70] Senator Swanson wondered, "Do we always have to accept the vote of the House as final?" He felt that the archives building must be fought for persistently; he continued, "We have tried and tried to get this proposition accepted. . . . We have had it up for 10 or 15 years and every time it comes up they take a vote in the House, and they have an idea [that] . . . if the matter has been voted down . . . it is the duty of the Senate to surrender to that vote." Swanson believed that as the "Senate is a coordinate branch of the Government," a vote in the Senate "should be entitled to as much respect as a vote in the House" and should receive as much consideration. The Virginia senator was voicing the age-old disagreement of the two houses on the primary locus of the power of the purse. He had hoped that Senator Smoot would have insisted, after the House's negative action, on sending the bill back to conference.[71]

Chairman Warren smoothed ruffled feathers and closed the discussion, telling Smoot that "his fellow conferees on the part of the Senate were in full sympathy and accord with him." He added, "We are also lamed by the fact that . . . the gentlemen of the House are somewhat sensitive about supplemental estimates that come in through the Senate . . . we had proceeded in a somewhat crosscut way."[72]

The *Evening Star* reported that Senator Smoot had declared that as long as he continued to be chairman of the Public Buildings Commission "he would try every year to reduce the expenses of the Government" but, concurrently, "to bring about the adoption of proper measures to safeguard the government records from destruction by fire."[73]

Shocked by the congressional impasse and consequent lack of progress, various organizations interested in the archives movement again publicly expressed their disappointments and their unalterable determination to press Congress for action. The National Genealogical Society, through its *Quarterly,* again called on every reader "to actively stimulate the *Nation wide demand* for . . . a National Hall of Archives," and especially to put pressure on the House of Representatives. "In this matter eternal vigilance is the price of success."[74] The Public Buildings Committee of the Washington Board of Trade, in its annual report, cited as the "most urgently needed public buildings," the Internal Revenue Bureau, the Comptroller General's Office, the Department of Justice, and "a building of approximately 3,000,000 cubic feet of storage capacity for an archives."[75]

The *New York Times* quoted Sen. David I. Walsh of Massachusetts as saying that "the Government is criminally neglecting its duty to future generations by making no effort to preserve motion pictures of great historical value." The senator pledged his support to patriotic societies "in a movement . . . which would place such films in the archives." He declared it unbelievable that films depicting the congressional declaration of war against Germany, the addresses of President Wilson, the burial of the unknown soldier, presidential inaugurations, and the like "should be left to the haphazard storage of commercial companies." The senator noted that the War Department was the only agency making an effort to collect historical films, but these were "housed in an inflammable wooden structure." He further declared that

Such a condition is intolerable. . . . The Government should no longer risk its invaluable records of all kinds in fire-traps, but should construct immediately an archives building, in which proper provision should also be made for the storage of historic motion pictures.[76]

In mid-February, Eben Putnam told Jameson that he realized "all hope is gone for this Congress with relation to any Archives Building." When the next Congress came in, however, he thought it best "to present a carefully drawn bill devoted to nothing but Archives . . . and force a showdown on that one point." He informed Jameson that the Massachusetts Legion had requested the Massachusetts legislature to send memorials to Congress on the subject. He thought that if enough other state legislatures would take similar action it should be very helpful to the cause. Putnam even criticized the National Legislative Committee of the Legion because, he said, it did not concentrate as much as it could have on influencing the members of the House. Putnam then asked Jameson a key question: Should not a separate Archives bill provide for both the building and the organization to administer it?[77]

Jameson's reply was characteristically shrewd, thorough, and technically informed. As to the next session of Congress, his impression was "that I ought first to get the Treasury to decide between two squares, both owned by the government, and then frame a careful estimate for as much construction as can be done in one fiscal year, $500,000 or more, and then concentrate all possible persuasion on the Director of the Budget." Jameson thought that if the proposal were passed by the budget director, a hearing before the House subcommittee on the Treasury appropriation bill was virtually ensured, and he felt that the archives item should be within the Treasury bill.[78]

To Putnam's suggestion of including archival organization and administration in an archives building construction item, Jameson was emphatically opposed. He explained the legislative facts of life. One could not get an appropriation outside of an appropriation bill; and if such a bill contained within it provisions for new legislation, "it would be subject to a point of order and would be thrown out." In short, Jameson told Putnam, an appropriation for the building, and the "organization of the [archival] service are in the procedure of Congress two

separate things." He therefore concluded, "let us get the building assured first" and leave the matter of "organization and rules" for another
session.[79]

After getting Jameson's instruction, Putnam again swung into action.
He sent a circular letter to all the department historians of the Legion,
informing them that it was the duty of the national historian "to report
on the condition in which our records are suffered to remain," and that
to him and to the National Legislative Committee "has fallen the particular duty to press the demand" of the American Legion that Congress
"provide for the safe keeping of our national records. *The only way possible
being by the erection of a suitable depository.*" He therefore urged department
historians to present the matter to their respective executive committees
with a view to having appropriate resolutions passed calling on Congress to act. Likewise, he asked that they send petitions requesting their
respective state legislatures to send memorials to Congress on the
subject.[80]

In the meantime, an important change occurred on the national scene.
President Harding suddenly died in San Francisco, on August 2, 1923;
he was succeeded by Vice President Calvin Coolidge. The views of the
late incumbent and the new president were virtually identical on economic, social, and political matters. They also agreed on the national
archives concept. Both favored it in principle. But the Republican administration had inherited a minor postwar depression, and was intent
on reversing the downward business cycle. The Harding-Coolidge for-
mula for business recovery was never a formalized document, but one
of its primary tenets was economy in federal expenditures. Harding
tolerated economy as a political necessity, but with Coolidge it was little
short of an article of faith. Consequently, as one writer remarked, "Budget directors took their duties seriously, and the normal peace-time
disbursements of the national government, if not actually reduced, were
given little opportunity to expand."[81]

In midsummer 1923, the Washington papers reported that President
Coolidge was strongly in favor "of a federal archives building, as well
as new structures to house the Department of Justice and the State
Department," but he would "not approve the passage at the next session
of Congress of a general public buildings bill." On August 17, Coolidge
had a lengthy conference with Chairman Langley and Rep. Frank Clark
of the House Public Buildings and Grounds Committee. After hearing
the president's views on legislation concerning buildings, the two representatives told him that unless there was a general public buildings bill
put through during the next session, there would be no chance for the
enactment of "bills providing for the archives building and for any other
individual government building."[82]

Later that day the president sent for Senator Smoot and Representative Madden and discussed with them the results of his various conferences with department heads, as well as his desire to keep the budget

(exclusive of the postal service and the service on the public debt) within $1.7 billion for the coming fiscal year. He asked them to let him know what the two appropriations committees would recommend for the expenditures of the executive departments. The next day the *Star,* in an editorial commentary, stated that there was little possibility of a national archives building in the immediate future.[83]

"The President," the paper said, "is believed to favor an archives building," but "two things stand in the way of an early erection" of the building. One was "the demand for retrenchment in public expenditures," and the other was that the archives building "is tied up with the need for government buildings in other parts of the country." Many congressmen would support an omnibus bill, but this would involve a large appropriation which, it was believed, would "call down much adverse criticism of the administration." It was thought that Coolidge's sensitivity to criticism on federal expenditures (aside from his personal bent) was very strongly influenced by the Daugherty, Fall, and other scandals of the Harding administration which had been but recently exposed. The president was, therefore, "opposed to a general building bill as it would require an appropriation estimated at between $150,000,000 and $200,000,000."[84]

Jameson, of course, was fully aware of the trends of thought and opinion in government circles, both in the White House and on Capitol Hill. He may have been disheartened, but he was not dismayed. He kept plugging away. Toward the end of September he informed Eben Putnam that the archives "estimates went from the Treasury to the Director of the Budget a few days ago." He did not like the estimates. The figures were for a total of $1 million: half a million for land and half a million for construction. Jameson had argued against the figures, which represented egregiously bad judgment on someone's part. "I urged what arguments I could put against this action," he told Putnam, "for it is perfectly plain that the House will turn down, by an enormous majority, any proposal of purchase of land, but I was not successful."[85]

He decided to do the next best thing, to "try to persuade the Director of the Budget not to throw out" the whole provision, but to keep in an item for construction "and to place the building on a certain square now owned by the government." Then he made a direct appeal to President Coolidge. Jameson told the chief executive that the heads of the executive departments had emphasized the need for an archival depository since 1879, but without success.

No member of Congress feels that it is a vital matter to him personally. No large body of voters is deeply excited on the subject. And yet . . . there is on the historical side, diffused throughout the country, a considerable force of opinion which would respond actively, and cause congressmen to respond actively, to an eloquent passage urging the matter, in the President's message [to Congress]. The American Legion, for instance, are to my knowledge actively interested in this better provision for the nation's records.[86]

Jameson concluded his letter with the observation that if the archival cause is to be advanced, "it needs a strong push from the Executive himself." And he hoped the president would "give appropriate instructions" to the director of the budget to put the matter in "the most favorable train for action on the part of the House Committee on Appropriations."[87]

The president and the budget director took note of the problem and projected a possible method of solution which is succinctly expressed in Jameson's own words to the Executive Council of the American Historical Association:

In respect to the session of Congress now approaching . . . a different turn is given to the matter by the probability that the President will try to end the deadlock about public buildings by requesting, so far as buildings in the District of Columbia are concerned, that an appropriation of perhaps $5,000,000 per annum for a term of years be entrusted to the Executive, for use in such work of construction. If such an appropriation is made, it seems likely that the national archives building will have a foremost place in any program which the Executive may frame.[88]

So Jameson, despite the disappointments of the year 1923 and those of the preceding decade, plus the loss of his staunchest congressional supporter, Sen. Miles Poindexter, looked forward to the new year with renewed confidence.

11

The First Appropriation

PRESIDENT COOLIDGE TAKES COMMAND

President Coolidge meant business. Though primarily interested in economizing on federal expenditures and reducing the wartime debt as rapidly as possible, he was not oblivious to some other urgent problems facing the government. Foremost among them was the need for properly housing federal departments and agencies in the national capital, including the safe housing of the national archives.

The president was aware of the sentiment in the House of Representatives for a nationwide public buildings program, but his frugal Yankee soul rebelled at the idea of "pork." One must admit, however, that the congressmen had a case because for an entire decade, during which the nation had grown rapidly, there had been no such program.

The principal cabinet officers, as well as other officials, earnestly urged upon the new president the building needs of the federal agencies in Washington. Herbert Hoover, the influential secretary of commerce, insistently raised his voice, pointing out that the "valuable records dating back to the founding of the Government," once destroyed, "could never be duplicated." He called attention to the near-impossibility of properly administering his own department, with two thousand employees scattered all over the city, and all the buildings badly overcrowded.[1] Edwin Denby, the secretary of the navy, spoke of the navy's historical section, which was receiving a rapidly increasing number of inquiries from "private individuals, historical and patriotic societies, State historians," government officials, the Veterans Bureau, and the Mixed Claims Commission. Denby further stated that although "9,000 pounds of material have been rejected and placed in storage," approximately thirty-five thousand documents were added "to the archives," which, of course, needed more space.[2]

Andrew Mellon, the secretary of the Treasury, whose department traditionally held primary responsibility in the area of public buildings, went into more detail, and particularly deplored the "lack of suitable fireproof space for storage" of records and the failure to provide for a national archives building. He pointed out that an archives building would release "approximately 450,000 square feet . . . urgently needed for clerical work." Once again he expressed hope for prompt legislation.[3]

As the urging of others accorded with his own views in the matter, President Coolidge, in his first State of the Union message, on December 6, 1923, called the legislators' attention to the matter of public buildings for the national capital.

Many of the departments in Washington need better housing facilities. Some are so crowded their work is impeded, others are so scattered that they lose their identity. While I do not favor at this time a general public building law, I believe it is necessary, in accordance with plans already sanctioned for a unified and orderly system for the development of this city, to begin the carrying out of those plans by authorizing the erection of three or four buildings most urgently needed by an annual appropriation of $5,000,000.[4]

This annual message reiterated the recommendation in the budget message which he had submitted to Congress a few days earlier.[5]

Soon after the yuletide holidays, Senator Smoot introduced a public buildings bill limited to the District of Columbia. It carried an authorization of $50 million, but not more than $10 million was to be appropriated in any fiscal year.[6] On April 24, the bill was favorably reported by Sen. Henry W. Keyes of New Hampshire, a member of the Committee on Public Buildings and Grounds, but with an amendment, the insertion of the phrase, "Subject to the approval of the President."[7]

The report included a passage from the acting supervising architect which was bound to arouse the ire of Jameson. In referring to past legislation on the subject of the national archives, James A. Wetmore stated, "it has been held in certain quarters that this legislation authorized the construction of the building, but the matter has not been passed upon officially by officers of the Government." The committee's report rather drily observed,

The committee believes, in view of the above circumstances, the most satisfactory way to solve the tangle in which this authorization has become involved is to authorize the Public Buildings Commission to acquire the site without regard to the provisions of existing legislation.[8]

The committee also remarked that "another strong reason" for the archives building was that a half million square feet of floor space now taken up by records would be released, which would provide "working room for 4,500 employees."[9] The bill ultimately got bogged down in a conflict between Smoot and Sen. Duncan U. Fletcher of Florida and never passed. This negative result came from Fletcher's efforts to amend the bill to include an additional sum of $15 million to help erect buildings elsewhere in the country (five in Florida), which had been authorized by the act of 1913 but never built.[10]

In accordance with the president's message, Rep. Richard N. Elliott of Indiana introduced two public buildings bills during 1924. The first, introduced May 27, was strictly in line with the president's wishes, limiting the provision for public buildings to the District of Columbia. But this effort died in committee for the obvious reason that it was not broad enough to satisfy the congressmen.[11] Several months later Elliott tried again, this time with a general public buildings bill applicable nationwide, carrying a price tag of $150 million, of which not more than $25 million was to be expended annually. The bill was referred to the Committee on Public Buildings and Grounds, but nothing more was heard of it thereafter.[12]

A DIFFERENT STRATEGY

Jameson, of course, was fully aware of these legislative efforts, but with 1924 also wending its fruitless way, as so many prior years had done, he became very pessimistic. He started playing with the idea of abandoning the quest for federal funding. Instead, he would try the route of privately financed memorial projects. Two memorial ideas seemed to have possibilities: those in behalf of George Washington and Theodore Roosevelt.

In corresponding with a fellow member of the Cosmos Club, John A. Stewart, Jameson related that "a young friend, Professor Samuel F. Bemis of Whitman College," was working in Jameson's office for the year, and Jameson had him writing on the current archives situation in Washington, particularly concerning the "proposed National Archive Building." Jameson intended to send this material to Stewart with the hope that he could help persuade congressmen to go along with the idea of authorizing a memorial to George Washington. He told Stewart that even though the coming Washington bicentennial would tend to "postpone the project to 1932," he would not mind, provided the project was started.[13]

In the meantime another possibility occupied Jameson's attention. Theodore Roosevelt, who had died on January 6, 1919, had been one of the most colorful and significant figures in early twentieth-century American political life. Now, five years later, there were movements to memorialize him in the nation's capital. His birthplace in New York City had been restored under the leadership of the Woman's Roosevelt Memorial Association. Ernest D. Lewis, editor of the *Roosevelt Quarterly*, published by the Woman's Association, had told Waldo G. Leland that he was much "impressed by the need of a special building" in Washington which, he understood, was "to be known as a National Archives Building." Lewis wondered "if it might not be possible for some committee of the American Historical Association" to get in touch with a committee of the Roosevelt Memorial Association, known as the Roosevelt Committee on a Memorial in Washington. He thought the Roosevelt memorial people could "be prevailed upon to make a memorial of practical use, such as a building for the storing of national archives."[14]

Leland promptly passed the idea on to Jameson. The latter thanked Lewis for the suggestion and wrote to James R. Garfield, son of the late president. Garfield was then president of the men's Roosevelt Memorial Association, an organization separate from the women's organization. Jameson told Garfield, "For fifteen years the American Historical Association has had a committee on the subject of a National Archive Building, and I have been chairman of it, and have been laboring with Congress in every session since 1908." Having set the stage, he continued,

Before the war we seemed to be making good progress, the necessary legislation was carried through, the building was duly authorized, a site was selected, and partial plans were drawn. All that is needed is the appropriations, for the purchase of the site, or, if it is possible to shift to a site already possessed by the government, for the erection of a building.[15]

The building, Jameson thought, "would be likely to cost $3,000,000." He was not aware, he said, of how much the Roosevelt association could spend.[16]

Garfield replied that he doubted "whether that character of memorial" would appeal to the committee. He would, however, present the matter to the executive committee of the association when it met in the "forepart of January" 1925. Garfield was true to his word. He did present the matter to the committee. In mid-January 1925, Jameson was apprised of the results by Hermann Hagedorn, director of the Roosevelt Memorial Association.

At a meeting of the Executive Committee of the Roosevelt Memorial Association held on January 7th, your suggestion to Mr. Garfield that a memorial to Mr. Roosevelt in the city of Washington take the form of a National Archives Building, was given consideration. I have been directed to inform you that it was the judgement of the committee that such a building should logically be erected by the Federal authorities, and that the subscribers to the Roosevelt Memorial fund would not approve of the assumption by this organization of a duty which clearly belonged to the national government.[17]

Hagedorn's letter seemed to convey a veiled rebuke to Jameson for straying from the straight and narrow path of federal appropriations. He was a proud man, and it may be surmised that he felt the rejection keenly. Once again, a dream had ended—a dream born of a feeling of near desperation. And, once again, Jameson was thrown back on the hitherto utterly bleak road of congressional appropriations.

THE NEED FOR BUILDINGS

Despite appearances, all was not quite as dark as it seemed to Jameson. The cause was now receiving powerful and persistent support at the highest executive level of government. In his second budget message to Congress, in December 1924, President Coolidge again urged a systematic program for the erection of public buildings in the District of Columbia. He told the national legislature,

In my message transmitting the Budget for the fiscal year 1925 I recommended . . . legislation which would authorize a reasonable progressive building program to meet the needs . . . of the Government in the District of Columbia. . . . An expenditure of $5,000,000 annually for a period of years would enable the present situation to be gradually relieved. . . . During the last session of Congress a bill was introduced authorizing a yearly appropriation of not exceeding $10,000,000 for . . . buildings in the District of Columbia. This bill has my endorsement. I earnestly recommend its enactment by Congress.[18]

In this message it will be observed that although Coolidge clearly recognized the building needs within the national capital, the desire for overall federal economy caused him to withhold his benison nationwide. Some weeks later, Representative Elliott introduced a general public buildings bill, with provisions far beyond the presidential plea, calling for a countrywide expenditure of $150 million, of which not more than $25 million was to be expended annually.[19] Elliott stated that there were pending before his Committee on Public Buildings and Grounds 869 public buildings bills involving a total expenditure of $225,891,016.59. Therefore, he felt, the sum called for in his measure was quite modest. This was the first serious public buildings bill for the entire country since 1913. The committee report mentioned, among other projects, the need for a national archives building.[20]

After hearings were held on January 22 and 23, 1925, the bill was favorably reported to the House, with amendments.[21] The bill passed the House on February 2, and was referred to the Senate Committee on Public Buildings and Grounds on February 3. Sen. Bert M. Fernald of Maine reported it to the Senate, with the recommendation that it be approved without amendment. Among other provisions, authority was granted in the bill to close portions of streets in the District of Columbia where the construction of buildings required the utilization of contiguous squares. This provision would clear the type of road block that had earlier bedeviled hapless Senator Poindexter.[22] In due course, hearings were held before the Senate Committee on Public Buildings and Grounds. Little time remained before the session ended, however, and the bill never became law.[23]

During all this time Jameson had been periodically in touch with his staunch ally, Eben Putnam. In answer to Putnam's query as to the status of the archives project, Jameson told him that the House "will never do a thing toward any building operations . . . in Washington until the Treasury and the President couple with it a substantial provision for post-offices." He went on to say that although the Public Buildings Act of 1913, "was then thought to be a monster in size," and had "contained many inequities," nevertheless there had not been such a measure since, and "members of the House are eager for one." Jameson was of the opinion that a general bill "can't be wholly delayed many years longer," but he thought "the expenditures for the bonus will hold down all spending for Washington buildings, and probably even for P.O.'s [Post Offices]." Jameson was here referring to the veterans bonus which was being promoted by the Legion and other veterans groups as "deferred compensation" to the service men and women of World War I. He felt that "the more sagacious members" of Congress appreciated "the value of the budget system, and of living within our means," but concluded that the "mass of the town-meeting," namely the congressmen, "will ignore such considerations rather than not be reelected, which local buildings will do much to achieve."[24]

In view of the depression of spirit that Jameson suffered, it was fortunate that he had so loyal a partner as Eben Putnam. At the seventh annual convention of the Legion at Omaha, Nebraska, October 5–9, 1925, the tocsin was sounded more vigorously than ever. The failure to pass the Elliott bill was given full airing by the Legion's legislative committee. It was noted that the Legion had thrown its influence behind it and that it had come very close to clearing all the legislative hurdles. "The administration favored the bill," the committee's report stated, "because it planned to do away with the old method of allocating public buildings." The bill "stipulated that the location and cost of the buildings would be determined by the Secretary of the Treasury." Secretary Andrew Mellon, in turn, had announced "that one of the first buildings to be erected under this measure would be an archives building in the city of Washington."[25]

The adverse minority report on the bill in the House had highlighted its weakness from the congressmen's point of view: "There is no guaranty, in fact no indication that each State will receive a part of the buildings for which the money was authorized herein." The minority report by Rep. Thomas J. Busby of Mississippi had further stated the basic objection that this bill proposed to change practically all existing law with regard to public buildings "which come under the supervision of the Treasury Department." Congress had always specifically provided for the "places where public buildings were to be constructed and the maximum amount which could be expended . . . at each place." Busby then quoted extensively from the last omnibus bill, the act of March 4, 1913, to show with "what care, precision, and thoroughness Congress defined its intentions as to what was to be done . . . the manner in which it was to be done, and the amount of money which was to be expended in each instance." Then he came to the root of his fears: "There is no provision where he shall spend the $150,000,000 authorized in this bill. It might all be spent in the District of Columbia." Moreover, even in the instance of the $100 million which was supposed to be spent outside of the District of Columbia, Busby feared that the funds would be allocated to the larger cities, "leaving the more sparsely settled sections of the country to get along as best they can." The congressman concluded that the Elliott bill "should not become law in its present form."[26]

The Legion committee viewed most seriously the repeated failures to obtain appropriations for the archives project. It had previously stated quite explicitly to the Legion membership that "the Legion, greatest of our patriotic societies, owes to the country an insistence upon the proper care and safe deposit of the national records."[27] The committee recited the past efforts of the Legion, maintaining that its interest went all the way back to its first convention in 1919. It was pointed out that annually strong resolutions were adopted by the membership "favoring the erection of an archives building at Washington, to protect and care for the priceless records of the World War and other valuable documents of a historical nature." Once again, and for the fourth time, the American Legion passed a resolution demanding a congressional appropriation for a national archives building.[28]

Though licking their wounds from the latest legislative battles, Smoot and Jameson were still full of fight. The *Evening Star,* looking forward to the legislative season of 1926, announced that "a drive to get the long-proposed archives building erected at the earliest possible date . . . will be made under the leadership of Senator Smoot . . . as soon as Congress meets."[29]

In the year-end accounting of his stewardship of the Committee on the National Archives, Jameson told the members of the American Historical Association that in "tardy pursuance of the recommendations made by President Coolidge in his Budget message of December, 1923," each house of Congress had a bill for the authorization of a large-scale building program, one for Washington, and the other for both Washington and the country at large. Because the two bills differed widely in character, "the result was a struggle between the two houses, so prolonged and inconclusive that neither bill passed and nothing was done." Jameson concluded with the self-evident observation that "the fortunes of the project for a National Archive Building are now closely tied up with the fate of the project for a general public buildings act."[30]

COOLIDGE TRIES AGAIN

In his third budget message to Congress, President Coolidge again urged Congress to take action on an appropriate public buildings bill. He reminded the legislators that he had repeatedly called their attention to the need for additional federal buildings "to protect employees and records at the seat of Government." Although he recognized the need in the country at large, the frugal president believed that that need was not as urgent as the need for buildings in the District of Columbia.[31]

Senator Smoot immediately seconded the presidential message with the introduction of two more bills: S. 778 on December 8, and S. 1720 on December 16, 1925. Again, both bills limited the provision of construction to buildings in the District of Columbia. Bill S. 778 specified new buildings for the Treasury, Justice, Agriculture, and Commerce departments and a site for the national archives. The bill placed the authority for carrying out the provisions of the measure in the Public Buildings Commission, authorized a study of the requirements of all government establishments, and lodged in the commission the selection of a site for each building. The commission would also allocate the preparation of plans, award contracts, and submit annual estimates to the Bureau of the Budget for the amounts proposed for each fiscal year. Fifty million dollars was authorized to be appropriated, with not more than $10 million to be made available in any fiscal year. Bill S. 1720 had similar provisions.[32] Both bills died in committee.

Concurrent with the introduction of the Senate bills, backup support was tendered by several annual reports that appeared in December 1925: those of the American Historical Association, the Fine Arts Commission, and the Public Buildings Commission. The Fine Arts Commission declared that it was determined that the new building program "shall begin with an archives building." The commission took the occasion to refer to the way in which the president's own files were kept in the White House offices, some in the basement and some in the attic. It deplored the practice of returning "most of the official correspondence" to former presidents or their families. The report concluded that some of the presidents' papers "by good fortune . . . found a place in the Library of Congress; but in most instances they have passed into private hands, to be purchased by Congress." It was further observed that "this lack of care of Government archives will go on until Congress shall provide a hall of records . . . and shall enact that every communication addressed to an officer of the Government in his official capacity shall be deemed a part of the public records and treated as such."[33]

The Public Buildings Commission in its year-end report referred to the specific needs of individual departments and bureaus and mentioned first and foremost the matter of housing the archives. The commission deplored the fact that the national government had never adopted a systematic plan for the care and preservation of the public archives. It went on to state the classic definition of archives, that they were more than just selected historical items but the permanently valuable records of the government, accumulated in the course of performing its functions and activities. The report detailed the administrative advantages of an archives building in promoting the orderly and expeditious administration of public affairs; and specific instances were given of research and reference problems arising from lack of central and accessible custody of records. Observing that "the need for an archives building . . . has long been recognized as urgent," the commission declared,

Many important organizations have for years been supporting the demand for an adequate archives building . . . for more than 15 years the council of the American Historical Association has been besieging Congress "in the interests of security, in the interests of economy, in the interest of system, in the interest of a rapid and efficient conduct of the public business and, not least, in the interests of American history," to make appropriations for purchase of a site and erection of a national archives building.[34]

THE FIRST POSTWAR PUBLIC BUILDINGS ACT

With the beginning of the sesquicentennial year of American independence, a simultaneous effort was pushed in both houses of Congress for a general public buildings program. Representative Richard N. Elliott introduced H.R. 6559 on January 4, 1926. The same day Sen. Bert M. Fernald introduced S. 2007. Both bills authorized the same total of expenditure, $150 million, and both applied to the District of Columbia and to the country at large. The Senate Committee on Public Buildings and Grounds a week later considered S. 2007, and promptly reported it out favorably. In view of the progress of the parallel bill in the House, further action on the Senate bill was indefinitely postponed.[35]

As not infrequently happens in human affairs, hope too long deferred may become hope lost. Constant defeat can try the most stouthearted so gravely that they no longer hope for the victory which may actually be near. The early spring of 1926 reveals Jameson in a pessimistic mood. In a letter to Roscoe Hill, an historian serving as an adviser to the Nicaraguan government, he expressed unhappiness about tying the fate of the archives project to a general public buildings program. He told Hill: "The President two years ago urged upon them [the Congress] the necessity of providing $50,000,000 in ten years for public buildings in Washington," but it was now amply clear that the only way to get this sum was "to let them add appropriations of $115,000,000 more for public buildings in the districts." Although he was willing to concede that the "enlargements of many post offices" were justifiable, still "nearly all the new ones added will be merely so much pie." On the other hand, Jameson said, the movement for an archives building was "likely to be carried along by the general eagerness of Congress for an omnibus public buildings bill."[36]

With the probable passage of public buildings legislation, Jameson now became seriously concerned lest the priority claims of the national archives should be lost in the shuffle as large agencies of the government seized the opportunity to acquire space for themselves. He conveyed his worries to Senator Smoot, observing that wartime legislation had "greatly increased the needs of the Internal Revenue Bureau and the Accounting Office, and some other branches of the government service." Then he came to the heart of the matter. "Such offices, with a definite headship, a large personnel, and duties whose importance is well known to everyone, have a great advantage, in making their needs felt, over a concern like the national archives, which have no organized existence, no head, no chief, no personnel." In frustration he cried out, "Because the national archives are everybody's business, they are in a sense nobody's business." In any event, Jameson continued, "it seems to be nobody's business, unless mine, to clamor to your Commission for an early place in your programme for the National Archive Building."[37]

Furthermore, as "one who for twenty years has watched with solicitude the interests of historical study in Washington," Jameson noted that recent years "have shown a remarkable . . . increase" in the number of students coming to Washington "for fresh investigations in American history." He thought it would be agreed "that the interests of our national history and those who pursue it are not an unimportant object of public consideration."[38]

But whatever were Jameson's tribulations, the fact remained that H.R. 6559 was to be the long-sought vehicle of victory. In view of the national significance of the bill, the House acted promptly. Hearings were held a few days after introduction. It was reported favorably to the House, with amendments,[39] and before the month was out it was passed by the House and referred to the Senate Committee on Public Buildings and Grounds.

On February 22, Senator Fernald reported the bill favorably, with amendments, to the Senate,[40] where it was subjected to a lengthy debate, further amended, and finally passed on May 3, 1926. As the amendments of the two houses were not identical, a conference committee was appointed, which rendered its report on May 17. The conference report was accepted by both houses and the measure went to the White House. President Coolidge signed it on May 25, 1926, and it became public law 281 of the Sixty-ninth Congress.[41]

This first public buildings act since 1913 was a triumph of equitable compromise. All parties got substantial results, but no one got everything. Though public buildings throughout the country were now ensured, the measure did not specifically mention individual projects. The administration was thus given a controlling voice in the allocation of future projects.

The act placed the contractual power in the hands of the secretary of the Treasury, who was authorized to expend a total of $165 million, of which $15 million was to be used for the construction of buildings authorized under previous acts but not yet erected. A total of $150 million was authorized for all new sites and construction. Of this sum, $100 million was allotted for federal buildings in the states, of which not more than $25 million could be expended in any one year; and $50 million was allotted for buildings in the District of Columbia, of which not more than $10 million could be expended in any one year. The act specified that in the District, sites should be acquired south of Pennsylvania Avenue and west of Maryland Avenue, that "suitable approaches" should be provided for the buildings, and that their surroundings should be beautified and embellished "as nearly in harmony with the plan of Peter Charles L'Enfant as may be practicable." The secretary of the Treasury was also authorized to close streets and alleys that lay between contiguous squares and were needed as parts of a site.[42]

All sites in the District were to be approved by "the commission created by the Act of March 1, 1919 . . . and said commission shall determine the order in which buildings or enlargement of buildings in the District of Columbia shall be constructed."[43] This last was the crucial provision of the act as far as Jameson was concerned, for Senator Smoot was chairman of the Public Buildings Commission, and he had repeatedly stated in the past that the national archives building would be first on the priority list for the District.

Though public law 281 was at last on the books—and to that extent Jameson could draw comfort—it was still, after all, an authorization and not an appropriation act. This was yet to come.

FIRST APPROPRIATION

Naturally, an authorization act that was so important to so many congressmen did not have long to wait to be implemented, and the first deficiency appropriation measure that came along was seized upon as the vehicle for the public buildings appropriation. As there was very little time left in the session, things moved with dramatic rapidity. Actions that would normally require weeks or even months were completed within hours.

On June 24, 1926, Rep. Martin B. Madden, chairman of the House Committee on Appropriations introduced the bill.[44] Five days later the measure was passed, with amendments, by the House of Representatives.[45] It was immediately referred to the Senate Committee on Appropriations, which just as promptly reported it, with amendments, to the Senate.[46] The upper house passed the bill on July 1, 1926.

As the House and Senate amendments were at variance, a conference committee was at once appointed, agreed on the amendments, and made its report the same day. The two houses accepted the conference report and thus finally passed the measure, also on the same day.[47] Two days later President Coolidge signed the measure and it became the law of the land. Included in the act was the following clause:

Washington, District of Columbia, *Archives Building:* Toward the construction of an extensible archives building and the acquisition of a site by purchase, condemnation, or otherwise, $1,000,000; and the Secretary of the Treasury is authorized to enter into contracts for the entire estimated cost of such building, including stacks, and site, for not to exceed $6,900,000.[48]

The National Archives Building was at last ensured. Jameson, with the aid of his allies and supporters, had achieved the second and most vital phase of his dream—the first appropriation! Came the hosannas. From private persons and public bodies, messages of congratulations flowed into Jameson's office. Replying to Eben Putnam's inquiry as to priorities, Jameson told him that at a recent meeting of the Public Buildings Commission, Smoot had announced that "the Archive Building would be the first to be taken up." Jameson, audibly sighing with relief after many years of tension, remarked, "I am now able to expect to see a National Archive Building here in Washington before I die."[49]

John C. Fitzpatrick, assistant chief of the Manuscript Division of the Library of Congress, wrote to Jameson offering his "sincere congratulations on the success of the archives building project" and declaring that "to you more than to any other man belongs the lion's share of the credit."[50] James G. McDonald of the Foreign Policy Association in New York City, added to the common refrain: "Many congratulations on your success . . . in securing an Archive Building!" he wrote. "Without your untiring zeal an indifferent Congress could never have been stirred to action. All of us are your debtors."[51]

Institutional reactions were no less enthusiastic than those of individuals. In October the American Legion held its annual convention in Philadelphia. In his annual report the national historian of the Legion, Eben Putnam, gave due credit to the American Historical Association, and inferentially to Jameson:

While the credit of initiating and persistently working for the erection of an archive building is especially due to the American Historical Association, yet unbiased opinion recognizes that the aid of the American Legion was a most important factor in obtaining the actual legislation required, including the appropriation to commence operations.[52]

Putnam further asserted that "this matter was never lost sight of by the legislative committee" headed by John Thomas Taylor, "nor by the national historian." But, said Putnam, what finally gave the project impetus was the support of the president. When Coolidge took office, "it became evident that the attainment of this objective was in sight."[53]

Yet, Putnam mused, how long it had taken! "For nearly twenty years the most active of our historical and patriotic societies have worked for the erection of an archive building and have been aided by far-sighted and appreciative members of Congress. . . . and although upon two or three occasions success seemed almost within grasp, there would intervene at the last moment an insurmountable obstacle." The Legion historian concluded that "the accomplishment of this objective should be a matter of great satisfaction," as "for one hundred and fifty years this nation has been making history; providing safe places in which to keep the records of those years is a far wiser and greater sesqui-centennial memorial than any other which could be thought of."[54]

The *Evening Star*, late in September, reported that "a conference of distinguished experts . . . was called by the Treasury to formulate general plans for the Government's great archives building to be erected here." The meeting was held in the office of Assistant Secretary of the Treasury Charles S. Dewey. The purpose was to determine how "the American Government can build its archives building" so as "to combine all the best features of the greatest archives of the world." The conference group included Acting Supervising Architect James A. Wetmore; Librarian of Congress Herbert Putnam; Chairman of the Fine Arts Commission Charles Moore; Worthington C. Ford of the Massachusetts Historical Society; and J. Franklin Jameson of the Carnegie Institution.[55]

The Public Buildings Commission in its annual report reiterated that "the Archives Building was placed first on the program because . . . it would provide more general relief than any other building." The commission also declared that it approved the location of the archives building (between Twelfth and Thirteenth and B and C streets, N.W.), but admitted that "the precise arrangement and area is at this time hard to determine." The estimates available prompted the commission to recommend "approximately 10,600,000 cubic feet of space."[56]

Treasury Secretary Mellon, in his 1926 report, noted that "steps have been taken to acquire the necessary sites, and work on the plans for the Internal Revenue, Archives, and Liberty Loan Buildings is well under way."[57]

It may be surmised that the most fervent rejoicing occurred at the annual meeting of the American Historical Association in Rochester, New York. The business meeting was held on December 29, 1926, and Leo F. Stock led off with the report of the Executive Council of the association: "We rejoice," he said, "that the campaign which the association, through its committee, has waged . . . for the erection of a national archives building in Washington, has at last met with success."[58]

Jameson, at the same meeting, rendering the report of the Committee on the National Archives, stated, "The committee on the national archives have the happiness to report, at last, that the erection of a national archive building in Washington is positively assured. By the terms of the Public Buildings bill passed in June 1926, authority is given to the Public Buildings Commission to provide such additional buildings in Washington for Government use as they may deem requisite, and a suitable lump-sum appropriation was made." Jameson went on to say that "important steps toward the acquisition of the site have been taken," and that "plans have been brought to an advanced stage of preparation in the Office of the Supervising Architect of the Treasury." As to plans, Jameson was perhaps a bit more enthusiastic than factual. Nevertheless, he was entitled to indulge in a happy display of hyperbole. He was fair, however, to others who aided in the movement:

. . . many persons, in and out of Congress, have cooperated in bringing about this welcome result. . . . It is a pleasure also to record that, during the more recent years of the campaign, the American Legion, awakened to the need of a national archive building, has exerted itself cordially and effectively in pushing the matter . . . through cooperation with our committee and also independently.[59]

Resolutions adopted by the American Historical Association that expressed its appreciation to Congress thriftily included reference to the importance of providing for the publication of the territorial papers "now preserved in the federal archives in Washington" and also to the need for speedily completing "the edition of the 'Journals of the Continental Congress,' prepared by the Library of Congress."[60] The historians were determined to keep Congress apprised of its responsibilities to the intellectual and cultural life of the nation.

It was left to President Coolidge, in his State of the Union message at the end of the year, to put in moving words the meaning of the congressional measures. Said the presumably laconic chief magistrate of the republic,

We are embarking on an ambitious building program for the city of Washington. The Memorial Bridge is under way with all that it holds for use and beauty. New buildings are soon contemplated. This program should represent the best that exists in the art and science of architecture. . . . Let it express the soul of America . . . a city of stately proportions, symmetrically laid out and adorned with the best that there is in architecture. . . . In the coming years Washington should be not only the art center of our country but the art center of the world. Around it should center all that is best in science, in learning, in letters, and in art. These are the results that justify the creation of those national resources with which we have been favored.[61]

National Archives Building
(National Archives)

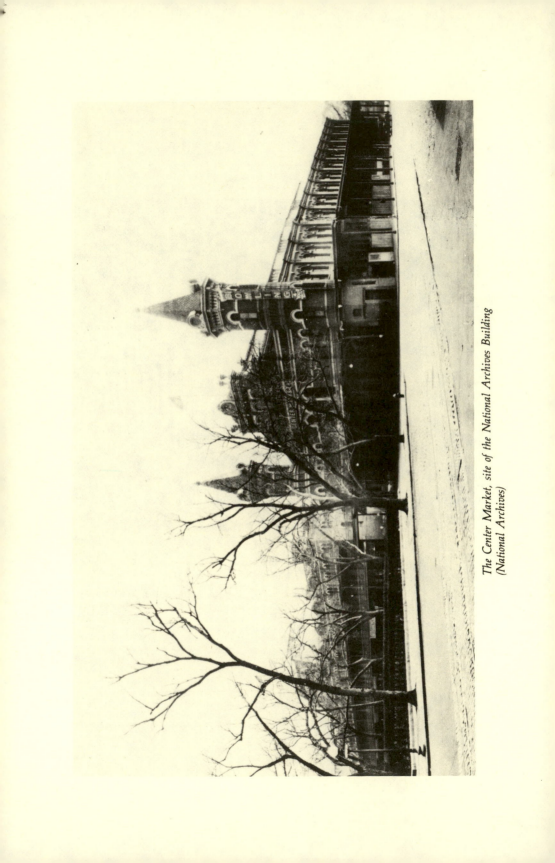

*The Center Market, site of the National Archives Building
(National Archives)*

12
Epilogue

The activities leading to the final consummation of the project—the construction of the building and the establishment of the National Archives of the United States—can be only briefly outlined here. The ultimate location of the building was tied in with the Federal Triangle concept planned by the Board of Architectural Consultants appointed by Treasury Secretary Mellon after the passage of the Public Buildings Act of 1926. The site of the archives was shifted from Twelfth and Thirteenth, B and C streets, N.W., as originally prescribed by the Public Buildings Commission, to a plot between Seventh and Ninth streets, and B Street and Pennsylvania Avenue, N.W., then occupied by the Center Market.

With the change of site and further study of the situation, the Treasury Department moved to increase the funds available for the archives building. An act of December 20, 1928, made an additional appropriation of $1.85 million for the national archives and authorized the secretary of the Treasury to construct the building on the finally designated site at a construction cost not to exceed $8.75 million.[1] Amounts already expended for the purchase of a site were charged against an appropriation of $25 million made under an act of January 13, 1928.[2] Eventually, the cost of the National Archives Building exceeded $12 million.[3]

At last, the depression year 1930 saw tangible progress in the development of the archives project. On July 3, exactly four years after the initial appropriation, the president signed the bill authorizing the construction of the National Archives on its present site.[4] Treasury Secretary Mellon appointed John Russell Pope of New York City to membership on the Board of Architectural Consultants and then se-

*National Archives Building under construction
(National Archives)*

*National Archives Building:
inner court, before completion
of stacks
(National Archives)*

lected Pope's firm to design the archives building. On July 7, President Hoover appointed an Advisory Committee on the National Archives Building to review the data previously gathered by the Treasury Department and to make final determinations for the programming of the new building so that definitive planning could proceed.[5] In further instructions to the advisory committee, the secretary of the Treasury declared that because it was "to occupy a conspicuous position in the Triangle . . . the National Archives Building . . . must present a completed artistic appearance and also admit deferred construction on . . . half the stack space . . . but with the inside courtyards invisible from the streets."[6]

The final plan and design of John Russell Pope carried out the spirit of the secretary's instructions to the letter. He created a rectangular building, completely enclosing a vacant inner court for future expansion. The outer shell of the building displayed a completed monumental edifice in the richest of the classical styles of architecture—the Corinthian order—marking the apex of the Triangle with an exclamatory terminal point.[7] The artistic effect desired by Secretary Mellon was enhanced by classical sculptural elements, executed by some of the foremost American sculptors of the time. The great exhibition hall was embellished by the paintings of the eminent muralist Barry Faulkner.

On September 9, 1931, building plans were sufficiently advanced for ground to be broken by Ferry K. Heath, assistant secretary of the Treasury. The contract for the original structure was awarded on December 1, 1932, to the George A. Fuller Company of Washington, D.C., in the sum of $5,284,000.[8] When the very difficult foundation work had advanced to the point where it was ready to receive the superstructure, the cornerstone was laid by President Hoover, on February 20, 1933. The original building was accepted by the government on October 15, 1935, and the assistant director of procurement of the Treasury advised the archivist of the United States that the building would be ready for occupancy by the National Archives staff on November 1. During the following week the small staff moved in and Archivist R. D. W. Connor declared the National Archives Building occupied as of November 8, 1935.[9]

Prior to the actual occupation of the new building, two events of the utmost importance transpired. The long-awaited organic act legally establishing the new archival agency, the National Archives Act, had been approved on June 19, 1934, by President Franklin Delano Roosevelt.[10] Several months later, on October 10, 1934, after a skillful campaign led by Jameson, President Roosevelt had appointed Professor R. D. W. Connor of the University of North Carolina as the first archivist of the United States.[11]

J. Franklin Jameson's quarter century of struggle was now history. He had achieved the three interlocking goals he had initiated during the administration of the first Roosevelt, and now completed with the cooperation of the second Roosevelt: first, the authorization of and appropriation for the National Archives Building; second, the conception and passage of the National Archives Act, establishing an independent institution; and, third, the selection and appointment of a highly qualified person as the first archivist of the United States.

With indefatigable persistence, with consummate skill, Jameson had accomplished these goals, and he had accomplished them just in time. Within three years death claimed him.

During the long years of frustration and failure, Jameson was wont to console himself and others with the thought that it had required 240 years to establish the Public Record Office in London. In view of the rapid rate of change in society and institutions in the contemporary world, it is difficult to feel charitable about the time lag of a century and a quarter, from proposal to fulfillment, in America.

Between 1810 and 1903, despite insistent agitation for adequate records protection and for a hall of records, mainly by government officials, only two statutes were actually enacted: the act of 1810, for some fireproof storage rooms, and that of 1903, for the purchase of a site. It is customary in certain circles to refer loosely to the act of April 28, 1810, as the first archives act of the federal government. This is wide of the mark. The act in no sense provided for an archival establishment or even for a simple hall of records. It merely provided for a few fireproof rooms for the slightly better protection of the older records of the State, War, and Navy departments.

Federal executives fought virtually alone during the nineteenth century for adequate facilities for the handling of permanently valuable noncurrent records. Until after the turn of the century there was no established historical lobby. That lobby had to await the creation of the American Historical Association, and its growth to a semblance of a historical profession in being, before pressure outside of the executive agencies could be mobilized and brought to bear on Congress.

It is singular that even after the AHA did start moving on the problem, by enlisting the efforts of hereditary societies and state and local historical societies, all the vocal support generated for the archival cause had a minimal influence on Congress. The reason for insufficient influence on the legislators was the lack of effective voter pressure. The federal executives had virtually no grass-roots constituency. The professional historians likewise lacked political clout. The lay historical societies and the patriotic organizations had slightly more political strength but not enough. It was not until the rise of the American Legion, able to claim thousands of votes in each congressional district, that any organization was in a position to compel a congressman to think twice about failing to support the archival demand.

The central question of why it took so long may be answered with the undramatic but essential reason—legislative sloth. The national legislators had too many other and more material interests than the archival problem to occupy and grip their attention. Here and there, some were willing to pay lip service to the problem, at least to the extent of recognizing its existence. But by and large, congressional ignorance of the values at stake, compounded by suspicion of the motives of the proponents, and congressional insistence on the time-honored pork barrel, hamstrung all efforts at archival progress. Even with the powerful support of the American Legion, Congress was slow to move off dead center until the first public buildings act in thirteen years offered the indispensable quid pro quo of pork, in the shape of a nationwide distribution of post offices, custom houses, and other federal edifices.

Would the result ultimately have been similar without the influence of Jameson? Probably not. The National Archives as it came into being and as it was to be for fifteen years, between 1934 and 1949, an independent, professionally oriented archival agency, staffed with and led by historically trained men, was the fulfillment of the Jameson concept.

Bibliography

BIBLIOGRAPHICAL TOOLS

Griffin, Grace G. et al., eds. *Writings on American History, 1906–40.* New York: Macmillan Publishing Co., 1908–1910; Washington, D.C.: U.S. Government Printing Office, 1911–1913, and 1921–1949; and New Haven: Yale University Press, 1914–1919.

Hamer, Philip M., ed. *A Guide to Archives and Manuscripts in the United States.* New Haven: Yale University Press, 1961.

Scisco, Louis D. *Analytical Index to the Records of the Columbia Historical Society, 1897–1907.* Washington, D.C.: Columbia Historical Society, 1955.

U.S., General Services Administration, National Archives and Records Service. Preliminary Inventories of Record Groups in the National Archives:

RG 29, *Records of the Bureau of the Census,* P.I. 161. Compiled by Katherine H. Davidson and Charlotte M. Ashby. Washington, D.C.: National Archives and Records Service, 1964.

RG 46, *Records of the United States Senate,* P.I. 23. Compiled by Harold E. Hufford and Watson G. Caudill. Washington, D.C.: National Archives and Records Service, 1950.

RG 56, *Records of the Department of the Treasury,* P.I. 187. Compiled by Carmelita S. Ryan and Hope K. Holdcamper. Washington, D.C.: National Archives and Records Service, 1977.

RG 59, *Records of the Department of State,* P.I. 157. Compiled by Daniel T. Goggin and H. Stephen Helton. Washington, D.C.: National Archives and Records Service, 1963.

RG 66, *Records of the Commission of Fine Arts,* P.I. 79. Compiled by Richard S. Maxwell. Washington, D.C.: National Archives and Records Service, 1955.

RG 121, *Records of the Public Buildings Service,* P.I. 110. Compiled by W. Lane

Van Neste and Virgil E. Baugh. Washington, D.C.: National Archives and Records Service, 1958.

RG 233, *Records of the United States House of Representatives, 1789–1946,* P.I. 113, vol. 1. Compiled by Buford Rowland, Handy B. Fant, and Harold E. Hufford. Washington, D.C.: National Archives and Records Service, 1959.

U.S., Library of Congress. *The National Union Catalog of Manuscript Collections, 1959– 1961.* Ann Arbor: J. W. Edwards, 1962.

———. "Report and Inventory, J. Franklin Jameson Papers." Washington, D.C.: 1956.

University of North Carolina Library, Southern Historical Collection. Inventory, Papers of R. D. W. Connor. Chapel Hill.

University of Virginia Library. Inventory of Miles Poindexter Papers, 1897– 1937. Charlottesville.

Van Tyne, Claude H., and Leland, Waldo G. *Guide to the Archives of the Government of the United States in Washington.* Carnegie Institution Publication no. 14. Washington, D.C.: Carnegie Institution, 1904.

PRIMARY MATERIALS

Manuscript Materials

American Legion Archives. The national headquarters of the American Legion is located in Indianapolis, Indiana, but a legislative headquarters is maintained in Washington, D.C. Both headquarters include libraries where printed materials are kept, but the correspondence files are kept only at the Indianapolis library, which serves as the archives of the Legion. Correspondence between Eben Putnam and American Legion officials and with others concerning the national archives building project is on file under the rubric, "Cooperation: Memorials: National Archives Building." The serials at the Washington headquarters, though incomplete, are readily available: American Legion Annual Reports, 1922–1934; Summary of Proceedings of National Conventions of the Legion, 1919–1934; Reports of the National Legislative Committee; the *American Legion Weekly,* 1919–1946; and *American Legion Magazine,* the complete set of which is on file at the New York City office of the Legion.

Connor Papers. Papers of Robert D. W. Connor, Southern Historical Collection, University of North Carolina Library, Chapel Hill. There are several dozen boxes of papers, chronologically arranged. Five boxes for the period 1930– 1935, were used. Included also is Connor's diary for the period 1934–1941, when he was archivist of the United States. The diary was restricted, but permission to see it was obtained. Restrictions have since been removed.

Flippin Collection. Percy Scott Flippin, compiler. "The Archives of the United States Government: A Documentary History, 1774–1934," 24 vols., loose leaf, National Archives Library, Washington, D.C. This is a scrapbook of photoreproductions and fair copies of documents, consisting of congressional hearings, reports, and bills; presidential messages; reports and messages from heads of executive departments; and newspaper items and magazine articles. Each volume averages about two hundred documents, giving a total of approximately forty-five hundred documents. The volumes are heavily weighted with repetitious official and newspaper accounts of fires in government buildings in Washington. The collection was compiled by direction of the first archivist of the United States, R. D. W. Connor.

Jameson Papers. Papers of J. Franklin Jameson, Manuscript Division, Library of Congress, Washington, D.C. These papers are mainly the files accumulated by Jameson in the Department of Historical Research of the Carnegie Institution for the period 1905–1928. There are some documents from before and after this period. They are said to number some fifty thousand pieces. The papers are rich in material on American historiography for the period 1890–1930 and are indispensable to any study on the crusade for the National Archives. Documents used for this study are mainly from the following boxes: box 52, American Historical Association and Public Archives Commission; box 57, Archives, National, Washington, 1906–1943; box 61, Solon J. Buck; box 71, Rosa P. Chiles; box 73, R. D. W. Connor; box 74, Daughters of the American Revolution; box 77, William E. Dodd; box 82, Simeon D. Fess; box 83, John C. Fitzpatrick and Percy Scott Flippin; box 87, Government Expenses for Historical Publications, and Evarts B. Greene; box 90, Guide to Washington Archives (Van Tyne and Leland); box 94, Historical Societies, State and Local; boxes 96 and 102, Waldo G. Leland; box 109, William F. Lingelbach, Henry Cabot Lodge, and the McCall Bill; and box 110, Andrew C. McLaughlin, John Bach McMaster, Alfred T. Mahan, and Thomas P. Martin.

Poindexter Papers. Papers of Miles Poindexter, 1897–1937, Manuscripts Department, University of Virginia Library, Charlottesville. There are several hundred boxes occupying over two hundred linear feet of shelving. The papers consist of correspondence, memorandums, charts, and the like. They relate mainly to Poindexter's service in the U.S. House of Representatives, from 1909 to 1911; in the U.S. Senate, from 1911 to 1923; and as American ambassador to Peru, from 1923 to 1928. There are also private personal papers relating to his law practice before 1909 and family papers after 1928. Papers useful for this study are mainly in Series III, "Code Filing System," 1912–1918, with some scattering of documents from other series through 1923.

Wilson Papers. Papers of Woodrow Wilson, 1880–1924, Library of Congress.

Records in the National Archives, Washington, D.C.:

Records of the Bureau of the Census, Record Group 29.

Records of the Office of Public Buildings and Grounds, Record Group 42.

Records relating to the Archives Building (File nos. 1100/2100 and 1250-15-5/210); the Apex Triangle (File no. 1460); and monthly and quarterly reports on the Triangle Group (File nos. 1555-50-20-60 and 1555-50-20-61).

Records of the United States Senate, Record Group 46. Materials on committees, hearings, bills, and reports.

Records of the Bureau of the Budget, Record Group 51. Materials in the Central File, 1921–1938; and the Subject File, National Archives, with letters and memorandums from Andrew W. Mellon, secretary of the Treasury, to Charles G. Dawes, director of the Bureau of the Budget, and from Daniel W. Bell, acting director of the bureau, to R. D. W. Connor.

Records of the Department of State, Record Group 59. Records of the Advisory Committee on the National Archives Building, authorized by President Hoover, July 7, 1930; correspondence of President Hoover with government departments relating to the National Archives; records of the historical adviser of the Department of State, Tyler Dennett; and reports of Natalia Summers on the European archival survey trip of 1929.

Records of the National Archives and Records Service, Record Group 64. Papers of Solon J. Buck and R. D. W. Connor; photographs of the National Archives, including sixteen hundred negatives and captioned prints of interior and exterior views, 1935–1945; the National Archives construction file, 1932–1942; and the National Archives depository file, 1936–1945, with illustrations of records in federal, state, and foreign archives.

Records of the Commission of Fine Arts, Record Group 66. Project Files, 1910–1952, consisting of correspondence, memorandums, clippings, maps, drawings, and plans relating to project artists, contractors, and government officials. There are also several folders of general correspondence, clippings, plans, sketches, and photostats, 1913–1937, relating to the archives building.

Records of the Public Buildings Service, Record Group 121. Records of the Advisory Committee on the National Archives Building, appointed by President Hoover to advise and assist the supervising architect of the Treasury Department in determining the size and character of the proposed building. The papers were assembled by Louis Simon, together with related correspondence and materials concerning archival depositories in Europe. Included are preliminary schemata from John Russell Pope, architect of the National Archives Building, 1929–1941.

Records of the United States House of Representatives, Record Group 233. Materials on committees, hearings, bills, and reports.

Printed Materials

General

American Historical Association. *Annual Report*[s] *of the American Historical Association for the Year*[s] *1891, 1893, 1896, 1899, 1901, 1908, 1909, 1910, 1911, 1912, 1913, 1915, 1917, 1918, 1919, 1921, 1922, 1923, 1925, 1926,* [and] *1927* [and] *1928.* Washington, D.C.: U.S. Government Printing Office, 1892–1929.

American State Papers: Documents, Legislative and Executive of the Congress of the United States, Miscellaneous. Vol. 2. Washington, D.C.: Gales and Seaton, 1834.

Carnegie Institution. *Report of the President of the Carnegie Institution of Washington, November 11, 1905.* Washington, D.C.: Carnegie Institution, 1905.

———. *Year Book for 1902.* Washington, D.C.: Carnegie Institution, 1902.

Daughters of the American Revolution. *Proceedings of the 20th Continental Congress.* Washington, D.C.: Daughters of the American Revolution, 1911.

Donnan, Elizabeth, and Stock, Leo F., eds. *An Historian's World: Selections from the Correspondence of John Franklin Jameson.* Memoirs of the American Philosophical Society, Vol. 42. Philadelphia: American Philosophical Society, 1956.

Israel, Fred L., ed. *The State of the Union Messages of the Presidents.* Vol. 3. New York: Chelsea House, Robert Hector, 1966.

Richardson, James D., comp. *A Compilation of the Messages and Papers of the Presidents.* Vols. 4, 7, 16, and 17. New York: Bureau of National Literature, 1897 and 1917.

U.S., Congress. *Annals of Congress.* 1810 and 1815.

U.S., Congress. *Congressional Record.* 1906, 1911–1914, 1916, 1917, 1919, 1921–1923, and 1925.

U.S., Department of Commerce. *Reports of the Department of Commerce, 1917, 1918, 1919,* [and] *1920.* Washington, D.C.: U.S. Government Printing Office, 1918–1921.

————. *Ninth, Tenth* [and] *Eleventh Annual Report* [s] *of the Secretary of Commerce, 1921, 1922,* [and] *1923.* Washington, D.C.: U.S. Government Printing Office, 1921–1923.

U.S., Department of the Treasury. *Annual Report* [s] *of the Secretary of the Treasury on the State of the Finances for the Fiscal Year* [s] *Ended June 30, 1904, 1905, 1906, 1919, 1923,* [and] *1926.* Washington, D.C.: U.S. Government Printing Office, 1905–1927.

U.S., Library of Congress. *Journals of the Continental Congress, 1774–1789.* Washington, D.C.: U.S. Government Printing Office, 1922.

U.S., National Archives. *Second* [and] *Third Annual Report* [s] *of the Archivist of the United States, for the Fiscal Year* [s] *Ending June 30, 1936* [and] *1937.* Washington, D.C.: U.S. Government Printing Office, 1936 and 1938.

U.S., National Commission of Fine Arts. *Ninth Report, July 1, 1919–June 30, 1921.* Washington, D.C.: U.S. Government Printing Office, 1921.

————. *Tenth Report, July 1, 1921–December 31, 1925.* Washington, D.C.: U.S. Government Printing Office, 1926.

U.S., Navy Department. *Annual Reports of the Navy Department for the Fiscal Year* [s] *1922* [and] *1923.* Washington, D.C.: U.S. Government Printing Office, 1923–1924.

U.S., Public Buildings Commission. *Report of the Public Buildings Commission, January 4, 1923.* Washington, D.C.: U.S. Government Printing Office, 1923.

U.S., *Statutes at Large.* Vols. 2, 32, 37–39, 44–46, and 48.

U.S., War Department. *Annual Report of the Secretary of War on the Operations of the Department for the Fiscal Year Ending June 30, 1875.* Washington, D.C.: U.S. Government Printing Office, 1875.

————. *Annual Report* [s] *of the Secretary of War for the Year* [s] *1878* [and] *1879.* Washington, D.C.: U.S. Government Printing Office, 1878–1879.

————. *Report of the Secretary of War.* Washington, D.C.: U.S. Government Printing Office, 1876.

Washington Board of Trade. *Thirty-first Annual Report of the Washington Board of Trade, 1921–1922.* Washington, D.C.: Gibson Brothers, n.d.

————. *Thirty-third Annual Report of the Washington Board of Trade, 1923.* Washington, D.C.: Charles H. Potter, 1923.

U.S. Congress

Senate

U.S., Congress, Senate. *Journal.* 46th Cong., 3d Sess.; and 69th Cong., 1st Sess.

BILLS

U.S., Congress, Senate. *A Bill Making Appropriation for the Purchase of Ground and Erection Thereon . . . of a . . . Hall of Records.* 46th Cong., 3d Sess., S. 1889, December 13, 1880.
————. *A Bill Making Appropriation for the Purchase of Ground and Erection Thereon . . . of a . . . Hall of Records.* 47th Cong., 1st Sess., S. 817, January 12, 1882.
————. *A Bill Making Appropriation for the Purchase of Ground and Erection Thereon . . . of a . . . Hall of Records.* 48th Cong., 1st Sess., S. 206, December 4, 1883.
————. *A Bill Making Appropriation for the Purchase of Ground and Erection Thereon . . . of a . . . Hall of Records.* 49th Cong., 2d Sess., S. 103, December 8, 1885.
————. *A Bill Making Appropriation for the Purchase of Ground and Erection Thereon . . . of a . . . Hall of Records.* 50th Cong., 1st Sess., S. 279, December 12, 1887.
————. *A Bill Making Appropriation for the Purchase of Ground and Erection Thereon . . . of a . . . Hall of Records.* 50th Cong., 1st Sess., S. 2305, March 8, 1888.
————. *A Bill Making Appropriation for the Purchase of Ground and Erection Thereon . . . of a . . . Hall of Records.* 51st Cong., 1st Sess., S. 490, December 4, 1889.
————. *A Bill Making Appropriation for the Purchase of Ground and Erection Thereon . . . of a . . . Hall of Records.* 52d Cong., 1st Sess., S. 430, December 10, 1891.
————. *A Bill to Authorize the Acquisition of Certain Real Estate in the City of Washington, D.C., and the Erection Thereon of Buildings to Be Used for a Hall of Records, a Folding Room for the House of Representatives, a Storage Warehouse, and for Other Purposes.* 55th Cong., 1st Sess., S. 421, March 16, 1897.
————. *A Bill to Authorize the Acquisition of Certain Real Estate in the City of Washington, District of Columbia, and Providing for a Hall of Records, and for Other Purposes.* 55th Cong., 1st Sess., S. 2795, December 15, 1897.
————. *A Bill for the Purchase of a Site for a Hall of Records.* 55th Cong., 1st Sess., S. 3796, February 17, 1898.
————. *A Bill to Authorize the Acquisition of Square No. 229, in the City of Washington, D.C., and Providing for a Hall of Records, and for Other Purposes.* 56th Cong., 1st Sess., S. 3546, March 12, 1900.
————. *A Bill for the Purchase of a Site for a Hall of Records.* 56th Cong., 1st Sess., S. 4227, April 16, 1900.
————. *A Bill to Provide for the Purchase of Square 862 in the District of Columbia for a Hall of Records.* 56th Cong., 2d Sess., S. 5674, January 21, 1901.
————. *A Bill to Provide for the Purchase of Square Bounded by Seventh and Eighth and D and E Streets, NW., in the District of Columbia, for a Hall of Records.* 56th Cong., 2d Sess., S. 5711, January 23, 1901.
————. *A Bill to Establish a Record Office.* 59th Cong., 2d Sess., S. 6728, December 5, 1906.

———. *A Bill Directing the Secretary of the Treasury to Prepare Designs and Estimates for and Report the Cost of a National Archives Building in the District of Columbia.* 62d Cong., 2d Sess., S. 5179, February 8, 1912.

———. *A Bill to Establish a Record Office.* 62d Cong., 2d Sess., S. 5274, February 14, 1912.

———. *A Bill to Repeal Paragraph 4 of Section 21 of the Public Buildings Act, Approved March 4, 1913, Providing for the Construction of a National Archives Building.* 64th Cong., 1st Sess., S. 5839, May 3, 1916.

———. *A Bill Amending Archive Building Act.* 64th Cong., 2d Sess., S. 7778, January 9, 1917.

———. *A Bill for the Erection of a National Archive Building.* 65th Cong., 2d Sess., S. 4538, May 15, 1918.

———. *A Bill to Provide for the Construction of Certain Public Buildings in the District of Columbia.* 68th Cong., 1st Sess., S. 2284, January 28, 1924.

———. *A Bill to Provide for the Construction of Certain Public Buildings in the District of Columbia.* 69th Cong., 1st Sess., S. 778, December 8, 1925.

———. *A Bill to Provide for the Construction of Certain Public Buildings in the District of Columbia.* 69th Cong., 1st Sess., S. 1720, December 16, 1925.

———. *A Bill for the Construction of Certain Public Buildings, and for Other Purposes.* 69th Cong., 1st Sess., S. 2007, January 4, 1926.

———. *A Bill to Create an Establishment to Be Known as the National Archives.* 70th Cong., 1st Sess., S. 1169, December 6, 1927.

———. *A Bill to Create an Establishment to Be Known as the National Archives, and for Other Purposes.* 71st Cong., 2d Sess., S. 3354, January 6, 1930.

———. *A Bill to Create an Establishment to Be Known as the National Archives, and for Other Purposes.* 73d Cong., 2d Sess., S. 3110, March 20, 1934.

———. *A Bill to Create an Establishment to Be Known as the National Archives, and for Other Purposes.* 73d Cong., 2d Sess., S. 3681, May 10, 1934.

DOCUMENTS

U.S., Congress, Senate, Committee on the Post Office and Post Roads. *Report of the Postmaster General, December 5, 1836.* 24th Cong., 2d Sess., S. Exec. Doc. 2, December 5, 1836.

———, Committee on the Post Office and Post Roads. *To Whom Was Referred the Resolution of the Senate Instructing Them to Inquire into the Cause of Destruction by Fire of the Building in Which Was the General Post Office, and the Patent Office. Report.* 24th Cong., 2d Sess., S. Doc. 215, March 2, 1837.

———, Committee on Public Buildings and Grounds. *Report to Accompany S. 304.* 25th Cong., 2d Sess., S. Doc. 435, April 17, 1838.

———, Committee on Public Buildings and Grounds. *Message from the President of the United States Transmitting a Letter from the Secretary of War of the 15th Instant . . . Setting Forth the Necessity for the Construction of a Fire-proof Building for the Storage of the Public Records.* 48th Cong., 1st Sess., S. Exec. Doc. 11, December 19, 1883.

———. *Letter from the Secretary of War Transmitting a Report Touching the Disposition of Useless Paper in the Department.* 50th Cong., 2d Sess., S. Doc. 133, February 27, 1889.

————, Committee on Appropriations. *Letter from the Secretary of the Treasury Transmitting a Report Relative to Certain Paper in the Files of the Department Not Needed in the Transaction of Business, and of No Permanent Value.* 51st Cong., 1st Sess., S. Exec. Doc. 44, January 29, 1890.

————. *Site for the Proposed Hall of Records.* 54th Cong., 2d Sess., S. Doc. 133, February 17, 1897.

————, Committee on Public Buildings and Grounds. *Secretary of the Treasury Urging the Necessity for the Construction of a Hall of Records in the City of Washington.* 57th Cong., 1st Sess., S. Doc. 236, March 5, 1902.

————, Committee on Public Buildings and Grounds. *Hall of Records for Treasury Department and Additional Quarters for the Post Office Department.* 59th Cong., 1st Sess., S. Doc. 508, June 26, 1906.

————. *Message from the President of the United States Transmitting a Report by the Committee on Department Methods of the Documentary Historical Publications of the United States Government.* 60th Cong., 2d Sess., S. Doc. 714, February 11, 1909.

————. *National Archive Building.* 61st Cong., 3d Sess., S. Doc. 838, February 25, 1911.

————. *Memorial of the Department of Archives and History of the States of Mississippi and Alabama, Respectively, Relative to a National Archives Building.* 62d Cong., 1st Sess., S. Doc. 64, July 11, 1911.

————. *History of the Movement for a National Archives Building in Washington, D.C.* 62d Cong., 2d Sess., S. Doc. 297, February 8, 1912.

————, Committee on Appropriations. *Estimates of Appropriations for Public Buildings for Fiscal Year Ending June 30, 1915.* 63d Cong., 2d Sess., S. Doc. 527, June 30, 1914.

————. *The National Archives: A Programme.* 63d Cong., 3d Sess., S. Doc. 717, December 21, 1914.

————. *Report of the Public Buildings Commission, Relating to Public Buildings in the District of Columbia.* 65th Cong., 2d Sess., S. Doc. 155, December 18, 1917.

————. *Assistant Secretary of War Benedict Crowell Transmits to the Congress, July 5, 1918, a Report on the Conditions of the State, War, and Navy Building.* 65th Cong., 3d Sess., S. Doc. 344, July 6, 1918.

————. *Report of the Public Buildings Commission.* 66th Cong., 1st Sess., S. Doc. 48, July 8, 1919.

————. *Annual Report of the Public Buildings Commission for the Year Ending December 31, 1925.* 69th Cong., 2d Sess., S. Doc. 179, December 18, 1926.

————. *Annual Report of the Public Buildings Commission for the Calendar Year of 1926.* 69th Cong., 2d Sess., S. Doc. 240, March 2, 1927.

————. *Washington the National Capital.* 71st Cong., 3d Sess., S. Doc. 332, December 1, 1930–March 4, 1931.

REPORTS

U.S., Congress, Senate, Select Committee of the United States Senate . . . to Inquire into . . . the Executive Departments. *Report of the Select Committee . . . to Inquire into . . . the Methods of Business and Work in the Executive Departments.* 50th Cong., 1st Sess., S. Rept. 507, March 8, 1888.

————, Committee on Public Buildings and Grounds. *National Archives Building.*

62d Cong., 3d Sess., S. Rept. 1191, to accompany S. 5179, February 5, 1913.

———, Committee on Public Buildings and Grounds. *To Provide for the Construction of Certain Public Buildings in the District of Columbia.* 68th Cong., 1st Sess., S. Rept. 493, to accompany S. 2284, April 24, 1924.

———, Committee on Public Buildings and Grounds. *Construction of Public Buildings.* 68th Cong., 2d Sess., S. Rept. 1089, to accompany H.R. 11791, February 3, 1925.

———, Committee on Public Buildings and Grounds. *For the Construction of Certain Public Buildings.* 69th Cong., 1st Sess., S. Rept. 197, to accompany H.R. 6559, February 22, 1926.

———, Committee on Appropriations. *Second Deficiency Appropriation Bill, 1926.* 69th Cong., 1st Sess., S. Rept. 1172, to accompany H.R. 13040, June 30, 1926.

———, Committee on the Library. *National Archives.* 73d Cong., 2d Sess., S. Rept. 1194, to accompany H.R. 8910, May 28, 1934.

HEARINGS

U.S., Congress, Senate, Committee on Public Buildings and Grounds. *Hearing on S. 5179, a Bill Directing the Secretary of the Treasury to Prepare Designs and Estimates for and Report the Cost of a National Archive Building in the District of Columbia.* 62d Cong., 2d Sess., March 1, 1912.

———, Public Buildings Commission. *Hearings Before the Public Buildings Commission.* 66th Cong., 1st Sess., Hearings, No. 2, October 13, 1919.

House of Representatives

U.S., Congress, House. *Journal.* 49th Cong., 1st Sess.; 53d Cong., 2d Sess.; 62d Cong., 3d Sess.; and 69th Cong., 1st Sess.

BILLS

U.S., Congress, House. *A Bill Making an Appropriation for the Purchase of Ground and the Erection Thereon in the City of Washington of a . . . Hall of Records.* 47th Cong., 1st Sess., H.R. 2788, January 12, 1882.

———. *A Bill to Extend Winder's Building for the Construction of a Hall of Records and for Other Purposes.* 49th Cong., 1st Sess., H.R. 7726, April 12, 1886.

———. *A Bill Authorizing the Secretary of the Treasury to Purchase Certain Lots and the Building Thereon Known as the Corcoran Gallery of Art, for . . . a Hall of Records.* 53d Cong., 2d Sess., H.R. 5385, January 22, 1894.

———. *A Bill to Authorize the Purchase of a Site for a Hall of Records, and Other Purposes.* 55th Cong., 1st Sess., H.R. 3515, June 21, 1897.

———. *A Bill to Authorize the Acquisition of Certain Real Estate in the City of Washington, D.C., and Providing for a Hall of Records, and for Other Purposes.* 55th Cong., 2d Sess., H.R. 5363, December 17, 1897.

———. *A Bill to Authorize the Secretary of the Treasury to Acquire Square 574 for the*

Erection Thereon of a Building to Be Used as a Bureau of Archives . . . and Other Purposes.
55th Cong., 2d Sess., H.R. 7202, January 25, 1898.

————. *A Bill for the Purchase of a Site for a Hall of Records.* 55th Cong., 2d Sess., H.R.
7211, January 25, 1898.

————. *A Bill for the Purchase of a Site for a Hall of Records.* 56th Cong., 1st Sess., H.R.
7083, January 25, 1900.

————. *A Bill to Authorize the Acquisition of Certain Real Estate for the Construction of a
Hall of Records.* 56th Cong., 1st Sess., H.R. 7655, January 29, 1900.

————. *A Bill for the Purchase of a Site for a Hall of Records.* 56th Cong., 1st Sess., H.R.
8022, February 3, 1900.

————. *A Bill to Authorize the Acquisition of Square No. 229, in the City of Washington
. . . for a Hall of Records.* 56th Cong., 1st Sess., H.R. 10042, March 27, 1900.

————. *A Bill Authorizing the President to Appoint a Commission on National Historical
Publications.* 61st Cong., 2d Sess., H.R. 15428, December 15, 1909.

————. *A Bill Directing the Secretary of the Treasury to Prepare Designs and Estimates for
and Report the Cost of a National Archives Building in the District of Columbia.* 62d
Cong., 1st Sess., H.R. 11850, June 19, 1911.

————. *A Bill to Limit the Cost of Certain Public Buildings . . . to Authorize the Erection
and Completion of Public Buildings, to Authorize the Purchase of Sites for Public Buildings,
and for Other Purposes.* 62d Cong., 3d Sess., H.R. 28766, February 15, 1913.

————. *A Bill to Amend Section 21 of . . . an Act to Increase the Limit of Cost of Certain
Public Buildings . . . to Authorize the Erection and Completion of Public Buildings; to
Authorize the Purchase of Sites for Public Buildings, and for Other Purposes, Approved
March 4, 1913.* 63d Cong., 2d Sess., H.R. 15653, April 14, 1914.

————. *A Bill Making Appropriations for Sundry Civil Expenses of the Government for the
Fiscal Year Ending June 30, 1915, and for Other Purposes.* 63d Cong., 2d Sess., H.R.
17041, August 3, 1914.

————. *A Bill Making Appropriations for the Treasury Department for the Fiscal Year Ending
June 30, 1923.* 67th Cong., 2d Sess., H.R. 9724, January 4, 1922.

————. *A Bill Making Appropriations for the Executive Office and for Sundry Independent
Executive Bureaus, Boards, Commissions, and Offices, for the Fiscal Year Ending June 30,
1924.* 67th Cong., 4th Sess., H.R. 13696, January 7, 1923.

————. *A Bill to Provide for the Construction of Certain Public Buildings in the District of
Columbia.* 68th Cong., 1st Sess., H.R. 9488, May 27, 1924.

————. *A Bill to Provide for the Construction of Certain Public Buildings in the District of
Columbia and the Several States, Territories, and Dependencies of the United States.* 68th
Cong., 2d Sess., H.R. 10406, December 6, 1924.

————. *A Bill to Provide for the Construction of Certain Public Buildings, and for Other
Purposes.* 68th Cong., 2d Sess., H.R. 11791, January 20, 1925.

————. *A Bill to Provide for the Construction of Certain Public Buildings, and for Other
Purposes.* 69th Cong., 1st Sess., H.R. 6559, January 4, 1926.

————. *A Bill Making Appropriations to Supply Deficiencies in Certain Appropriations for
the Fiscal Year Ending June 30, 1926, and Prior Fiscal Years, and . . . to Provide
Supplemental Appropriations for the Fiscal Years Ending June 30, 1926 and June 30,
1927, and for Other Purposes.* 69th Cong., 1st Sess., H.R. 13040, June 24, 1926.

————. *A Bill to Establish a Department of National Archives of the United States of America.*
73d Cong., 2d Sess., H.R. 6216, January 3, 1934.

————. *A Bill to Establish a Bureau of National Archives of the United States Government.*
73d Cong., 2d Sess., H.R. 8340, February 28, 1934.

————. *A Bill to Establish a National Archives of the United States Government, and for Other Purposes.* 73d Cong., 2d Sess., H.R. 8910, April 2, 1934.

DOCUMENTS

U.S., Congress, House. *Burning of the Treasury Building.* 23d Cong., 2d Sess., H. Doc. 22, December 12, 1834.
————. *Treasury Building.* 25th Cong., 2d Sess., H. Doc. 38, December 21, 1837.
————. *Fire-Proof Building for the War and Navy Departments.* 29th Cong., 1st Sess., H. Exec. Doc. 186, April 15, 1846.
————, Committee on Ways and Means. *Letter from the Secretary of the Treasury Transmitting His Annual Report on the State of the Finances.* 30th Cong., 2d Sess., H. Exec. Doc. 7, December 11, 1848.
————. Committee on Public Buildings and Grounds. *Security of Public Buildings against Fire.* 45th Cong., 2d Sess., H. Exec. Doc. 10, December 10, 1877.
————, Committee on Expenditures in the War Department. *Useless Paper in the Departments.* 51st Cong., 1st Sess., H. Exec. Doc. 197, February 14, 1890.
————, Committee on Public Buildings and Grounds. *Letter from the Secretary of the Treasury in Regard to a Proposed Hall of Records.* 55th Cong., 2d Sess., H. Doc. 226, January 15, 1898.
————, Committee on Ways and Means. *Rents Received from Property in Washington, D.C., Purchased as a Site for Hall of Records.* 59th Cong., 2d Sess., H. Doc. 698, February 8, 1907.
————, Committee on Expenditures in the Treasury Department. *Rents Received from Property Purchased for a Hall of Records.* 60th Cong., 2d Sess., H. Doc. 1332, January 16, 1909.
————, Committee on Appropriations. *Letter from the Secretary of the Treasury Submitting Estimates . . . for the Patent Office and National Archives Buildings, Washington, D.C.,* 63d Cong., 2d Sess., H. Doc. 903, April 17, 1914.
————. *Archives Building, Washington, D.C.* 64th Cong., 2d Sess., H. Doc. 1918, January 11, 1917.
————. *National Archives Building, Washington, D.C.* 65th Cong., 3d Sess., H. Doc. 1772, February 7, 1919.
————. *Construction of a National Archives Building.* 66th Cong., 1st Sess., H. Doc. 200, August 25, 1919.
————. *Message of the President of the United States Transmitting the Budget for the . . . Fiscal Year Ending June 30, 1925.* 68th Cong., 1st Sess., H. Doc. 76, December 3, 1923.
————. *Message of the President of the United States Transmitting the Budget for the . . . Fiscal Year Ending June 30, 1926.* 68th Cong., 2d Sess., H. Doc. 444, December 1, 1924.
————. *Message of the President of the United States Transmitting the Budget for the . . . Fiscal Year Ending June 30, 1927.* 69th Cong., 1st Sess., H. Doc. 65, December 7, 1925.

REPORTS

U.S., Congress, House. *Report of the Committee Appointed to Inquire into the State of the Ancient Public Records and Archives of the United States.* 11th Cong., 2d Sess., H. Rept. 125, April 2, 1810.

———, Committee on the Post Office and Post Roads. *Report on Conflagration— Post Office Building.* 24th Cong., 2d Sess., H. Rept. 134, January 20, 1837.

———. *Erection of a Hall of Records in the City of Washington.* 47th Cong., 1st Sess., H. Rept. 778, to accompany S. 817, March 16, 1882.

———, Committee on the Library. *Report on Commission on National Historical Publications.* 61st Cong., 2d Sess., H. Rept. 1000, April 13, 1910.

———, Committee on Public Buildings and Grounds. *To Amend Section 21 of the Public Buildings Act.* 63d Cong., 2d Sess., H. Rept. 539, to accompany H.R. 15653, April 16, 1914.

———, Committee on Public Buildings and Grounds. *National Archives Building.* 64th Cong., 1st Sess., H. Rept. 753, to accompany S. 5839, May 24, 1916.

———, Committee on Public Buildings and Grounds. *Public Buildings Bill.* 68th Cong., 2d Sess., H. Rept. 1285, to accompany H.R. 11791, January 27, 1925.

———, Committee on Public Buildings and Grounds. *Public Buildings Bill.* 69th Cong., 1st Sess., H. Rept. 132, to accompany H.R. 6559, January 21, 1926.

———, Committee on Appropriations. *Report on Second Deficiency Appropriation Bill, Fiscal Year 1926.* 69th Cong., 1st Sess., H. Rept. 1536, to accompany H.R. 13040, June 24, 1926.

———, Committee on the Library. *Report on National Archives of the United States Government.* 73d Cong., 2d Sess., H. Rept. 1156, to accompany H.R. 8910, April 9, 1934.

HEARINGS

U.S., Congress, House, Committee on Public Buildings and Grounds. *Preservation of Government Archives.* 62d Cong., 1st Sess., Hearings, No. 2, May 12, 1911.

———, Subcommittee of the Committee on Public Buildings and Grounds. *Fire Precautions in Public Buildings and Safety of Government Records.* 62d Cong., 1st Sess., Hearings, No. 9, May 23, 1911.

———, Committee on Public Buildings and Grounds. *Fire Precautions in Public Buildings and the Preservation of Government Records.* 62d Cong., 1st Sess., Hearings, No. 11, May 30, 1911.

———, Committee on Public Buildings and Grounds. *Preservation of Government Archives. Memorial from the Departments of Archives and History of the States of Mississippi and Alabama.* 62d Cong., 1st Sess., Hearings, No. 18, July 10, 1911.

———, Committee on Public Buildings and Grounds. *Preservation of Government Archives. Appendix.* 62d Cong., 2d Sess., Hearings, No. 2, February 14, 1912.

———, Committee on Public Buildings and Grounds. *National Archives Bill.* 62d Cong., 2d Sess., Hearings on S. 5179, March 1, 1912.

———, Committee on Public Buildings and Grounds. *National Archives Building.* 64th Cong., 1st Sess., Hearings, No. 19, May 17, 1916.

———, Committee on Appropriations, Subcommittee on Legislative, Executive, and Judicial Appropriations for Fiscal Year 1922. *Statement of Bainbridge Colby.* 66th Cong., 3d Sess., Hearings, November 23, 1920.

———, Committee on Public Buildings and Grounds. *George Washington Memorial Hall.* 67th Cong., 1st Sess., Hearings on H.J. Res. 142, December 16, 1921.

———, Committee on Public Buildings and Grounds. *Public Buildings Bill.* 68th Cong., 2d Sess., Hearings on H.R. 11791, January 22–23, 1925.

Newspapers

Daily American Telegraph (Washington, D.C.). December 24, 1851.

Daily National Intelligencer (Washington, D.C.). April 1, 1833; December 16, 1836; December 25, 1851.

Evening Star (Washington, D.C.). March 29, 1916; January 14, 1921; February 7 and 10, 1921; February 3 and 9, 1922; January 25, 1923; February 11, 1923; August 17 and 18, 1923; July 7, 1925; September 24, 1926; March 24, 1930; February 19 and 20, 1933.

Georgetown (D.C.) *Advocate.* December 27, 1851.

Globe (Washington, D.C.). April 1, 1833; December 17, 1836.

Independent (Washington, D.C.). July 20, 1893.

New York Times. May 4, 1919; January 12, 1921; February 9 and 13, 1922; January 21, 1923; March 19, 1923; June 6, 1926.

Sunday Star (Washington, D.C.). January 22, 1922; February 3, 1935.

United States Telegraph (Washington, D.C.). April 1, 1833.

Universal Gazette (Washington, D.C.). November 13, 1800; January 22, 1801.

Washington Herald. January 5, 6, 8–13, 17, 20, 22, 23, 29, and 30, 1923; February 1, 1923.

Washington Post. August 1, 1910; November 10, 1920; January 11 and 18, 1921; February 5, 1921; February 3 and 9, 1922; January 3, 1932; April 8, 1934.

Washington Times. September 15, 1920.

Secondary Materials

Books

American Institute of Architects, Washington Metropolitan Chapter. *A Guide to the Architecture of Washington, D.C.* Washington, D.C.: American Institute of Architects, Washington Metropolitan Chapter, 1965.

Burnett, Edmund Cody. *The Continental Congress.* New York: W. W. Norton and Co., 1964.

Butterfield, Lyman H., and Boyd, Julian P. *Historical Editing in the United States.* Worcester, Mass.: American Antiquarian Society, 1963.

Chamberlain, Mellen. *John Adams, the Statesman of the Revolution.* Boston: Houghton Mifflin, 1898.

Deutrich, Mabel E. *The Struggle for Supremacy: The Career of General Fred C. Ainsworth.* Washington, D.C.: Public Affairs Press, 1962.

Fisher, Ruth Anna, and Fox, William Lloyd, eds. *J. Franklin Jameson: A Tribute.* Washington, D.C.: Catholic University of America Press, 1965.

Gallagher, H. M. Pierce. *Robert Mills.* New York: Columbia University Press, 1935.

Harley, Lewis R. *Life of Charles Thomson.* Philadelphia: George W. Jacobs and Co., 1900.

Hesseltine, William B., and McNeil, Donald R., eds. *In Support of Clio: Essays in Memory of Herbert A. Kellar.* Madison: State Historical Society of Wisconsin, 1955.

Hicks, John D. *The American Nation.* 3d ed. Cambridge: Houghton Mifflin, 1955.

Higham, John; Krieger, Leonard; and Gilbert, Felix. *History.* Princeton Studies in Humanistic Scholarship in America. Englewood Cliffs, N.J.: Prentice-Hall, 1965.

Hollaender, A. E. J., ed. *Essays in Memory of Sir Hilary Jenkinson.* Chichester, Sussex: Moore and Tillyer, 1962.

James, Marquis. *A History of the American Legion.* New York: W. Green, 1923.

Jones, H. G. *For History's Sake.* Chapel Hill: University of North Carolina Press, 1966.

————. *The Records of a Nation.* New York: Atheneum, 1969.

Lord, Clifford, ed. *Keepers of the Past.* Chapel Hill: University of North Carolina Press, 1965.

McCoy, Donald R. *The National Archives: America's Ministry of Documents, 1934–1968.* Chapel Hill: University of North Carolina Press, 1978.

Posner, Ernst. *American State Archives.* Chicago: University of Chicago Press, 1964.

————. *Archives and the Public Interest: Selected Essays by Ernst Posner.* Edited by Ken Munden. Washington, D.C.: Public Affairs Press, 1967.

Van Tassel, David D. *Recording America's Past: An Interpretation of the Development of Historical Studies in America, 1607–1884.* Chicago: University of Chicago Press, 1960.

U.S., Congress, House. *Biographical Directory of the American Congress, 1774–1949.* Compiled by James L. Harrison. Washington, D.C.: U.S. Government Printing Office, 1950.

————, Department of the Interior, National Park Service. *Historic American Buildings Survey Catalog.* Washington, D.C.: U.S. Government Printing Office, 1941.

————, General Services Administration. *Executive Office Bulding.* General Services Administration Historical Study No. 3, compiled by Donald J. Lehman. Washington, D.C.: U.S. Government Printing Office, 1970.

————, General Services Administration. *The Pension Building.* General Services Administration Historical Study No. 1, compiled by Donald J. Lehman. Washington, D.C.: U.S. Government Printing Office, 1964.

————, National Archives and Records Service. *The Appraisal of Modern Public Records.* National Archives Bulletin No. 8, compiled by Theodore R. Schellenberg. Washington, D.C.: U.S. Government Printing Office, 1956.

————, Library of Congress. *A Guide to the Study of the United States of America.* Compiled by Donald H. Mugridge and Blanche P. McCrumb. Washington, D.C.: U.S. Government Printing Office, 1960.

————, Works Progress Administration, Federal Writers' Project. *Washington, City and Capital.* American Guide Series. Washington, D.C.: U.S. Government Printing Office, 1937.

White, Leonard D. *The Federalists: A Study in Administrative History.* New York: Macmillan Publishing Co., 1948.

Young, Jeremiah S.; Manning, John W.; and Arnold, Joseph I. *Government of the American People.* Boston: D. C. Heath, 1947.

Articles

Beers, Henry P. "Historical Development of the Records Disposal Policy of the Federal Government Prior to 1934." *American Archivist* 7:181–201.
Cappon, Lester J. "Waldo Gifford Leland, 1879–1966." *American Archivist* 30: 125–28.
Chiles, Rosa P. "The National Archives: Are They in Peril?" *Review of Reviews* 45:209–13.
Editorial. *National Genealogical Quarterly* 6:59.
———. *National Genealogical Quarterly* 12:16.
Glenn, Bess. "The Taft Commission and the Government's Record Practices." *American Archivist* 21:277–303.
J. Franklin Jameson. "The Need of a National Archive Building." *Bulletin of the American Library Association* 8:130–40.
Leland, Waldo G. "The Archives of the Federal Government." *Records of the Columbia Historical Society, Washington, D.C.* 11:71–100.
———. "The National Archives Again." *Nation* 95:426–27.
———. "The National Archives: A Programme." *American Historical Review* 18: 5–25.
Lokke, Carl L. "The Continental Congress Papers: Their History, 1789–1952." *National Archives Accessions* 51 (June 1954):1–19.
Martin, Thomas P. "The National Archives Building." *Historical Outlook* 24: 177–79.
"Meeting of the American Historical Association at Charleston and Columbia, The." *American Historical Review* 19:486.
Moore, Charles. "The Transformation of Washington." *National Geographic* 43: 569–95.
"National Archives, The." *Outlook* 112:174–75.
"National Archives in Danger." *Scientific American* 104:562.
"Our National Archives." *Nation* 92:109.
"Our War Documents." *Military Historian and Economist* 3:1–6.
Paltsits, Victor H. "Pioneering for a Science of Archives in the United States." *Proceedings of the Society of American Archivists, 1936 and 1937,* pp. 41–46. Processed. Urbana, Ill.: 1937.
Paullin, Charles O. "History of the Movement for a National Archives Building in Washington." *Congressional Record,* 64th Cong., 1st Sess., 1916, 53, pt. 14:1116–19.
Pinkett, Harold T. "Investigations of Federal Recordkeeping, 1887–1906." *American Archivist* 21:163–92.
———. "New York as the Temporary National Capital, 1785–1790: The Archival Heritage." *National Archives Accessions* 60 (December 1967):1–11.
"Proceedings, Swampscott Conference, June 20–25, 1921." *Bulletin of the American Library Association* 15:165.
Riepma, Siert F. "Portrait of an Adjutant General." *Journal of the American Military History Foundation* 2:26–35.

Rowe, Lily Lykes. "Archives Hall Planned by Congress." *Daughters of the American Revolution Magazine* 55:138–40.
Shelley, Fred. "The Interest of J. Franklin Jameson in the National Archives: 1908–1934." *American Archivist* 12:99–130.
U.S., Federal Works Agency, Public Buildings Administration. "The National Archives Building." *Bulletin, Office of Buildings Manager,* June 1940, p. 2.
Withington, Lothrop. "Housing of Federal Archives." *Nation* 92:165–66.
Wood, Richard G. "Richard Bartlett, Minor Archival Prophet." *American Archivist* 17:13–18.
Wriston, Henry Gerritt. "An Archive Building at Washington." *Review of Reviews* 70:191–92.

Unpublished Secondary Material

Pomrenze, Seymour J. "The Records Problem: Significant Congressional and Presidential Solutions, 1789–Present." Unpublished typescript, n.d.

Notes

1. U.S., National Archives, *Third Annual Report of the Archivist of the United States for the Fiscal Year Ending June 30, 1937* (Washington, D.C.: U.S. Government Printing Office, 1938), pp. 3–4. See also a loose-leaf volume entitled "Journal/ A Chronological Order of Events/ Affecting the National Archives/ from the passage of the Act of/ May 25, 1926 to June 30, 1936," in Record Group 64, Records of the National Archives and Records Service, National Archives, Washington, D.C. The entry for July 1, 1935, p. 15, states, "Work was started in the Division of Research in compiling data on fires and other incidents establishing the necessity of a National Archives and the various steps that were taken to bring about The National Archives."
2. Leo F. Stock to Solon J. Buck, August 18, 1943; and Buck to Stock, August 19, 1943, J. Franklin Jameson Papers, Library of Congress, Washington, D.C.
3. See Ernst Posner, "What, Then, Is the American Archivist, This New Man," *Archives and the Public Interest: Selected Essays by Ernst Posner*, ed. Ken Munden (Washington, D.C.: Public Affairs Press, 1967), p. 167.
4. Memorandum of interview of Victor Gondos, Jr., with Waldo G. Leland, March 12, 1964.

CHAPTER 1

1. Typescript of address entitled "Remarks of President at the laying of the Corner-stone of the National Archives Building, Washington, D.C., Monday, February 20, 1933, at 2:30 o'clock," in Percy Scott Flippin,

193

comp., "The Archives of the United States Government: A Documentary History, 1774–1934" (unpublished typescript and scrapbook in 24 vols., loose-leaf, plus index vols., in the National Archives Library, Washington, D.C.) 22:63 (hereafter cited as Flippin Collection).

2. The address of Secretary of the Treasury Ogden Mills is attached to Memo. 111, W. R. Willoughby to Thomas M. Owen, Jr., June 7, 1937; annexed also to Memo. 111 are other relevant correspondence and memorandums: program for laying of the cornerstone; lists of invitees to the ceremony; and correspondence of Ferry K. Heath as follows: Heath to Ben H. Fuller, February 7 and 9, 1933; Heath to James E. Freeman, February 9, 1933, and Freeman to Heath, February 11, 1933; Heath to Michael J. Curley, February 9, 1933, and Curley to Heath, February 10, 1933. All the cited documents are in the Functional Classification File, 71–72, Box 13, of a series informally referred to as the "Buck Papers," Record Group 64, Records of the National Archives and Records Service. Hereafter, all record groups in the National Archives will be cited as RG ____, National Archives. See also the *Evening Star* (Washington, D.C.), and other Washington newspapers for February 19 and 20, 1933.

3. Radio address of R. D. W. Connor, "Our Federal Archives," on network of the National Broadcasting Co., November 25, 1935, in a series informally referred to as the "Connor Papers," RG 64, National Archives.

4. Lewis R. Harley, *Life of Charles Thomson* (Philadelphia: George W. Jacobs and Co., 1900), pp. 86–88.

5. Carl L. Lokke, "The Continental Congress Papers: Their History, 1789–1952," *National Archives Accessions* 51 (June 1954):1–19. For further data on records of the Confederation period see the following: U.S., Library of Congress, *Journals of the Continental Congress, 1774–1789* (Washington, D.C.: U.S. Government Printing Office, 1922), 24:517; Edmund Cody Burnett, *The Continental Congress* (New York: W. W. Norton and Co., 1964); Leonard D. White, *The Federalists: A Study in Administrative History* (New York: Macmillan Publishing Co., 1948); Harold T. Pinkett, "New York as the Temporary National Capital, 1785–1790: The Archival Heritage," *National Archives Accessions* 60 (December 1962):1–11; and Seymour J. Pomrenze, "The Records Problem: Significant Congressional and Presidential Solutions, 1789–Present" (unpublished typescript, n.d.).

6. Wayne C. Grover, "Introduction," in H. G. Jones, *The Records of a Nation* (New York: Atheneum, 1969), p. viii.

7. U.S., General Services Administration, *Executive Office Building,* General Services Administration Historical Study No. 3, comp. Donald J. Lehman (Washington, D.C.: U.S. Government Printing Office, 1970), pp. 4–5.

8. *Universal Gazette* (Washington, D.C.), November 13, 1800, reporting the War Department fire, and January 22, 1801, reporting the Treasury fire; both in Flippin Collection, 1:69–70, 72.

9. U.S., Congress, House, *Report of the Committee Appointed to Inquire into the State of the Ancient Public Records and Archives of the United States,* 11th Cong., 2d Sess., H. Rept. 125, April 2, 1810. See also U.S., Congress, *Annals of Congress,* 11th Cong., 2d Sess., 21:1427, 1633, 1704, 1771–72, 1791–92; and U.S., *Statutes at Large,* vol. 2, pp. 589–90.

10. U.S., Congress, *Annals of Congress,* 13th Cong., 3d Sess., 28:305–8, 872–76; and reports to the 13th Cong., printed in *American State Papers: Documents, Legislative and Executive, of the Congress of the United States, Miscellaneous* (Washington, D.C.: Gales and Seaton, 1834) 2:246–52.

11. G. Philip Bauer, "Public Archives in the United States," In *Support of Clio: Essays in Memory of Herbert A. Kellar,* ed. William B. Hesseltine and Donald R. McNeil (Madison: State Historical Society of Wisconsin, 1958), pp. 62–63.

12. See Bauer, "Public Archives," pp. 63–64. See also Clifford Lord, ed., *Keepers of the Past* (Chapel Hill: University of North Carolina Press, 1965), pp. 7–8.

13. Richard G. Wood, "Richard Bartlett, Minor Archival Prophet," *American Archivist* 17:14–15. For a brief survey of American documentary publications, see Lyman H. Butterfield and Julian P. Boyd, *Historical Editing in the United States* (Worcester, Mass.: American Antiquarian Society, 1963), pp. 3–28. See also David D. Van Tassel, *Recording America's Past: An Interpretation of the Development of Historical Studies in America, 1607–1884* (Chicago: University of Chicago Press, 1960).

14. Descriptions of the Treasury Building conflagrations are reported in several Washington newspapers of the period: the *Daily National Intelligencer,* the *United States Telegraph,* and the *Globe,* all April 1, 1833.

15. U.S., Congress, House, *Burning of the Treasury Building,* 23d Cong., 2d Sess., H. Doc. 22, December 12, 1834.

16. H. M. Pierce Gallagher, *Robert Mills* (New York: Columbia University Press, 1935), p. 60. Mills, who had come to Washington, D.C., from Charleston, S.C., in 1830, was then employed in the General Land Office of the Treasury Department drafting plans for federal buildings in New England and the South.

17. U.S., Congress, Senate, Committee on the Post Office and Post Roads, *Report of the Postmaster General, December 5, 1836,* 24th Cong., 2d Sess., S. Exec. Doc. 2, December 5, 1836.

18. "Message of Andrew Jackson to the Congress, Dec. 5, 1836," in *A Compilation of the Messages and Papers of the Presidents,* comp. James D. Richardson (New York: Bureau of National Literature, 1897) 4:1477 (hereafter cited as *Messages and Papers).*

19. *Daily National Intelligencer,* December 16, 1836; and the *Globe,* December 17, 1836.

20. "Message of Andrew Jackson to the Senate and House of Representatives," December 20, 1836, *Messages and Papers* 4:1483–84.

21. U.S., Congress, Senate, Committee on Public Buildings and Grounds, *Report to Accompany S. 304,* 25th Cong., 2d Sess., S. Doc. 435, April 17, 1838; and U.S., Congress, House, *Fire-Proof Building for the War and Navy Departments,* 29th Cong., 1st Sess., H. Exec. Doc. 186, April 15, 1846.

22. U.S., Congress, House, *Letter from the Secretary of the Treasury Transmitting His Annual Report on the State of the Finances,* 30th Cong., 2d Sess., H. Exec. Doc. 7, December 11, 1848.

23. Connor, "Our Federal Archives," radio broadcast, November 25, 1935, "Connor Papers," RG 64, National Archives.

24. U.S., Congress, Senate, Select Committee of the United States Senate . . . to Inquire into . . . the Executive Departments, *Report of the Select*

Committee . . . to Inquire into . . . the Methods of Business and Work in the Executive Departments, 50th Cong., 1st Sess., S. Rept. 507, pt. 3, March 8, 1888, pp. 117–21, 239–54.

25. U.S., War Department, *Annual Report of the Secretary of War on the Operations of the Department for the Fiscal Year Ending June 30, 1875* (Washington, D.C.: U.S. Government Printing Office, 1875) 1:200.

26. U.S., Congress, House, Committee on Public Buildings and Grounds, *Security of Public Buildings Against Fire,* 45th Cong., 2d Sess., H. Exec. Doc. 10, December 10, 1877, p. 9.

27. U.S., War Department, *Annual Report of the Secretary of War for the Year 1878* (Washington, D.C.: U.S. Government Printing Office, 1878), pp. 257–58; and Montgomery C. Meigs to Justin S. Morrill, January 13, 1879, in U.S., Congress, House, *Erection of a Hall of Records in the City of Washington,* 47th Cong., 1st Sess., H. Rept. 778, to accompany S. 817, March 16, 1882, pp. 1–2.

28. "Second Annual Message of Rutherford B. Hayes, Dec. 2, 1878," *Messages and Papers* 7:500; and "Third Annual Message of Rutherford B. Hayes, Dec. 1, 1879," *Messages and Papers* 7:572.

29. U.S., Congress, Senate, *A Bill Making Appropriation for the Purchase of Ground and Erection Thereon . . . of a . . . Hall of Records,* 46th Cong., 3d Sess., S. 1889, December 13, 1880.

30. Senator Vest introduced the following bills, each similarly entitled, *A Bill Making Appropriation for the Purchase of Ground and Erection Thereon . . . of a . . . Hall of Records,* each referred to the Committee on Public Buildings and Grounds: 47th Cong., 1st Sess., S. 817, January 12, 1882; 48th Cong., 1st Sess., S. 206, December 4, 1883; 49th Cong., 2d Sess., S. 103, December 8, 1885; 50th Cong., 1st Sess., S. 279, December 12, 1887; 50th Cong., 1st Sess., S. 2305, March 8, 1888; 51st Cong., 1st Sess., S. 490, December 4, 1889; and 52nd Cong., 1st Sess., S. 430, December 10, 1891.

31. U.S., Congress, Senate, Committee on Public Buildings and Grounds, *History of the Movement for a National Archives Building in Washington, D.C.,* 62d Cong., 2d Sess., S. Doc. 297, February 8, 1912, p. 4. This brief history of fifteen pages relates to the hall of records movement of the late nineteenth century rather than to that of the national archives.

32. U.S., Congress, House, *A Bill to Extend Winder's Building for the Construction of a Hall of Records, and for Other Purposes,* 49th Cong., 1st Sess., H.R. 7726, April 12, 1886.

33. Bauer, "Public Archives," p. 63; and Lord, *Keepers of the Past,* pp. 7–8.

34. Mabel E. Deutrich, *The Struggle for Supremacy: The Career of General Fred C. Ainsworth* (Washington, D.C.: Public Affairs Press, 1962), pp. 36–48, 52–75; and Siert F. Reipma, "Portrait of an Adjutant General," *Journal of the American Military History Foundation* 2:26–35.

35. Harold T. Pinkett, "Investigations of Federal Record Keeping, 1881–1906," *American Archivist* 21:163–92; and Henry P. Beers, "Historical Development of the Records Disposal Policy of the Federal Government Prior to 1934," *American Archivist* 7:181–201.

36. U.S., Congress, House, Committee on Public Buildings and Grounds, *A Bill Authorizing the Secretary of the Treasury to Purchase Certain Lots and the Building*

Thereon Known as the Corcoran Gallery of Art, for . . . a Hall of Records, 53d Cong., 2d Sess., H.R. 5385, January 22, 1894.

37. U.S., Congress, Senate, *Site for the Proposed Hall of Records,* 54th Cong., 2d Sess., S. Doc. 133, February 17, 1897.

38. U.S., Congress, Senate, *Urging the Necessity for the Construction of a Hall of Records in the City of Washington, D.C.,* 57th Cong., 1st Sess., S. Doc. 236, March 5, 1902, p. 6.

39. *Statutes at Large,* vol. 32, pt. 1, pp. 1212, 1039.

40. U.S., Department of the Treasury, *Annual Report of the Secretary of the Treasury on the State of the Finances for the Fiscal Year Ended June 30, 1904* (Washington, D.C.: U.S. Government Printing Office, 1905), p. 27; *Annual Report of the Secretary of the Treasury on the State of the Finances for the Fiscal Year Ended June 30, 1905* (Washington, D.C.: U.S. Government Printing Office, 1906), p. 22; and *Annual Report of the Secretary of the Treasury on the State of the Finances for the Fiscal Year Ended June 30, 1906* (Washington, D.C.: U.S. Government Printing Office, 1906), p. 50.

41. Ernst Posner, "Archival Administration in the United States," in *Archives and the Public Interest, Selected Essays by Ernst Posner,* ed. Ken Munden (Washington, D.C.: Public Affairs Press, 1967), p. 116.

42. American Historical Association, *Annual Report of the American Historical Association for the Year 1893* (Washington, D.C.: U.S. Government Printing Office, 1894), pp. iv, 3 (hereafter cited as AHA, *Annual Report*); Jones, *Records of a Nation,* p. 6.

43. AHA, *Annual Report,* 1893, p. 4. Mrs. Walworth's paper was published in the same report with the shorter title, "The Value of a National Archives," pp. 27–32.

44. "Report of the Proceedings of the Eleventh Annual Meeting . . . Washington, D.C., December 26, 27, 1895," in AHA, *Annual Report,* 1896, p. 10; and David D. Van Tassel, "John Franklin Jameson," in *Keepers of the Past,* pp. 86–87.

45. Posner, *Archives and the Public Interest,* p. 116; AHA, *Annual Report,* 1899, 1:27–28. See also Victor H. Paltsits, "An Historical Resume of the Public Archives Commission from 1899 to 1921," AHA, *Annual Report,* 1922, 1:152–60.

46. AHA, *Annual Report,* 1901, 1:36. The same report also included a paper by Herbert Putnam, "The Relation of the National Library to Historical Research in the United States," 1:113–30.

CHAPTER 2

1. David D. Van Tassel, "John Franklin Jameson," *Keepers of the Past,* ed. Clifford L. Lord (Chapel Hill: University of North Carolina Press, 1965), p. 88.

2. J. Franklin Jameson to Francis A. Christie, March 6, 1903, *An Historian's World: Selections from the Correspondence of John Franklin Jameson,* ed. Elizabeth Donnan and Leo F. Stock (Philadelphia: American Philosophical Society, 1956), p. 85 (hereafter cited as *Jameson Correspondence*).

3. Claude H. Van Tyne and Waldo G. Leland, *Guide to the Archives of the Government of the United States in Washington,* Carnegie Institution

Publication no. 14 (Washington, D.C.: Carnegie Institution, 1904).
4. Robert S. Woodward to Jameson, April 11, 1905, in which Woodward tells Jameson that the Executive Committee offers him the post of director of the Bureau of Historical Research at a salary of $6,000, J. Franklin Jameson Papers, Library of Congress, Washington, D.C. (hereafter cited as JFJ). After his arrival on the job, Jameson changed the title of his office to Department of Historical Research. He so designates the office in his first budget in 1906, which lists seven other employees of both a professional and clerical type, including Waldo G. Leland at a salary of $1,300. See Jameson to Woodward, October 9, 1906, JFJ.
5. Carnegie Institution, *Year Book for 1902* (Washington, D.C.: Carnegie Institution, 1903), p. 227; and Elizabeth Donnan, "Introduction," *Jameson Correspondence*, pp. 7–8.
6. Donnan, "Introduction," *Jameson Correspondence*, p. 8.
7. Ibid., pp. 1, 12.
8. Ibid.
9. Waldo G. Leland, "J. Franklin Jameson and the Origin of the National Historical Publications Commission," *J. Franklin Jameson: A Tribute*, ed. Ruth Anna Fisher and William Lloyd Fox (Washington, D.C.: The Catholic University of American Press, 1965), p. 29.
10. U.S., Library of Congress, *A Guide to the Study of the United States of America*, comp. Donald H. Mugridge and Blanche P. McCrumb (Washington, D.C.: U.S. Government Printing Office, 1960), p. 307.
11. Jameson to Woodward, February 1, 1906; and Jameson to Leland, May 13, 1906; *Jameson Correspondence*, pp. 94–96.
12. See Fred Shelley, "John Franklin Jameson and the National Archives," *Jameson: A Tribute*, p. 85; H. G. Jones, *The Records of a Nation* (New York: Atheneum, 1969), p. 6; and Van Tassel, "John Franklin Jameson," *Keepers of the Past*, p. 90.
13. John Higham, Leonard Krieger, and Felix Gilbert, *History*, Princeton Studies in Humanistic Scholarship in America (Englewood Cliffs, N.J.: Prentice-Hall, 1965), p. 14. In those days all noncurrent records in storage were called archives, without any distinction between materials of ephemeral or transitory value and those of permanent value. The concept of archives, as later refined, relates solely to permanently valuable records, usually a fraction of the total holdings of an agency or institution. With the development of a program of evaluation, segregation, and eventual disposal of records of temporary value, the true archival program becomes more realistic in both quantitative and qualitative terms.
14. The activities of the commission were summarized by Victor H. Paltsits in "An Historical Resume of the Public Archives Commission from 1899 to 1921," *Annual Report of the American Historical Association for the Year 1922* (Washington, D.C.: U.S. Government Printing Office, 1926) 1:152–60 (hereafter cited as AHA, *Annual Report*). The periodic reports of the commission were also published in the various annual reports of the association. Higham notes that the commission methodically surveyed "the records of one state after another and published its findings each year. Within ten years the commission's reports had stimulated twenty-four states to make formal provisions for the preservation and custody of their unpublished records," Higham et al., *History*, p. 17.

15. George C. Hazelton to Miles Poindexter, March 1, 1912, Miles Poindexter Papers, Series III, File 16, Manuscripts Department, University of Virginia Library, Charlottesville.

16. Elihu Root to Jameson, May 26, 1911, JFJ. Six years after the purchase of square 143, in 1909, Secretary of the Treasury George B. Cortelyou reported to the Speaker of the House that "the rents received from the property for a Hall of Records" netted some $11,000. See U.S., Congress, House, Committee on Expenditures in the Treasury Department, *Rents Received from Property Purchased for a Hall of Records,* 60th Cong., 2d Sess., H. Doc. 1332, January 16, 1909.

17. U.S., Congress, Senate, Committee on Public Buildings and Grounds, *Hall of Records for Treasury Department and Additional Quarters for the Post Office Department,* 50th Cong., 1st Sess., S. Doc. 508, June 26, 1906.

18. U.S., Congress, House, *Congressional Record,* 59th Cong., 1st Sess., 1906, 40, pt. 10:9751.

19. For example, see Charles H. Keep, acting secretary of the Treasury, to the secretary of commerce and labor, August 6, 1906; and Lawrence O. Murray, assistant secretary of commerce and labor to the secretary of the Treasury, November 13, 1906, JFJ.

20. Lothrop Withington, "Housing of Federal Archives," letter to the editor of the *Nation* 92:165–66, February 16, 1911. This was inspired by an editorial in the *Nation,* February 2, 1911, entitled, "Our National Archives."

21. Ibid. Withington was born of an old New England family in Newbury, Massachusetts, January 31, 1856. When eighteen years old, he went abroad and lived in London and Paris as a free-lance correspondent for newspapers and magazines and learned the printing trade. Returning to America he worked as a printer at the Government Printing Office in Washington (1873–1874, and again in 1885–1886), and at the University Press in Cambridge, Massachusetts. From his boyhood he was interested in genealogy and worked as a professional genealogist with his headquarters in London. He made frequent trips to New England and contributed to various genealogical publications in the United States. He was returning to London from one of his genealogical trips to the United States when he took passage on the ill-fated *Lusitania* and perished when it sank on May 7, 1915. See "Proceedings at the Annual Meeting, 2 February 1916," *New England Historical and Genealogical Register,* supplement to April 1916, p. xliii.

22. U.S., Congress, Senate, *A Bill to Establish a Record Office,* 59th Cong., 2d Sess., S. 6728, December 5, 1906.

23. Ibid.

24. Withington, "Housing of Federal Archives," *Nation,* 92:165–66.

25. Ibid.

26. Ibid.

27. Leland, "The Archives of the Federal Government," *Records of the Columbia Historical Society, Washington, D.C.* 11:71–100.

28. Ibid.

29. Jameson to Theodore Roosevelt, December 12, 1907, JFJ.

30. Ibid.

31. James Wilson to the president, December 16, 1907, JFJ.
32. Martin A. Knapp to William Loeb, Jr., secretary to the president, December 23, 1907, JFJ.
33. Charles Walcott to Loeb, December 27, 1907, JFJ.
34. Charles J. Bonaparte to the president, December 16, 1907, JFJ.
35. George von L. Meyer to Loeb, December 19, 1907, JFJ.
36. Robert Shaw Oliver to the president, January 10, 1908, JFJ. Oliver identified the specific needs of the several bureaus. Those with the largest requirements were the Office of the Chief of Ordnance, 126,000 cubic feet; and the Adjutant General's office, 75,000 cubic feet.
37. Victor H. Metcalf to Loeb, February 20, 1908, JFJ. Metcalf also took occasion to refer to the Office of Naval War Records and Library, which had about one thousand volumes of papers concerning officers of the Union and Confederate navies, which had been lent to the department, as well as other records on naval operations which were on loan. None of these, he said, could be released to a hall of records.
38. Beekman Winthrop to Loeb, December 24, 1907, JFJ.
39. Herbert Putnam to the president, December 20, 1907, JFJ.
40. Ibid.
41. Ibid.
42. For a similar opinion see Shelley, "Jameson and the National Archives," *Jameson: A Tribute,* p. 86.
43. AHA, *Annual Report,* 1908, 1:30.
44. Jameson to Alfred T. Mahan, December 8, 1908; and Jameson to John Bach McMaster, December 9, 1908, JFJ.
45. Mahan to Jameson, December 10, 1908, JFJ.
46. McMaster to Jameson, December 15, 1908, JFJ.
47. The Round Table was an informal luncheon group of men distinguished in affairs and in scholarship, which centered on Herbert Putnam, the librarian of Congress. It provided a forum for the exchange of ideas and opinions of men who carried weight in their respective fields. As in this instance with McMaster, Jameson used the Round Table as an element in his educational campaign to establish a national archives. See also Shelley, "The Interest of J. Franklin Jameson in the National Archives: 1908–1934," *American Archivist* 12:99–130.
48. Jameson to McMaster, December 17, 1908, JFJ.
49. Jameson to H. B. Gardner, January 22, 1919, cited in Shelley, "Jameson," *American Archivist* 12:105.
50. Jameson to George B. Cortelyou, December 17, 1908; and Cortelyou to Jameson, January 8, 1909, JFJ.
51. Jameson to E. C. Heald, October 17, 1909, JFJ.
52. Jameson to Heald, October 27, 1909, JFJ.
53. Heald to Jameson, November 5, 1909, JFJ.
54. AHA, *Annual Report,* 1909, p. 354.
55. Ibid., pp. 342–48.
56. Van Tassel, "John Franklin Jameson," *Keepers of the Past,* p. 87.

CHAPTER 3

1. *Washington Post,* August 1, 1910.

2. Ernst Posner, *American State Archives* (Chicago: University of Chicago Press, 1964), p. 194.

3. *Washington Post,* August 1, 1910. Smith also emphasized that the fire illustrated "the wisdom of Congress in authorizing at its last session the preparation of plans for a government building that will not only be better adapted" to the needs of his scientific and map-making bureau "but will insure the safety of the public records that have been five times endangered by fire destruction since 1903."

4. As an example, the Modern Historic Records Association addressed a letter to James Sherman, vice president of the United States, citing "the irreparable loss of historical documents by fire," in New York State and also in Missouri, and petitioning that Congress should take warning and hasten to provide a fireproof building for government records. It was the association's purpose to select records "upon competent advice . . . deemed worthy of preservation in the National Archives," and these records would be "offered to the National government for its custody and ownership, as an aid to Historians of future generations." Among the names listed on the letterhead were William Howard Taft, Frederick Dent Grant, Robert E. Peary, Alexander Konta, Oswald Garrison Villard, Melvil Dewey, Hamilton Holt, and over two dozen other persons of contemporary distinction. See Herbert L. Bridgman and William T. Larned to James S. Sherman, December 30, 1911, in Percy Scott Flippin, comp., "The Archives of the United States Government: A Documentary History, 1774–1934," 13:121a, National Archives Library, Washington, D.C.

5. J. Franklin Jameson to Charles D. Norton, September 7, 1910, J. Franklin Jameson Papers, Library of Congress, Washington, D.C. (hereafter cited as JFJ).

6. Norton to Jameson, November 9, 1910, JFJ.

7. Norton to Jameson, November 9, 1910, fair copy, JFJ.

8. Jameson to Norton, November 21, 1910, JFJ. See also Jameson to Waldo G. Leland, November 21, 1910, *An Historian's World: Selections from the Correspondence of John Franklin Jameson,* ed. Elizabeth Donnan and Leo F. Stock (Philadelphia: American Philosophical Society, 1956), p. 138 (hereafter cited as *Jameson Correspondence*).

9. William Howard Taft, "Second Annual Message," December 6, 1910, *A Compilation of the Messages and Papers of the Presidents,* comp. James D. Richardson (New York: Bureau of National Literature, 1917) 16:7510 (hereafter cited as *Messages and Papers*).

10. Jameson to Leland, December 12, 1910, *Jameson Correspondence,* p. 140.

11. American Historical Association, *Annual Report of the American Historical Association for the Year 1910* (Washington, D.C.: U.S. Government Printing Office, 1911), pp. 294–95 (hereafter cited as AHA, *Annual Report*).

12. Ibid., pp. 298–301.

13. Ibid.

14. Ibid.

15. Ibid., p. 43. See also *American Historical Review* 16:473.

16. Jameson to John Bach McMaster, February 10, 1911; and Jameson to Alfred T. Mahan, February 10, 1911, JFJ.
17. Jameson to Mahan, February 10, 1911, JFJ.
18. McMaster to Jameson, February 21, 1911; and Mahan to Jameson, February 2, 1911, JFJ.
19. Jameson to Mahan, February 25, 1911, JFJ.
20. U.S., Congress, Senate, *National Archive Building,* 61st Cong., 3d Sess., S. Doc. 838, February 25, 1911; U.S., Congress, Senate, *Congressional Record,* 61st Cong., 3d Sess., 1911, 46, pt. 4:3383; *American Historical Review* 16: 473; and Jameson to McMaster, November 3, 1911, JFJ.
21. "Our National Archives," *Nation* 92:109.
22. Ibid.
23. Ibid.
24. Ibid.
25. Jameson to Leland, April 25, 1911, *Jameson Correspondence,* pp. 143–44. Lowry was the Washington correspondent of the New York *Evening Post* during the period 1904–1911, and it was during this service that he became acquainted with the efforts of Jameson and the expertise of Leland.
26. U.S., Congress, House, *Biographical Directory of the American Congress, 1774–1949,* comp. James L. Harrison (Washington, D.C.: U.S. Government Printing Office, 1950), p. 1689.
27. Jameson to Leland, May 3, 1911, *Jameson Correspondence,* p. 144.
28. Ibid. That week, Jameson had "put in quite a little time among the statesmen" on Capitol Hill. He had been in contact with Sen. Reed Smoot concerning the printing of the annual reports of the AHA, and overseeing the prospects of the "National Historical Commission" bill then "in the hands of Providence and the new House Library Committee," whose chairman was Rep. James L. Slayden of Texas.
29. U.S., Congress, House, *Biographical Directory,* p. 1805.
30. *Jameson Correspondence,* p. 15.
31. Jameson to Miles Poindexter, June 12, 1911, Miles Poindexter Papers, Series III, File 16, Manuscripts Department, University of Virginia Library, Charlottesville.
32. Jameson to James A. Wetmore, June 13, 1911, JFJ.
33. Elihu Root to Jameson, May 26, 1911, JFJ.
34. Jameson to Root, May 30, 1911, JFJ.
35. French was a fellow in political science at the University of Chicago, 1901–1903, when Jameson taught there. See Jameson to Leland, May 17, 1911, *Jameson Correspondence,* p. 145.
36. Morris Sheppard to Jameson, May 8, 1911, JFJ.
37. Jameson to Sheppard, May 10, 1911, JFJ.
38. U.S., Congress, House, Committee on Public Buildings and Grounds, *Preservation of Government Archives,* 62d Cong., 1st Sess., Hearings, No. 2, May 12, 1911.
39. Jameson to Leland, May 12, 1911, *Jameson Correspondence,* p. 144.
40. Ibid.
41. Jameson to Leland, May 17, 1911, *Jameson Correspondence,* p. 145.
42. Jameson to Gaillard Hunt, May 13, 1911, JFJ.
43. Hunt to Jameson, May 15, 1911, JFJ.

44. Jameson to David Jayne Hill, May 22, 1911, JFJ.
45. Ibid. Jameson asked the ambassador for some highly technical data: (1) plans of the buildings at Berlin and Dresden; (2) materials used in their construction; (3) general dimensions; (4) provisions for future expansion; (5) administrative changes that will be caused by removal to new facilities; and (6) length of time needed for construction.
46. Jameson to Charles Moore, May 13, 1911, JFJ.
47. Jameson to J. Campbell Cantrill, May 22, 1911; and Cantrill to Jameson, May 23, 1911, JFJ.
48. Jameson to Lawrence O. Murray, May 30, 1911; and Murray to Jameson, June 3, 1911, JFJ.
49. Moore to Jameson, May 16, 1911, JFJ.
50. Ibid.
51. Jameson to Moore, May 13, 1911, JFJ.
52. U.S., Congress, House, Committee on Public Buildings and Grounds, *Fire Precautions in Public Buildings and the Preservation of Government Records*, 62d Congress, 1st Sess., Hearings, No. 11, May 30, 1911, pp. 131–47.
53. It may be noted that these recommendations sparked a revolution in the design and construction of library stacks and, consequently, archival stacks as well. Prior to that time stacks were of light steel construction, with the steel rising unprotected through multistoried decks, often with open steel gratings for deck floors. A better condition for fire flues could hardly be imagined. The Ohio State University Library and others similarly constructed simply collapsed when fire broke out, as the steel structure became bent by the heat. By the time the National Archives of the United States was built, this type of steel stack structure was no longer designed. As late as 1960, this writer saw these dangerous types of stacks in use in the Palais de Soubisse of the *Archives nationales* in Paris. Ernst Posner told the writer that the "Haus-, Hof-, und Staats archiv in Vienna is a prime example" also "of the use of open steel gratings for nine floors of stacks."
54. Jameson to Leland, May 3, 1911, *Jameson Correspondence*, p. 144.
55. "National Archives in Danger," *Scientific American* 104:562.
56. George P. Wetmore to Jameson, June 28, 1911, JFJ; U.S., Congress, House, *A Bill Directing the Secretary of the Treasury to Prepare Designs and Estimates for and Report the Cost of a National Archives Building in the District of Columbia*, 62d Cong., 1st Sess., H.R. 11850, June 19, 1911. See also Fred Shelley, "The Interest of J. Franklin Jameson in the National Archives: 1908–1934," *American Archivist* 12:110. Shelley, citing a letter of June 30, 1911, from Jameson to Senator Wetmore, as his source, refers to a conference that Jameson had with Bernard R. Greene, superintendent of the Library of Congress Building. In this conference, Jameson became convinced that the usual plan allowing for a courtyard to admit daylight to the stacks was both wasteful and unnecessary. Shelley quotes Jameson, that "the stacks may as well rely solely upon artificial light, as has been done in the new stacks of the Library of Congress, provided that the working rooms for the archivists, file clerks, and historical workers shall be placed at the outside and have daylight. Under these circumstances we could figure upon a solid cubical structure." A better statement of modern practice could hardly be given. The National Archives Build-

ing as well as various state archival buildings built since 1930 follow this prescription.

57. U.S., Congress, Senate, *Memorial of the Department of Archives and History, of the States of Mississippi and Alabama, Respectively, Relative to a National Archives Building,* 62d Cong., 1st Sess., S. Doc. 64, July 11, 1911.

58. AHA, *Annual Report,* 1911, 1:55, 58–60.

59. Ibid., 1:43–44.

60. Ibid.

61. Jameson to McMaster, February 10, 1911, JFJ.

62. McMaster to Jameson, February 21, 1911, JFJ.

63. Mahan to Jameson, February 21, 1911; and Mahan to Jameson, n.d. (ca. March 1911), JFJ.

64. Charles D. Hilles to Jameson, June 15, 1911; and Jameson to Hilles, June 22, 1911, JFJ.

65. Jameson to Hilles, June 14, 1911, JFJ.

66. Jameson to Hilles, August 25, 1911, JFJ.

67. Jameson to McMaster, and Jameson to Mahan, both November 7, 1911, JFJ. See also Jameson to Taft, October 30, 1911, JFJ.

68. Taft, "Third Annual Message," December 5, 7, 20, and 21, 1911, *Messages and Papers* 17:7619–8098.

CHAPTER 4

1. J. Franklin Jameson, "Address to the Daughters of the American Revolution," *Proceedings of the 20th Continental Congress* (Washington, D.C.: Daughters of the American Revolution, 1911), pp. 90–93.

2. Jameson, circular letter addressed to each state regent and officer of the DAR, January 15, 1912, J. Franklin Jameson Papers, Library of Congress, Washington, D.C. (hereafter cited as JFJ). In the letter he inserted a list of the members of the Committee on Public Buildings and Grounds, and especially asked that letters be written to House leaders, such as Oscar W. Underwood of Alabama, John J. Fitzgerald of New York, A. S. Burleson and R. L. Henry of Texas, and to the committee chairman, Morris Sheppard of Texas.

3. Mrs. William Cummings Story to Jameson, January 18, 1912. JFJ.

4. Mrs. Samuel W. Jamison to Jameson, January 20, 1912, JFJ.

5. Mrs. Edwin A. Richardson to Jameson, January 22, 1912, JFJ.

6. Mrs. Chalmers Meek Williamson to Jameson, January 23, 1912, JFJ.

7. Mrs. W. S. Moore to Jameson, March 14, 1912, JFJ.

8. Jameson to Mrs. Matthew T. Scott, February 1, 1912, JFJ.

9. Jameson to Mrs. Albert B. Cumming, March 25, 1912, JFJ.

10. Jameson to Charles H. McCarthy, January 25, 1912, JFJ.

11. Charles F. D. Belden and George Seymour Godard to George P. Wetmore, July 29, 1912, Miles Poindexter Papers, Series III, File 16, Manuscripts Department, University of Virginia Library, Charlottesville (hereafter cited as MP). Belden and Godard were president and secretary, respectively, of the National Association of State Libraries.

12. Jameson to J. C. Welliver, March 6, 1912, JFJ.

13. Ibid.

14. Jameson to J. Stewart Bryan, November 19, 1912; and Bryan to Jameson, November 25, 1912, JFJ.
15. Waldo G. Leland, "The National Archives Again," *Nation* 95:426–27.
16. Memorial from the State Historical Society of Wisconsin and the Department of History of the University of Wisconsin, n.d., referred to the Senate Committee on Public Buildings and Grounds, April 15, 1912, in Percy Scott Flippin, comp., "The Archives of the United States Government: A Documentary History, 1774–1934," 14:25a, National Archives Library, Washington, D.C. (hereafter cited as Flippin Collection).
17. Clarence W. Alvord to Jameson, November 18, 1912; and Alvord to Jameson, November 26, 1912, JFJ.
18. Herman V. Ames to Jameson, November 20, 1912; Jameson to Ames, November 22, 1912; and Ames to Jameson, December 10, 1912, JFJ.
19. R. D. W. Connor to Jameson, November 18, 1912, JFJ.
20. O. G. Libby to Jameson, November 21, 1912, JFJ.
21. William MacDonald to Jameson, November 20, 1912, JFJ.
22. Thomas M. Owen to Jameson, November 22, 1912, JFJ.
23. Franklin L. Riley to Jameson, November 19, 1912, JFJ.
24. Reuben G. Thwaites to Jameson, November 19, and December 14 and 21, 1912, JFJ.
25. A. S. Salley, Jr. to Jameson, December 4, 1912, JFJ.
26. See letters addressed to Jameson from Robert H. Kelsey, New York Historical Society, November 18, 1912; William Nelson, New Jersey Historical Society, November 18, 1912; E. O. Randall, Ohio State Archaeological and Historical Society, November 21, 1912; George W. Martin, Kansas State Historical Society, December 5, 1912; and Eugene C. Barker, Texas State Historical Association, November 21, 1912, all in JFJ.
27. Jameson to S. S. McClure, November 3, 1911; and Jameson to Albert Shaw, November 10, 1911, JFJ.
28. Jameson to McClure, November 3, 1911, JFJ.
29. Jameson to Shaw, November 10, 1911, JFJ.
30. Shaw to Jameson, January 4, 1912; and Jameson to Shaw, January 8, 1912, JFJ.
31. Rosa P. Chiles, "The National Archives: Are They in Peril?" *Review of Reviews* 45:209–13.
32. Burton L. French to Jameson, January 30, 1912, JFJ.
33. U.S., Congress, House, Committee on Public Buildings and Grounds, *Preservation of Government Archives,* Appendix, 62d Cong., 2d Sess., Hearings, No. 2, February 14, 1912.
34. Ibid.
35. Ibid.
36. Ibid.
37. Ibid.
38. Leland, "The National Archives: A Programme," *American Historical Review* 18:5–25. See also U.S., Congress, Senate, *The National Archives: A Programme,* 63d Cong., 3d Sess., S. Doc. 717, December 21, 1914.
39. Jameson to Oscar Callaway, December 14, 1912, JFJ.
40. U.S., Congress, Senate, *A Bill Directing the Secretary of the Treasury to Prepare Designs and Estimates for and Report the Cost of a National Archives Building in*

the District of Columbia, 62d Cong., 2d Sess., S. 5179, February 8, 1912.

41. U.S., Congress, Senate, *History of the Movement for a National Archives Building in Washington, D.C.,* 62d Cong., 2d Sess., S. Doc. 297, February 8, 1912. See also U.S., Congress, Senate, *Congressional Record,* 62d Cong., 2d Sess., 1912, 48, pt. 2:1833.

42. F. W. Fitzpatrick to Miles Poindexter, February 9, 1912, MP, III, 16.

43. Ibid.

44. Lothrop Withington to Poindexter, February 15, 1912, MP, III, 16.

45. U.S., Congress, Senate, *A Bill to Establish a Record Office,* 62d Cong., 2d Sess., S. 5274, February 14, 1912.

46. Jameson to Poindexter, February 10, 1912; and Poindexter to Jameson, February 14, 1912, MP, III, 16.

47. Jameson to the following: Charles M. Andrews and Ames, February 21, 1912; Alfred T. Mahan and John B. McMaster, February 23, 1912; Gaillard Hunt and Rosa P. Chiles, February 24, 1912, all in JFJ. For invitations to Leland, Fred Dennett, and James L. Wilmeth, see Jameson to Poindexter, February 21 and 28, 1912, MP, III, 16.

48. Andrews to Jameson, February 27, 1912, JFJ.

49. Jameson to Ames, February 21, 1912; Ames to Jameson, February 23, 1912; and Jameson to Ames, February 24, 1912, all in JFJ.

50. Mahan to Jameson, February 25, 1912, JFJ.

51. Jameson to Poindexter, February 21 and 28, 1912, MP, III, 16; and Jameson to George Sutherland, February 28, 1912, JFJ.

52. U.S., Congress, Senate, Committee on Public Buildings and Grounds, *Hearings on S. 5179, A Bill Directing the Secretary of the Treasury to Prepare Designs and Estimates for and Report the Cost of a National Archive Building in the District of Columbia,* 62d Cong., 2d Sess., March 1, 1912, pp. 11–16.

53. Ibid., pp. 21–23. Miss Chiles's statement was prescient. Although it occurred a decade later, the records under the roof of the Treasury Building were gravely endangered by a fire. By prompt and heroic action, the fire was limited to a comparatively small loss, but it again underlined the need for better protection. See the *Evening Star* (Washington, D.C.), the *New York Times,* and the *Washington Post,* February 9, 1922. There were, of course, many other actual and incipient fires in government buildings in the interim.

54. *Hearings on S. 5179, National Archives Bill,* pp. 27–28.

55. Ibid., pp. 29–30. Leland's comment on the Dominion archives being in a safe place was strikingly demonstrated four years later when, by sabotage or otherwise, the Dominion Parliament Building was burned to the ground. Fortunately, the library, which contained the archives, was in a virtually separate, round, chapel-like structure directly to the rear of the main building, connected to it by a corridor. It escaped completely unscathed. Interview of the writer with W. Kaye Lamb, Dominion archivist, October 1, 1968.

56. Ibid., p. 31. Leland here provided a background of the records disposal practices of the federal government, "regulated by the law of February 16, 1889," and "passed after the investigation of the Cockrell Committee of the Senate in 1889, which inquired into the methods of the Government departments at that time." See also Henry P. Beers, "His-

torical Development of the Records Disposal Policy of the Federal Government to 1934," *American Archivist* 8:181–201.

57. *Hearings on S. 5179, National Archives Bill*, p. 31.
58. Ibid., p. 34. For an excellent historical article on the construction of the Public Record Office, see Roger H. Ellis, "The Building of the Public Record Office," in *Essays in Memory of Sir Hilary Jenkinson*, ed. Albert E. J. Hollaender (Chichester, Sussex: Society of Archivists, 1962), pp. 9–30.
59. *Hearings on S. 5179, National Archives Bill*, p. 35.
60. Jameson to Frances G. Davenport, March 4, 1912, *An Historian's World: Selections from the Correspondence of John Franklin Jameson*, ed. Elizabeth Donnan and Leo F. Stock (Philadelphia: American Philosophical Society, 1956), p. 148 (hereafter cited as *Jameson Correspondence*).
61. *Hearings on S. 5179, National Archives Bill*, pp. 36–37.
62. Ibid., p. 37. Withington's guess as to the cost of the building he envisioned was well informed. The first appropriation for the national archives building, the Second Deficiency Act, approved July 3, 1926, was for $6.9 million. This was increased to $8.75 million the following year, and when the original building (without the subsequent inner court annex) was completed in 1936, the cost exceeded $12 million. The comparative modesty of these costs for so monumental a building reflects the unusually low prices during the Great Depression.
63. Ibid., p. 38.
64. Ibid., p. 39. A message from the secretary of the Treasury gave the following data: a building with suitable entrance and vestibule, five stories and basement, of fireproof construction, granite faced, and containing not less than 1.5 million cubic feet would cost approximately $700,000; if, however, the building included 4 million cubic feet, the estimated cost would be $1.95 million; the design would permit an extension to approximately 8.9 million cubic feet, to cost an estimated $4.1 million. The estimates were based upon the very moderate unit cost of fifty cents per cubic foot. (*Hearings*, p. 40.)
65. Ford's Theater, after the assassination of President Lincoln, was for decades utilized by the War Department, mainly by its Record and Pension Office.
66. *Hearings on S. 5179, National Archives Bill*, pp. 12–13. But see Jameson to Leland, May 12, 1911, *Jameson Correspondence*, p. 144: "I . . . told you that in July 1910 the Committee on Appropriations succeeded in giving away Square 143 to the Geological Survey; but as the architect's plans for their building would cost two or three times as much as was stipulated (queer lot, architects!) the matter is still at a pause, and the square cannot be said to have been definitely removed from the list of archive possibilities."
67. American Historical Association, *Annual Report of the American Historical Association for the Year 1912* (Washington, D.C.: U.S. Government Printing Office, 1914), p. 51.
68. Jameson to Henry Cabot Lodge, December 24, 1912; and Lodge to Jameson, December 26, 1912, JFJ.
69. Jameson to William Howard Taft, October 30, 1911, JFJ.
70. Taft, "Message concerning the work of the Interior Department and other matters," February 2, 1912, *A Compilation of the Messages and Papers*

of the Presidents, comp. James D. Richardson (New York: Bureau of National Literature, 1917) 17:7728 (hereafter cited as *Messages and Papers*).

71. Jameson to Taft, February 5, 1912, *Jameson Correspondence,* pp. 146–47.
72. William Howard Taft, *Executive Order 1567,* July 19, 1912, in Flippin Collection, 14:27. The order specified the data desired: earliest year of the archives and their subject matter, up to the year 1873; for what years, if any, the records are missing; their condition, where kept, and cause of destruction if destroyed; and whether they are accessible for use and the extent of use.
73. Elihu Root to Jameson, December 29, 1911, JFJ.
74. Jameson to Taft, October 24, 1912, JFJ. As the president was away on a speaking trip, Rudolph Forster, executive clerk of the White House, acknowledged Jameson's letter and promised to call it to the president's attention when he returned. Forster to Jameson, November 5, 1912, JFJ.
75. Jameson to Taft, November 26, 1912, *Jameson Correspondence,* pp. 152–53. But see also John L. Burnett to Jameson, November 30, 1912, JFJ, for a contrary view. Representative Burnett of Alabama, a member of the House Committee on Public Buildings and Grounds, took exception to Jameson's statement that the House committee was unanimously in favor of a national archives building. Burnett wrote, "I do not know where you got the impression that our Committee . . . are unanimously of the opinion that such a building ought to be started forthwith." On the contrary, he stated, "I am of the opinion that there are many buildings needed worse than the one you refer to. . . . I am opposed to any appropriation for the Archives Building at this session."
76. Taft, "Fourth Annual Message," December 19, 1912, *Messages and Papers* 17:7822.

CHAPTER 5

1. J. Franklin Jameson to Woodrow Wilson, August 26, 1912, *An Historian's World: Selections from the Correspondence of John Franklin Jameson,* ed. Elizabeth Donnan and Leo F. Stock (Philadelphia: American Philosophical Society, 1956), pp. 150–51 (hereafter cited as *Jameson Correspondence*).
2. Jameson to Henry Adams, October 8, 1912, *Jameson Correspondence,* p. 155.
3. U.S., Congress, Senate, *Congressional Record,* 62d Cong., 3d Sess., 1912, 49, pt. 1:912. The letter is dated December 16, 1912.
4. *Congressional Record,* 62d Cong., 3d Sess., 1913, 49, pt. 2:1481.
5. S. P. Heilman to George Sutherland, January 17, 1913, in Percy Scott Flippin, comp., "The Archives of the United States Government: A Documentary History, 1774–1934," 14:45b, National Archives Library, Washington, D.C. (hereafter cited as Flippin Collection).
6. U.S., Congress, Senate, Committee on Public Buildings and Grounds, *National Archives Building,* 62d Cong., 3d Sess., S. Rept. 1191, to accompany S. 5179, February 5, 1913. As the raison d'être for increasing the initial space requirement to 3 million cubic feet, the report noted that "by order of the President, December 14, 1907, the heads of executive departments reported the need at that time for 1,317,760 cubic feet of space for storing records and archives." As the annual increase was

estimated at near sixty thousand cubic feet, it was evident that a forward projection for even ten years would require the larger figure.

7. *Congressional Record,* 62d Cong., 3d Sess., 1913, 50, pt. 4:3294, 3304. See U.S., Congress, House, *A Bill to Limit the Cost of Certain Public Buildings . . . to Authorize the Erection and Completion of Public Buildings, to Authorize the Purchase of Sites for Public Buildings, and for Other Purposes,* 62d Cong., 3d Sess., H.R. 28766, February 15, 1913.

8. A two-thirds vote is required to suspend the rules of the House. Debate is limited to forty minutes, and no floor amendments are permitted.

9. U.S., Congress, House, *Journal,* 62d Cong., 3d Sess., December 2, 1912, pp. 313, 314, 319, 328, 340, 346, 356, 364.

10. U.S., *Statutes at Large,* vol. 37, p. 884.

11. Herman V. Ames to Jameson, March 11, 1913, J. Franklin Jameson Papers, Library of Congress, Washington, D.C. (hereafter cited as JFJ).

12. Jameson to Miles Poindexter, March 5, 1913, Miles Poindexter Papers, Series III, File 16, Manuscripts Department, University of Virginia Library, Charlottesville (hereafter cited as MP).

13. Poindexter to Jameson, March 8, 1913; and Jameson to Poindexter, March 11, 1913, MP, III, 16.

14. American Historical Association, *Annual Report of the American Historical Association for the Year 1913* (Washington, D.C.: U.S. Government Printing Office, 1915) 1:266–68 (hereafter cited as AHA, *Annual Report*). Jameson stated that so far as "the preparation of plans is concerned," the act marks only a stage in advancement, but not substantive action. Jameson also thought that another obstacle militating against obtaining archives plans was that the "office of the Supervising Architect is overwhelmed with its existing work."

15. Ibid. Jameson further remarked that the congressional representation on the commission would be chosen from the Public Buildings and Grounds Committees of the Senate and of the House, the chairman and one minority member from each chamber. It may be noted that the act actually provided for two commissions: one, as described above, in section 36, to consider and recommend on the whole field of government buildings; the other, in section 21, the archives section, provided for a commission to select a site for the archives building.

16. Jameson to Oscar Wenderoth, March 17, 1913, JFJ.

17. Sherman Allen to Poindexter, May 24, 1913, MP, III, 16.

18. Jameson to William Gibbs McAdoo, June 11, 1913, JFJ.

19. Byron R. Newton to Jameson, June 12, 1913, JFJ.

20. Poindexter to John J. Fitzgerald, June 21, 1913, MP, III, 16.

21. Allen to Poindexter, July 12, 1913, MP, III, 16.

22. Jameson to Edward G. Lowry, September 27, 1913, JFJ.

23. Lowry to Jameson, September 29, 1913, JFJ.

24. Jameson to the postmaster general; the attorney general; Senators Claude A. Swanson and George Sutherland; and Representatives Richard W. Austin and Frank Clark, all October 28, 1913, JFJ.

25. Sutherland to Jameson, October 30, 1913, JFJ.

26. Austin to Jameson, October 30, 1913, JFJ.

27. "The Meeting of the American Historical Association at Charleston and Columbia," *American Historical Review* 19:486.

28. Gaillard Hunt to Wilson, March 4, 1914, Woodrow Wilson Papers, Library of Congress.
29. Harry A. Garfield to Wilson, March 7, 1914, Wilson Papers.
30. Wilson to Garfield, March 10, 1914, in Flippin Collection, 15:6.
31. McAdoo to Clark, April 10, 1914, MP, III, 16.
32. U.S., Congress, House, *A Bill to Amend Section 21 of . . . an Act to Increase the Limit of Cost of Certain Public Buildings . . . to Authorize the Erection and Completion of Public Buildings; to Authorize the Purchase of Sites for Public Buildings, and for Other Purposes, Approved March 4, 1913*, 63d Cong., 2d Sess., H.R. 15653, April 14, 1914.
33. U.S., Congress, House, Committee on Public Buildings and Grounds, *To Amend Section 21 of the Public Buildings Act*, 63d Cong., 2d Sess., H. Rept. 539, to accompany H.R. 15653, April 16, 1914.
34. Jameson to Poindexter, May 5, 1914; and Poindexter to Jameson, May 6, 1914, MP, III, 16.
35. Jameson to Poindexter, June 6, 1914, MP, III, 16.
36. Jameson to Poindexter, June 8, 1914, MP, III, 16.
37. Ibid.
38. Poindexter to Jameson, June 9, 1914, MP, III, 16.
39. Newton to Poindexter, July 2, 1914, MP, III, 16. The Treasury letter is in U.S., Congress, Senate, Committee on Appropriations, *Estimates of Appropriations for Public Buildings for Fiscal Year Ending June 30, 1915*, 63d Cong., 2d Sess., S. Doc. 527, June 30, 1914.
40. Poindexter to Newton, July 3, 1914, MP, III, 16.
41. *Congressional Record*, 63d Cong., 2d Sess., 1914, 51, pt. 12:11810–11.
42. Poindexter to Jameson, July 9, 1914, MP, III, 16.
43. R. C. Ballard Thruston to the American Historical Association (attention of Jameson), May 7, 1914, JFJ.
44. Jameson to Thruston, May 12, 1914, JFJ.
45. Jameson, "The Need of a National Archive Building," *Bulletin of the American Library Association* 8:134.
46. Ibid., pp. 135–36.
47. Ibid., p. 137.
48. Ibid., p. 140.
49. Ibid., pp. 185–86.
50. Ibid., p. 324.
51. Ibid.
52. Jameson to Representatives Fitzgerald and Frank W. Mondell; and to Senators Lee S. Overman, Thomas S. Martin, and Francis E. Warren, all July 20, 1914, JFJ.
53. Fitzgerald to Jameson, July 21, 1914, JFJ.
54. Overman to Jameson, July 22, 1914, JFJ.
55. Jameson to Overman, July 27, 1914, JFJ.
56. U.S., Congress, House, *A Bill Making Appropriation for Sundry Civil Expenses of the Government for the Fiscal Year Ending June 30, 1915, and for Other Purposes*, 63d Cong. 2d Sess., H.R. 17041, August 3, 1914; and *Statutes at Large*, vol. 38, p. 614.
57. Newton to Poindexter, January 30, 1915 (with enclosure, McAdoo to chairman, House Committee on Public Buildings and Grounds, December 17, 1914), MP, III, 16.

58. Poindexter to Jameson, February 2, 1915; and Jameson to Poindexter, February 5, 1915, MP, III, 16.
59. Jameson to Poindexter, May 27, 1914, MP, III, 16.
60. Ibid.
61. Poindexter to Jameson, June 1, 1915, MP, III, 16.
62. Jameson to Poindexter, November 15, 1915, MP, III, 16. James A. Wetmore served as *acting* supervising architect of the Treasury for approximately twenty years, from 1915 to 1934.
63. Poindexter to Jameson, November 19, 1915, MP, III, 16.
64. Ibid.
65. Newton to Poindexter, April 5, 1916, MP, III, 16.
66. Poindexter to Jameson, November 19, 1915, MP, III, 16.
67. Jameson to Poindexter, November 15, 1915, MP, III, 16.
68. AHA, *Annual Report,* 1915, pp. 261–64. See also *American Historical Review* 21:443–44; and Leland to Hunt, November 10, 1915, in Flippin Collection, 15:107–8.
69. AHA, *Annual Report,* 1915, p. 262.
70. Leland to Poindexter, November 5, 1915; and Poindexter to Leland, November 17, 1915, MP, III, 16.
71. AHA, *Annual Report,* 1915, pp. 262–63. See also *American Historical Review* 21:443–44.
72. *American Historical Review* 21:443–44.
73. AHA, *Annual Report,* 1915, p. 264.
74. "The National Archives," *Outlook* 112:174–75.
75. *Evening Star* (Washington, D.C.), March 29, 1916.
76. Victor H. Paltsits to Poindexter, January 5 and 18, 1916, MP, III, 16.
77. Newton to Poindexter, April 5, 1916, MP, III, 16.
78. Jameson to Poindexter, April 26, 1916, MP, III, 16.
79. Jameson to Poindexter, April 24, 1916, MP, III, 16.
80. Poindexter to Jameson, April 25, 1916, MP, III, 16.
81. *Congressional Record,* 64th Cong., 1st Sess., 1916, 53, pt. 8:7625, 8070; and U.S., Congress, Senate, *A Bill to Repeal Paragraph 4 of Section 21 of the Public Buildings Act, Approved March 4, 1913, Providing for the Construction of a National Archives Building,* 64th Cong., 1st Sess., S. 5839, May 3, 1916.
82. U.S., Congress, House, Committee on Public Buildings and Grounds, *National Archives Building,* 64th Cong., 1st Sess., Hearings, No. 19, May 17, 1916, pp. 23–24.
83. Ibid.
84. U.S., Congress, House, Committee on Public Buildings and Grounds, *National Archives Building,* 64th Cong., 1st Sess., H. Rept. 753, to accompany S. 5839, May 24, 1916, p. 2.
85. *Congressional Record,* 64th Cong., 1st Sess., 1916, 53, pt. 10:9439. See also *Statutes at Large,* vol. 39, p. 241.

CHAPTER 6

1. J. Franklin Jameson to Woodrow Wilson, November 15, 1916, J. Franklin Jameson Papers, Library of Congress, Washington, D.C. (hereafter cited as JFJ).

2. Ibid.
3. Wilson to Jameson, November 16, 1916, JFJ.
4. Jameson to Wilson, November 15, 1916, JFJ.
5. Jameson to Andrew C. McLaughlin, November 20, 1916, *An Historian's World: Selections from the Correspondence of John Franklin Jameson,* ed. Elizabeth Donnan and Leo F. Stock (Philadelphia: American Philosophical Society, 1956), p. 202 (hereafter cited as *Jameson Correspondence*).
6. U.S., Congress, House, *Archives Building, Washington, D.C.,* 64th Cong., 2d Sess., H. Doc. 1918, January 11, 1917.
7. U.S., Congress, Senate, *A Bill Amending Archive Building Act,* 64th Cong., 2d Sess., S. 7778, January 9, 1917. See also U.S., Congress, Senate, *Congressional Record,* 64th Cong., 2d Sess., 1917, 54, pt. 2:1067.
8. It will be recalled that the Public Buildings Commission of the act of 1913 (to distinguish if from other like-named bodies), consisted of the vice president, the Speaker, and the secretaries of the Treasury, War, and Interior.
9. Jameson to Thomas R. Marshall, January 12, 1917, JFJ.
10. Marshall to Jameson, January 19, 1917; and Jameson to Marshall, January 22, 1917, JFJ.
11. Marshall to the secretary of the Treasury, February 6, 1917, JFJ. Jameson continued to chip away at Marshall's armor of indifference. In the fall of the year, he addressed Prof. Samuel B. Harding of Indiana University, asking him to influence Marshall "in favor of the archive building." (Jameson to Harding, October 19, 1917.) Harding replied, "We at the State University did not get along very well with Marshall while he was Governor," and consequently they would have little weight with him "in the matter of the archives building." (Harding to Jameson, October 21, 1917.) But Jameson would not let Harding wriggle off the hook that easily. He countered with the proposal that Harding get in touch with Jacob P. Dunn and Meredith Nicholson, for, he said, "Both are good Democrats and both are interested in history." (Jameson to Harding, October 23, 1917.) All the foregoing letters are in JFJ.
12. U.S., Department of Commerce, *Reports of the Department of Commerce, 1917* (Washington, D.C.: U.S. Government Printing Office, 1918), pp. 16–17.
13. Sarah E. Guernsey to Herbert Putnam, July 20, 1917; and Putnam to Guernsey, July 23, 1917, JFJ.
14. Jameson to Guernsey, August 1, 1917, JFJ.
15. Ibid.
16. G. M. Brumbaugh to Jameson, October 22, 1917, JFJ.
17. Jameson to Brumbaugh, October 24, 1917, JFJ.
18. Jameson to Miles Poindexter, August 9, 1917; and Poindexter to Jameson, August 11, 1917, JFJ.
19. *National Genealogical Society Quarterly* 6:59.
20. American Historical Association, *Annual Report of the American Historical Association for the Year 1917* (Washington, D.C.: U.S. Government Printing Office, 1920), pp. 181–82 (hereafter cited as AHA, *Annual Report*).
21. Ibid., pp. 129–30.
22. "Our War Documents," *Military Historian and Economist* 3:1–6.
23. Ibid., p. 1.
24. Ibid., pp. 2, 4.

25. Ibid., p. 5.
26. Ibid., p. 6.
27. Ibid., p. 5.
28. AHA, *Annual Report,* 1917, p. 119.
29. Jameson, "Memorandum Concerning Sites for a National Archive Building," in Percy Scott Flippin, comp., "The Archives of the United States Government: A Documentary History, 1774–1934," 16:51–82, National Archives Library, Washington, D.C. (hereafter cited as Flippin Collection).
30. Poindexter to Jameson, September 15, 1917, JFJ.
31. Jameson to Poindexter, September 24, 1917, JFJ.
32. Poindexter to Jameson, May 27, 1918, JFJ.
33. Jameson to David H. Parker, October 31, 1918, *Jameson Correspondence,* pp. 227–28.
34. Ibid.
35. Jameson to Henry Jones Ford, January 22, 1919, JFJ.
36. Ibid.
37. Jameson to Henry B. Gardner, January 22, 1919; and Gardner to Jameson, March 11, 1919, JFJ. Gardner was president of Brown University.
38. Jameson to Oliver L. Spaulding, Jr., January 13, 1921, JFJ.
39. U.S., Congress, Senate, *A Bill for the Erection of a National Archive Building,* 65th Cong., 2d Sess., S. 4538, May 15, 1918.
40. *Congressional Record,* 65th Cong., 3d Sess., 1919, 57, pt. 5:4307.
41. Poindexter to Harry A. Garfield, December 24, 1918, in Flippin Collection, 16:121.
42. Garfield to Poindexter, January 4, 1919; and Poindexter to Garfield, January 10, 1919, in Flippin Collection, 16:123–24.
43. Garfield to Poindexter, January 14, 1919, in Flippin Collection, 16:125. The truth of this statement was amply attested by experience after the American entry into the Second World War, but particularly so with the outbreak of the Korean War, as the National Archives then had the advantage of half a decade between the two wars to winnow, accession, arrange, and make available the agency records of the Second World War.
44. Ibid.
45. U.S., Department of the Treasury, *Annual Report of the Secretary of the Treasury on the State of the Finances for the Fiscal Year Ended June 30, 1919* (Washington, D.C.: U.S. Government Printing Office, 1920), p. 168.
46. U.S., Department of Commerce, *Reports of the Department of Commerce, 1919* (Washington, D.C.: U.S. Government Printing Office, 1920), p. 21.
47. U.S., Congress, House, *National Archives Building, Washington, D.C.,* 65th Cong., 3d Sess., H. Doc. 1772, February 7, 1919. The secretary noted that "no appropriation is asked for furnishings at this time because the plan is to utilize so far as practicable the steel filing cases already in use and simply transfer them to the new building."
48. U.S., Congress, House, *Construction of a National Archives Building,* 66th Cong., 1st Sess., H. Doc. 200, August 25, 1919.
49. *New York Times,* May 4, 1919. Assistant Secretary of War Benedict Crowell, on July 5, 1918, transmitted to the Congress a report on the fire hazards in the State, War, and Navy Building, compiled by the National

Board of Fire Underwriters. See U.S., Congress, Senate, *Condition of the State, War, and Navy Building,* 65th Cong., 3d Sess., S. Doc. 344, July 6, 1918. The report concluded that it was "the obvious duty of the Government . . . to provide an absolutely invulnerable hall of records."

50. "Statement of the Hon. Franklin D. Roosevelt, Assistant Secretary of the Navy," October 13, 1919, U.S., Senate, Public Buildings Commission, *Hearings before the Public Buildings Commission,* 66th Cong., 1st Sess., Hearings, No. 2, October 13, 1919, p. 8.

51. Josephus Daniels to Reed Smoot, n.d., *Hearings before the Public Buildings Commission,* October 13, 1919, pp. 8–10.

52. Ibid.

53. Ibid.

54. For example, see U.S., Department of Commerce, *Reports of the Department of Commerce, 1920* (Washington, D.C.: U.S. Government Printing Office, 1921), p. 33.

55. U.S., Congress, House, Committee on Appropriations, Subcommittee on Appropriations for the Legislative, Executive, and Judicial Appropriations for Fiscal Year 1922, *Statement of Bainbridge Colby,* 66th Cong., 3d Sess., Hearings, November 23, 1920.

56. Ibid. The informal committee consisted of Gaillard Hunt, former chief of the Manuscript Division of the Library of Congress and, since the war, historian with the State Department; Worthington C. Ford, editor of the Massachusetts Historical Society; and R. D. W. Connor, secretary of the North Carolina Historical Commission. See Flippin Collection, 16:209.

57. Jameson to Graham Botha, April 12, 1920, JFJ. Jameson tells Botha to see Victor H. Paltsits of the New York Public Library, chairman of the Public Archives Commission of the AHA, as "he can tell you more about American archives than any one else" except "my assistant Mr. Waldo G. Leland."

58. AHA, *Annual Report,* 1919, 1:75–76.

59. Ibid.

60. Jameson to Spaulding, January 13, 1921, JFJ.

61. AHA, *Annual Report,* 1920, 1:88.

CHAPTER 7

1. *New York Times,* January 12, 1921; and *Washington Post,* January 11, 1921. See also U.S., General Services Administration, National Archives and Records Service, *Preliminary Inventory of the Records of the Bureau of the Census,* RG 29 (P.I. 161). In an interview on July 8, 1968, with W. Neil Franklin, former chief of the Central Reference branch of the National Archives, Franklin stated to the writer that "only some 6 thousand names were saved out of the millions in the 1890 census." These were on pages interleaved in volumes relating to a scattering of state enumerations.

2. J. Franklin Jameson to Carter Glass, Wesley L. Jones, Francis E. Warren, and Lee S. Overman, all January 12, 1921, J. Franklin Jameson Papers, Library of Congress, Washington, D.C. (hereafter cited as JFJ).

3. Jameson to Miles Poindexter, January 12, 1921, JFJ.

4. *New York Times,* January 12, 1921.
5. U.S., Department of Commerce, *Ninth Annual Report of the Secretary of Commerce, 1921* (Washington, D.C.: U.S. Government Printing Office, 1921), p. 8.
6. *Washington Post,* January 18, 1921.
7. U.S., Congress, Senate, *Congressional Record,* 66th Cong., 3d Sess., 1921, 60, pt. 2:1491.
8. Jameson to Wilfred H. Munro, January 19, 1921, JFJ.
9. *Congressional Record,* 66th Cong., 3d Sess., 1921, 60, pt. 2:1491, 1553.
10. Ibid.
11. *Washington Post,* February 5, 1921.
12. *Evening Star* (Washington, D.C.), February 7, 1921.
13. *Congressional Record,* 66th Cong., 3d Sess., 1921, 60, pt. 3:2698–702.
14. Ibid.
15. Ibid.
16. Ibid.
17. Ibid.
18. Ibid. The War and Navy buildings referred to in Underwood's remarks were razed in 1970. The old State, War, and Navy Building, now the Old Executive Office Building, is just west of the White House, on the southeast corner of Pennsylvania Avenue and Seventeenth Street, N.W.
19. Ibid.
20. Ibid.
21. Ibid. Poli's Theater, one of Washington's leading amusement places, was then located there.
22. Ibid.
23. Ibid.
24. *Congressional Record,* 66th Cong., 3d Sess., 1921, 60, pt. 3:2851–54.
25. Ibid.
26. Ibid.
27. Ibid.
28. Senator King was referring to the Treasury Annex Building, opposite the Treasury Building, on the corner of Pennsylvania Avenue and Madison Place, N.W., fronting Lafayette Square.
29. Ibid.
30. Ibid.
31. Ibid. The Star Building was on the north side of Pennsylvania Avenue, directly opposite the Post Office Building. The Washington Post Building was several blocks up the avenue, near Fourteenth Street.
32. Ibid.
33. Ibid.
34. Ibid.
35. Jameson to Poindexter, February 5, 1921, JFJ.
36. Jameson to Poindexter, February 8, 1921, JFJ. Those referred to were Rep. Simeon D. Fess of Ohio and Acting Supervising Architect James A. Wetmore.
37. *Evening Star,* February 10, 1921.
38. Lily Lykes Rowe, "Archives Hall Planned by Congress," *Daughters of the American Revolution Magazine* 55:138–40.

39. Ibid.
40. Herbert Hoover to Poindexter, April 14, 1921, JFJ.
41. Poindexter to Jameson, June 10, 1921, JFJ.
42. Rowe, "Archives Hall Planned by Congress," *DAR Magazine* 55:149.

CHAPTER 8

1. For an early history of the Legion, see Marquis James, *A History of the American Legion* (New York: W. Green, 1923).
2. Report of the National Memorials Committee to the third annual convention of the American Legion, Kansas City, Missouri, October 31–November 2, 1921; and minutes of the American Legion Executive Committee, October 30, 1921, American Legion Archives, Indianapolis, Indiana. T. Semmes Walmsley of Louisiana was made chairman of the Memorials Committee.
3. The biographical information on Eben Putnam is derived from memorandums from Thomas V. Hull, national librarian of the American Legion to Victor Gondos, Jr., May–July 1968; and the following materials from the American Legion Archives: "Eben Putnam—National Historian of the American Legion," May 18, 1929; the military record of Eben Putnam, August 22, 1919; and "Eben Putnam, American Legion Historian, Dead," *Indianapolis News,* January 23, 1933.
4. American Historical Association, *Annual Report of the American Historical Association for the Year 1921* (Washington, D.C.: U.S. Government Printing Office, 1926), pp. 19, 51, 69–70 (hereafter cited as AHA, *Annual Report*).
5. Report of the National Memorials Committee, 1921, American Legion Archives.
6. AHA, *Annual Report,* 1921, pp. 69–70.
7. Report of the National Memorials Committee, 1921, American Legion Archives.
8. Eben Putnam to Lemuel Bolles, April 3, 1921, American Legion Archives. As early as January, Putnam had written to Bolles's secretary, Miss Sickels, asking her to be sure to bring the archival matter to the attention of Bolles and, through him, to the Legion's Executive Committee. See Putnam to Sickels, January 13, 1921, American Legion Archives.
9. Putnam to R. G. Creviston, April 10, 1921, American Legion Archives.
10. Ibid.
11. Putnam to T. Semmes Walmsley, n.d. (ca. May 1921), American Legion Archives.
12. Ibid.
13. Putnam to Walmsley, June 21, 1921, American Legion Archives.
14. Ibid. See also U.S., Congress, House, Committee on Public Buildings and Grounds, *George Washington Memorial Hall,* 67th Cong., 1st Sess., Hearings on H.J. Res. 142, December 16, 1921.
15. Putnam to Walmsley, June 21, 1921, American Legion Archives.
16. Ibid.
17. Ibid.
18. Ibid.
19. Putnam to Creviston, August 25, 1921, American Legion Archives.

20. Ibid.
21. Putnam to B. M. Roszel, June 30, 1921, American Legion Archives.
22. Putnam to Waldo G. Leland, July 14, 1921, J. Franklin Jameson Papers, Library of Congress, Washington, D.C. (hereafter cited as JFJ).
23. Report of the National Memorials Committee, 1921, American Legion Archives.
24. Ibid.
25. Ibid.
26. Ibid.
27. Ibid.
28. Ibid.
29. Ibid. While the Memorials Committee report was being prepared in midsummer 1921, Putnam made an educated guess based upon figures he probably got from Jameson and Leland, that it was "safe to say the Government archives have doubled since 1915 . . . it is roughly estimated that at least 20,000,000 cubic feet would be now required," Putnam to Walmsley, June 21, 1921, American Legion Archives. This figure, of course, was meant to represent all federal records, active and inactive.
30. Summary of Proceedings, Third National Convention, pp. 34–35; and Thomas V. Hull to John Andreola, November 19, 1964, American Legion Archives.
31. Putnam to Leland, November 25, 1921, JFJ.
32. AHA, *Annual Report,* 1921, p. 60.
33. Ibid.
34. Ibid. See also John C. Parish to Oscar W. Underwood, January 10, 1922; and Victor H. Paltsits to Jameson, February 15, 1922, JFJ. Parish was the secretary of the Conference of Historical Societies.
35. Paltsits to Jameson, February 15 and 22, and March 10, 1922, JFJ.
36. "Proceedings, Swampscott Conference, June 20–25, 1921," *Bulletin of the American Library Association* 15:165.
37. Washington Board of Trade, *Thirty-First Annual Report of the Washington Board of Trade, 1921–1922* (Washington, D.C.: Gibson Brothers, n.d.), p. 16.
38. U.S., Congress, House, *Congressional Record,* 67th Cong., 1st Sess., 1921, 61, pt. 7:6628.
39. U.S., Navy Department, *Annual Reports of the Navy Department for the Fiscal Year 1922* (Washington, D.C.: U.S. Government Printing Office, 1923), p. 37.
40. U.S., Department of Commerce, *Ninth Annual Report of the Secretary of Commerce, 1921* (Washington, D.C.: U.S. Government Printing Office, 1921), p. 47.
41. Ibid.
42. U.S., National Commission of Fine Arts, *Ninth Report, July 1, 1919–June 30, 1921* (Washington, D.C.: U.S. Government Printing Office, 1921), p. 86.

CHAPTER 9

1. J. Franklin Jameson to Victor H. Paltsits, February 2, 1922, J. Franklin Jameson Papers, Library of Congress, Washington, D.C. (hereafter cited as JFJ).
2. Jameson to Reed Smoot, January 10, 1922, in Percy Scott Flippin, comp., "The Archives of the United States Government: A Documentary History, 1774–1934," 17:86–92, National Archives Library, Washington, D.C. (hereafter cited as Flippin Collection).
3. Ibid.
4. Jameson to Andrew C. McLaughlin, January 11, 1922; and Jameson to Paltsits, February 10, 1922, JFJ.
5. Jameson to McLaughlin, January 11, 1922; and Jameson to Paltsits, February 10, 1922, JFJ.
6. Jameson to Smoot, January 10, 1922, in Flippin Collection, 17:86–92. At this time, Eben Putnam, the American Legion national historian, had come to Washington and was actively helping to recruit congressmen for a round table at which Jameson was to talk to them on the archives problem. See Jameson to McLaughlin, January 11, 1922, JFJ.
7. Jameson to Smoot, January 10, 1922, in Flippin Collection, 17:86–92. Jameson further noted that Secretary McAdoo's letter was "in the *Congressional Record,* February 7, 1921, page 2806," and, moreover, the commission's approving report "was at that time . . . in the Senate . . . on the desk of Senator Poindexter."
8. Ibid.
9. Ibid.
10. Ibid. See also Jameson to McLaughlin, January 11, 1922, JFJ. In this letter, Jameson told McLaughlin that despite his strenuous efforts, he was pessimistic about the results. "I don't think we shall get the thing this session. Perhaps in 1923, perhaps in 1933, or in 1943. Francis Bacon proposed the British Public Record Office in 1616, and they got it in 1856."
11. U.S., Congress, Senate, *Congressional Record,* 67th Cong., 1st Sess., 1922, 62, pt. 2:1505–7.
12. Ibid.
13. Ibid.
14. Ibid.
15. Ibid.
16. *Congressional Record,* 67th Cong., 1st Sess., 1922, 62, pt. 2:2073–77.
17. *Evening Star* (Washington, D.C.), February 3, 1922. The memorial project referred to above was Mrs. Dimock's project. Actually, only the cornerstone had been laid.
18. *Congressional Record,* 67th Cong., 1st Sess., 1922, 62, pt. 2:2073–77.
19. Ibid.
20. Ibid.
21. Ibid.
22. Ibid.
23. Ibid.
24. Ibid.
25. Ibid.

26. *Washington Post,* February 3, 1922. See also the *Evening Star,* February 3, 1922, for an able summary of the debate in the House.
27. *Washington Post,* February 3, 1922.
28. *Congressional Record,* 67th Cong., 1st Sess., 1922, 62, pt. 2:2214–16.
29. Ibid.
30. Ibid.
31. Jameson to Paltsits, February 10, 1922, JFJ.
32. Ibid.
33. Paltsits to Jameson, February 15, 1922, JFJ.
34. Jameson to Paltsits, February 17, 1922, JFJ.
35. C. O. Sherrill to Smoot, February 13, 1922, in Flippin Collection, 17: 129–40.
36. Ibid.
37. Ibid.
38. Ibid.
39. Ibid.
40. Ibid.
41. Ibid.
42. Ibid.
43. Ibid.
44. *New York Times,* February 13, 1922.
45. Ibid.
46. *Evening Star,* February 9, 1922.
47. Jameson to Smoot, February 23, 1922, JFJ.
48. Jameson to Waldo G. Leland, May 29, 1922, *An Historian's World: Selections from the Correspondence of John Franklin Jameson,* ed. Elizabeth Donnan and Leo F. Stock (Philadelphia: American Philosophical Society, 1956), p. 274, n. 401 (hereafter cited as *Jameson Correspondence*).
49. Jameson to Leland, April 25, 1922, *Jameson Correspondence,* p. 268. In this letter Jameson facetiously noted, "As further signs of progress to cheer you on your voyage, I may mention that the old house of Senator Kean at Seventeenth and I [streets] now bears an enormous sign, about 30 feet by 5 feet, designating it as the headquarters of the Victory Memorial Committee." This was a reference to the old Dimock project, the George Washington memorial, which now metamorphosed under what seemed to be a more popular designation. President Harding in January 1922 had endorsed the Victory memorial project.
50. Jameson to Leland, May 29, 1922, *Jameson Correspondence,* p. 274.
51. Jameson to Leland, April 25, 1922, *Jameson Correspondence,* p. 268.
52. Eben Putnam to Jameson, September 7, 1922, JFJ.
53. Ibid.
54. Jameson to Putnam, September 9, 1922, JFJ. Jameson had had a conference with Budget Director H. M. Lord on August 16, 1922, and the following day wrote him a letter detailing the whole range of events relevant to efforts to obtain an archival depository, noting that "appeals for such a building from the departments" were made "in almost every session . . . beginning in 1879 . . . [yet] conditions grow worse." He made some invidious comparisons with archival situations in the states and corporations, claiming that "ten of our states have separate fire-proof state archive buildings." He goes on to say, "Railroads and banking

corporations . . . have model buildings of the sort. Every European country has a good National Archive Building, and Canada has an especially excellent one." Jameson concluded his letter with a recitation of the abortive efforts in Congress in 1921 and 1922 and stated that he hoped "an appropriation may be made this time." See Jameson to H. M. Lord, August 17, 1922, JFJ.

55. Putnam to Jameson, September 20, 1920, JFJ.

56. Sons of Veterans, U.S.A., Division of Maryland, November 11, 1922, in Flippin Collection, 17:163–64.

57. Resolution, President's Own Garrison, No. 104, Army and Navy Union, U.S.A., November 11, 1922, JFJ.

58. Report of the National Legislative Committee to the Fourth National Convention of the American Legion, October 16–20, 1922, New Orleans, in Flippin Collection, 17:161–62. The report noted that "your National Legislative Committee has actively cooperated with Mr. Eben Putnam, National Historian." John Thomas Taylor, long-time legislative head of the Legion headquarters in the national capital, consistently cooperated with Putnam on the national archives project.

59. Leland to Jameson, November 14, 1922, *Jameson Correspondence*, p. 278, n. 428.

60. Jameson to Leland, November 27, 1922, *Jameson Correspondence*, p. 278.

CHAPTER 10

1. U.S., Congress, House, Committee on Appropriations, *A Bill Making Appropriations for the Executive Office and for Sundry Independent Executive Bureaus, Boards, Commissions, and Offices for the Fiscal Year Ending June 30, 1924,* 67th Cong., 4th Sess., H.R. 13696, January 7, 1923. See also memorandum, "Steel Stacks in Pension Office," n.d., Miles Poindexter Papers, Series VI, File 30 (1922–1923), Manuscripts Department, University of Virginia Library, Charlottesville.

2. U.S., Public Buildings Commission, *Report of the Public Buildings Commission, January 4, 1923* (Washington, D.C.: U.S. Government Printing Office, 1923).

3. J. Franklin Jameson to Eben Putnam, January 5, 1923; and Jameson to Clode Byars, February 8, 1923, J. Franklin Jameson Papers, Library of Congress, Washington, D.C. (hereafter cited as JFJ). See also Jameson to Waldo G. Leland, January 9, 1923, *An Historian's World: Selections from the Correspondence of John Franklin Jameson,* ed. Elizabeth Donnan and Leo F. Stock (Philadelphia: American Philosophical Society, 1956), p. 285, n. 455 (hereafter cited as *Jameson Correspondence*).

4. *Washington Herald,* January 5, 1923.

5. Ibid.

6. Ibid.

7. Ibid.

8. Ibid.

9. Ibid.

10. *Washington Herald,* January 6, 1923. Introducing Leland's comments, the

report asserted that Leland was "described by Dr. Jameson . . . as the 'best archivist in the world.'"

11. Ibid.
12. *Washington Herald,* January 8, 1923.
13. *Washington Herald,* January 9, 1923.
14. Ibid.
15. *Washington Herald,* January 10, 1923.
16. *Washington Herald,* January 11, 1923.
17. *Washington Herald,* January 12, 1923.
18. *Washington Herald,* January 11, 1923.
19. *Washington Herald,* January 17, 1923.
20. *Washington Herald,* January 13, 1923. The Department of Commerce Building, which forms the base of the Federal Triangle, now occupies this location. Herbert Hoover, as secretary of commerce, undoubtedly had a major voice in locating his department on that preferred site.
21. Jameson to Putnam, February 8, 1923, American Legion Archives, Indianapolis, Indiana.
22. The need for a planned national budget had long been acknowledged. In both houses of Congress, numerous committees could authorize (as distinguished from appropriate) expenditures without any reference to what other committees might be doing. Appropriations committees would then appropriate for these authorizations or refuse to do so as they saw fit, but without consciously planning that the expenditures and receipts of the government would be in balance. President Taft, in 1911, had appointed a Commission on Economy and Efficiency which recommended a budget system. Ten years later, in June 1921, the Budget and Accounting Act became law. President Harding appointed Charles G. Dawes, a Chicago banker, who later became vice president of the United States, as the first director of the budget. All agency proposals for expenditures came under the scrutiny of the director, who made every effort to eliminate duplication and pare down unreasonable requests before the chief executive's budget was presented to Congress. See Jeremiah S. Young, John W. Manning, and Joseph I. Arnold, *Government of the American People* (Boston: D. C. Heath, 1947), pp. 189–203.
23. U.S., Congress, Senate, *Congressional Record,* 67th Cong., 4th Sess., 1923, 64, pt. 2:2007–9.
24. Ibid.
25. Jameson to Leland, January 30, 1923, *Jameson Correspondence,* p. 282.
26. *Congressional Record,* 67th Cong., 4th Sess., 1923, 64, pt. 2:2007–9.
27. *Congressional Record,* 67th Cong., 4th Sess., 1923, 64, pt. 2:1986.
28. *Washington Herald,* January 20, 1923. Smoot's amendment to H.R. 13696, the independent offices appropriation bill, was numbered 25, and Poindexter's was numbered 26.
29. *Congressional Record,* 67th Cong., 4th Sess., 1923, 64, pt. 2:2007–9. See also U.S., General Services Administration, *Pension Building,* GSA Historical Study No. 1, comp. Donald J. Lehman (Washington, D.C.: U.S. Government Printing Office, 1964).
30. *Congressional Record,* 67th Cong., 4th Sess., 1923, 64, pt. 2:2064–69.
31. Ibid.
32. Ibid.

33. Ibid.
34. Ibid.
35. Ibid.
36. Ibid.
37. Ibid.
38. Ibid.
39. Ibid.
40. Ibid.
41. Ibid.
42. Ibid.
43. Ibid.
44. Ibid.
45. Ibid.
46. Ibid.
47. Ibid.
48. Ibid.
49. Ibid.
50. Ibid.
51. Putnam to Jameson, January 22, 1923, JFJ.
52. Jameson to Putnam, February 8, 1923, American Legion Archives. See also Jameson to Leland, January 30, 1923, *Jameson Correspondence,* p. 282.
53. *Washington Herald,* January 22, 1923.
54. *Washington Herald,* January 29, 1923.
55. Ibid.
56. *Evening Star* (Washington, D.C.), January 25, 1923.
57. *Washington Herald,* January 30 and February 1, 1923.
58. *Evening Star,* January 25, 1923.
59. Jameson to Leland, January 30, 1923, *Jameson Correspondence,* p. 282.
60. *Congressional Record,* 67th Cong., 4th Sess., 1923, 64, pt. 3:2898–900.
61. Ibid.
62. Ibid.
63. Jameson to Putnam, February 8, 1923, American Legion Archives. In this letter he acknowledged the aid received from the American Legion: "Your people worked valiantly in the cause . . . but did not succeed." He intimated it would be a different story at a later time.
64. Jameson to Leland, January 30, 1923, *Jameson Correspondence,* p. 282.
65. Ibid.
66. Jameson to Putnam, February 8, 1923, JFJ.
67. Jameson to Leland, January 30, 1923, *Jameson Correspondence,* p. 282.
68. Jameson to Putnam, February 8, 1923, JFJ.
69. Ibid., and Jameson to Leland, January 30, 1923, *Jameson Correspondence,* p. 282.
70. *Congressional Record,* 67th Cong., 4th Sess., 1923, 64, pt. 4:3413–14. Smoot was particularly bitter about some unnamed "clerk or official," who, he said, furnished ammunition to one of the critical House conferees. He accused the official of being more "concerned about his own particular desires than the good of the Government," that he did not want to be deprived of some "particular . . . place that he is now occupying in the Pension Building. His view would no doubt be interrupted . . . but the

gentleman did not want his view interrupted, and therefore the Government is deprived of saving $1,000,000 in two years."

71. Ibid.
72. Ibid.
73. *Evening Star,* February 11, 1923.
74. *National Genealogical Quarterly* 12:16.
75. Washington Board of Trade, *Thirty-Third Annual Report of the Washington Board of Trade* (Washington, D.C.: Charles H. Potter, 1923), p. 109.
76. *New York Times,* March 19, 1923.
77. Putnam to Jameson, February 14, 1923, American Legion Archives.
78. Jameson to Putnam, February 15, 1923, JFJ.
79. Ibid.
80. Putnam, "Memorandum to Department Historians," February 21, 1923, American Legion Archives. The italics are Putnam's.
81. John D. Hicks, *The American Nation,* 3d ed. (Cambridge: Houghton Mifflin, 1955), p. 491.
82. *Evening Star,* August 17, 1923.
83. *Evening Star,* August 18, 1923.
84. Ibid.
85. Jameson to Putnam, September 25, 1923, JFJ.
86. Ibid., and Jameson to Calvin Coolidge, September 29, 1923, JFJ.
87. Jameson to Coolidge, September 29, 1923, JFJ.
88. American Historical Association, *Annual Report of the American Historical Association for the Year 1923* (Washington, D.C.: U.S. Government Printing Office, 1929) 1:79–80.

CHAPTER 11

1. U.S., Department of Commerce, *Eleventh Annual Report of the Secretary of Commerce, 1923* (Washington, D.C.: U.S. Government Printing Office, 1923), pp. 40–41.
2. U.S., Navy Department, *Annual Reports of the Navy Department for the Fiscal Year 1923* (Washington, D.C.: U.S. Government Printing Office, 1924), p. 68.
3. U.S., Department of the Treasury, *Annual Report of the Secretary of the Treasury on the State of the Finances for the Fiscal Year Ended June 30, 1923* (Washington, D.C.: U.S. Government Printing Office, 1924), pp. 84–85.
4. Calvin Coolidge, "First Annual Message," *The State of the Union Messages of the Presidents,* ed. Fred L. Israel (New York: Chelsea House, Robert Hector, 1966) 3:2649.
5. U.S., Congress, House, *Message of the President of the United States Transmitting the Budget for the . . . Fiscal Year Ending June 30, 1925,* 68th Cong., 1st Sess., H. Doc. 76, December 3, 1923.
6. U.S., Congress, Senate, *A Bill to Provide for the Construction of Certain Public Buildings in the District of Columbia,* 68th Cong., 1st Sess., S. 2284, January 28, 1924.
7. U.S., Congress, Senate, Committee on Public Buildings and Grounds, *To Provide for the Construction of Certain Public Buildings in the District of Columbia,*

68th Cong., 1st Sess., S. Rept. 493, to accompany S. 2284, April 24, 1924.

8.   Ibid.

9.   Ibid.

10.   U.S., Congress, Senate, *Congressional Record*, 68th Cong., 1st Sess., 1925, 66, pt. 3:2448–56.

11.   U.S., Congress, House, *A Bill to Provide for the Construction of Certain Public Buildings in the District of Columbia*, 68th Cong., 1st Sess., H.R. 9488, May 27, 1924.

12.   U.S., Congress, House, *A Bill to Provide for the Construction of Certain Public Buildings in the District of Columbia and the Several States, Territories, and Dependencies of the United States*, 68th Cong., 2d Sess., H.R. 10406, December 6, 1924.

13.   J. Franklin Jameson to John A. Stewart, February 18, 1924, J. Franklin Jameson Papers, Library of Congress, Washington, D.C. (hereafter cited as JFJ).

14.   Ernest D. Lewis to Waldo G. Leland, October 21, 1924, JFJ.

15.   Jameson to James R. Garfield, December 3, 1924, JFJ.

16.   Ibid.

17.   Garfield to Jameson, December 6, 1924; and Hermann Hagedorn to Jameson, January 12, 1925, JFJ.

18.   U.S., Congress, House, *Message of the President of the United States Transmitting the Budget for the . . . Fiscal Year Ending June 30, 1926*, 68th Cong., 2d Sess., H. Doc. 444, December 1, 1924.

19.   U.S., Congress, House, *A Bill to Provide for the Construction of Certain Public Buildings, and for Other Purposes*, 68th Cong., 2d Sess., H.R. 11791, January 20, 1925. Of the total sum, $50 million was to be allocated to federal projects in the District of Columbia.

20.   U.S., Congress, House, Committee on Public Buildings and Grounds, *Public Buildings Bill*, 68th Cong., 2d Sess., Hearing on H.R. 11791, January 22–23, 1925. The national archives is mentioned on p. 51, and the site on p. 54.

21.   U.S., Congress, House, Committee on Public Buildings and Grounds, *Public Buildings Bill*, 68th Cong., 2d Sess., H. Rept. 1285, to accompany H.R. 11791, January 27, 1925.

22.   U.S., Congress, Senate, Committee on Public Buildings and Grounds, *Construction of Public Buildings*, 68th Cong., 2d Sess., S. Rept. 1089, to accompany H.R. 11791, February 3, 1925.

23.   On January 31, Senator Smoot had introduced S. 2758. The bill was again limited to buildings to be constructed in the District of Columbia. When Senator Fletcher of Florida attempted to amend it, Smoot refused to debate it, and nothing more was heard of it in the session. See *Congressional Record*, 68th Cong., 2d Sess., 1925, 66, pt. 3:2758–59.

24.   Eben Putnam to Jameson, July 9 and 20, 1924; and Jameson to Putnam, July 22, 1924, JFJ.

25.   Reports to the Seventh Annual Convention of the American Legion, October 5–9, 1925, Omaha, Nebraska, pp. 63–64, American Legion Archives, Indianapolis, Indiana.

26.   U.S., Congress, House, Committee on Public Buildings and Grounds,

Public Buildings Bill, 68th Cong., 2d Sess., H. Rept. 1285, to accompany H.R. 11791, January 27, 1925, pp. 5–9.

27. Proceedings of the Sixth National Convention of the American Legion, September 15–19, 1924, St. Paul, Minnesota, p. 97, American Legion Archives.

28. Reports of the Seventh National Convention of the American Legion, October 5–9, 1925, Omaha, Nebraska, pp. 63–64, American Legion Archives.

29. *Evening Star* (Washington, D.C.), July 7, 1925.

30. American Historical Association, *Annual Report of the American Historical Association for the Year 1925* (Washington, D.C.: U.S. Government Printing Office, 1929), p. 79 (hereafter cited as AHA, *Annual Report*).

31. U.S., Congress, House, *Message of the President of the United States Transmitting the Budget for the . . . Fiscal Year Ending June 30, 1927,* 69th Cong., 1st Sess., H. Doc. 65, December 7, 1925.

32. U.S., Congress, Senate, *A Bill to Provide for the Construction of Certain Public Buildings in the District of Columbia,* 69th Cong., 1st Sess., S. 778, December 8, 1925; and *A Bill to Provide for the Construction of Certain Public Buildings in the District of Columbia,* 69th Cong., 1st Sess., S. 1720, December 16, 1925. Successive bills introduced on the same subject usually mean variations in provisions. In both bills the national archives provisions were identical.

33. U.S., National Commission of Fine Arts, *Tenth Report, July 1, 1921–December 31, 1925* (Washington, D.C.: U.S. Government Printing Office, 1926), p. 24.

34. U.S., Congress, Senate, *Annual Report of the Public Buildings Commission for the Year Ending December 31, 1925,* 69th Cong., 2d Sess., S. Doc. 179, December 18, 1926, pp. 6–11.

35. U.S., Congress, House, *A Bill to Provide for the Construction of Certain Public Buildings, and for Other Purposes,* 69th Cong., 1st Sess., H.R. 6559, January 4, 1926; and U.S., Congress, Senate, *A Bill for the Construction of Certain Public Buildings and for Other Purposes,* 69th Cong., 1st Sess., S. 2007, January 4, 1926.

36. Jameson to Roscoe R. Hill, February 9, 1926, *An Historian's World: Selections from the Correspondence of John Franklin Jameson,* ed. Elizabeth Donnan and Leo F. Stock (Philadelphia: American Philosophical Society, 1956), p. 316.

37. Jameson to Reed Smoot, April 2, 1926, in Percy Scott Flippin, comp., "The Archives of the United States Government: A Documentary History, 1774–1934," 19:154–56, National Archives Library, Washington, D.C.

38. Ibid.

39. U.S., Congress, House, Committee on Public Buildings and Grounds, *Public Buildings Bill,* 69th Cong., 1st Sess., H. Rept. 132, to accompany H.R. 6559, January 21, 1926.

40. U.S., Congress, Senate, Committee on Public Buildings and Grounds, *For the Construction of Certain Public Buildings,* 69th Cong., 1st Sess., S. Rept. 197, to accompany H.R. 6559, February 22, 1926.

41. U.S., *Statutes at Large,* vol. 44, p. 630.

42. Ibid.

43. Ibid.

44. U.S., Congress, House, Committee on Appropriations, *A Bill Making Appropriations to Supply Deficiencies in Certain Appropriations for the Fiscal Year Ending June 30, 1926, and Prior Fiscal Years, and . . . to Provide Supplemental Appropriations for the Fiscal Years Ending June 30, 1926, and June 30, 1927, and for Other Purposes*, 69th Cong., 1st Sess., H.R. 13040, June 24, 1926.

45. U.S., Congress, House, *Journal*, 69th Cong., 1st Sess., December 7, 1925, p. 841.

46. U.S., Congress, Senate, Committee on Appropriations, *Second Deficiency Appropriation Bill, 1926*, 69th Cong., 1st Sess., S. Rept. 1172, to accompany H.R. 13040, June 30, 1926.

47. U.S., Congress, Senate, *Journal*, 69th Cong., 1st Sess., December 7, 1925, p. 5570.

48. *Statutes at Large*, vol. 44, p. 841.

49. Jameson to Putnam, June 4, 1926, JFJ.

50. John C. Fitzpatrick to Jameson, June 15, 1926, JFJ.

51. James G. McDonald to Jameson, July 2, 1926, JFJ.

52. Reports to the Eighth National Convention of the American Legion, Philadelphia, October 11–15, 1926, pp. 38–39, American Legion Archives.

53. Ibid.

54. Ibid.

55. *Evening Star*, September 24, 1926.

56. U.S., Congress, Senate, *Annual Report of the Public Buildings Commission for the Calendar Year of 1926*, 69th Cong., 2d Sess., S. Doc. 240, March 2, 1927, pp. 6–7.

57. U.S., Department of the Treasury, *Annual Report of the Secretary of the Treasury on the State of the Finances for the Fiscal Year Ended June 30, 1926* (Washington, D.C.: U.S. Government Printing Office, 1927), pp. 156–57.

58. AHA, *Annual Report*, 1926, p. 54.

59. Ibid., pp. 69–70.

60. Ibid., p. 70.

61. Coolidge, "Fourth Annual Message," *The State of the Union Messages of the Presidents* 3:2708–9.

CHAPTER 12

1. U.S., *Statutes at Large*, Vol. 45, p. 1044.

2. Ibid., pp. 51–52.

3. U.S., National Archives, *Third Annual Report of the Archivist of the United States for the Fiscal Year Ending June 30, 1937* (Washington, D.C.: U.S. Government Printing Office, 1938), p. 2.

4. *Statutes at Large*, Vol. 46, p. 906.

5. Herbert Hoover to the heads of executive departments and independent establishments, July 7, 1930; and Seymour Lowman to J. Franklin Jameson, July 16, 1930; both in Percy Scott Flippin, comp., "The Archives of the United States Government: A Documentary History, 1774–1934," 21:40a, National Archives Library, Washington, D.C.

6. Thomas P. Martin, "The National Archives Building, 1930," *Historical Outlook* 24:177–79.

7. After Pope's preliminary design had been passed by the Board of Architectural Consultants, the design was submitted to the Fine Arts Commission and to the Public Buildings Commission, which approved the plans on July 1 and August 4, 1931, respectively. The architect then proceeded with the working drawings and specifications, which were completed on May 16, 1932, and approved by the Treasury Department on August 24. See W. E. Reynolds to R. D. W. Connor, November 4, 1937, in folder "A–Z, by date, 1935," RG 64, Records of the National Archives and Records Service, National Archives.

8. Ibid.

9. U.S., National Archives, *Second Annual Report of the Archivist of the United States for the Fiscal Year Ending June 30, 1936* (Washington, D.C.: U.S. Government Printing Office, 1936), p. 1.

10. *Statutes at Large,* vol. 48, p. 1122.

11. For excellent accounts of the legislative maneuvering that led to the enactment of the National Archives Act, and the appointment of Connor, see Donald R. McCoy, *The National Archives: America's Ministry of Documents, 1934–1968* (Chapel Hill: University of North Carolina Press, 1978), pp. 8–26.

Index